To

DR. ADEMOLA O. DASYLVA

of the University of Ibadan, Nigeria

The embodiment of what Nigeria needs to succeed

CONTENTS

PREFACE

The theme of this book is the ways that the imposition of colonial rule and the British governance of Nigeria created conditions for violence from the second half of the nineteenth century to the early 1950s. I define violence in terms of its most basic elements: the use of force to damage people and objects; the use of force to maintain control; and the use of humiliating words to generate violent reactions. As the chapters in this book show, violence is based on intentions, political calculations, and expected consequences. In many ways, violence is thus connected with the larger issues of power, resistance, terrorism, and nationalism. While the meaning and outcome of violence are not necessarily the same from one era to another or from one historical event to another, the goals are not difficult to analyze.[1] For instance, chapters 6 and 7 consider verbal warfare and radical unionism as acts of violence, precisely because angry Nigerians were looking for ways to humiliate colonial officers and instigate protest and violence. They threatened violence and used words that suggested the possibility of terrorism against the colonial state. In addition, the very conquest of Nigerian groups was an exercise in humiliation, a domination made possible by violence.

Violence has a political purpose: to dominate, to resist domination, to create conditions for negotiation, and to target people and objects that symbolize oppression. If one party—the colonialists—saw violence to achieve conquest and ensure domination as "legitimate," the other party—the Nigerian groups—saw it as one aspect of resistance. Thus, to both sides, the use of violence was legitimate, and each side painted the other as aggressive. There were two orientations to the use and characterization of violence: visible violence, as in the case of attacks, wars, and injuries; and invisible violence, as in the use of violence as a metaphor (for instance, trade unionists and nationalists saw their anti-colonial efforts as a form of asymmetric warfare, or what they called "battles"). The colonial power imposed violence during the two world wars by drafting Nigerians as involuntary allies.

The inequality of power was glaring. The colonial state had greater resources with which to unleash violence. Thus, colonial soldiers with guns might be found confronting Nigerians carrying clubs and machetes. When it had established itself, the colonial state had the power to criminalize and punish. The state was above the law, which meant that the legitimacy of its own violence could not be questioned. Of course the activities of the agents of the state could be investigated, but this did not mean that the basis of institutional power was threatened. On the other hand, the violence of the Nigerian groups was treated as illegitimate—as acts of terrorism to be put down by the legitimate power of colonial law enforcement. This power inequality is reflected in the protesting Nigerians' targets—court buildings, court clerks, individual policemen—symbols that became victims. When the colonial state fought back, it intimidated its enemies, sometimes using maximum violence. The resulting anger provoked the creation of songs, dramas, and rituals of violence. Angry words communicated threats of violence. Violent tactics included killing, destroying houses, arson, and physical assault. In the encounters relating to the conquest and the consolidation of colonial power, the strategies of violence were actually similar to those of warfare. Burning houses and villages and killing those resisting conquest fall into the category of atrocities. Documentation does not exist to count the dead and injured people, the damage to property, and the destruction of villages and farms.

This book dwells on two phases of Nigerian history that stretch from the last quarter of the nineteenth century to the middle of the twentieth century. Chapters 1 and 2 capture the key elements of the first phase, which was characterized by violent confrontations between the British and Nigerian groups. The British wanted to conquer and the multiple Nigerian nations wanted to defend their sovereignty. Violence in this phase was largely an unlawful use of force by an imperialist power to obtain political dominance and was characterized by episodes of conquest and resistance. African leaders responded on the basis of their understanding of what the invading armies were trying to do. In spite of the gallant efforts of many Nigerian groups, they lost the wars of resistance. Colonial rule was thus established in part by violence, although the British said that the legal basis of their colonial power was based on treaties of surrender signed by kings and chiefs.

Violent resistance cannot be interpreted solely in terms of its final out-come. As a process of political engagement between various parties, resist-ance provides an opportunity for Africans, scholars, and policymakers to understand politics, power, leadership, and the organization of society. Leaders and their armies did not anticipate failures; they believed in their forces, their resources, and the willpower to overcome colonial conquest. Even when crushed, violent resistance was a tool with which to negotiate power relations, and some chiefs and kings gained important concessions and even enhanced their power when the colonial administration was estab-lished. The failure of violent resistance in no way indicates a failure of polit-ical leadership or a failure of the energy of the fighting forces.

The second phase spanned the period from the turn of the century to the late 1940s, a period when Nigeria was under colonial rule and Nigerians re-sisted the forces of colonial domination. Violent resistance revolved around policies on such issues as taxation and the consolidation of colonial rule and involved resistance to exploitation, domination, and inequality. In many cases, the state defined violence against it as unlawful, while defining its own violence, which it used to suppress rebellions, as a legitimate state function. In some ways, the violent actions of this period continued along the same lines as the previous resistance to the conquest. Groups that had previously welcomed the British, including some Yoruba city-states, reacted violently against certain British policies. In the north,[2] the colonial govern-ment was afraid of the extent to which Islam could be used as an ideology of violent resistance. The Igbo continued to resist in some areas, and the Women's War of 1929 marked a decisive turning point in Anglo-Nigerian relations that led to the reorganization of local administration. In the Mid-dle Belt, the British had to subdue a number of groups many times.[3] At the root of the protests and violence of this period were political and economic grievances against the colonial power. Many of the protest movements and "wars" were led by the precolonial leaders—the "warrior class" of aristo-crats and others who saw their power on the decline. While the majority of the Western-educated elements did not join in violent protests, they orchestrated them by other means—by making comments in the media, by expressing anticolonial sentiments, and by forming elite-based political associations. Where violent resistance was dramatic, it did impact upon politics. As noted in some previous studies, violence, or the anticipation of violent resistance, shaped the ways European officers behaved; it forced them to negotiate with or to respect many of their subjects.[4] The anti-tax protests are an example; they compelled the colonial administration to re-examine its methods.

In countries such as Mozambique and Angola, some scholars have concluded that it is not always useful to separate one trend or phase from the other, since protests continued over a long period.[5] These scholars argue that political consciousness was fostered by the politics and histories of resistance and created a historical memory with political implications.[6] Although Nigeria's wars of the nineteenth century to prevent colonial conquest were not necessarily connected with the violence of the colonial era, they tend to be regarded as "the origins of nationalism," events that served as an inspiration to later nationalists.[7] Nigeria did not witness violence on a massive enough scale to support Frantz Fanon's thesis on the necessity and psychology of violence in a colonial order,[8] but the emerging political elite resisted in conventional ways, ably analyzed by J. S. Coleman.[9] While it was the kings and chiefs who organized the resistance of the nineteenth century, new leaders and centers of power began to emerge in the twentieth century. Women leaders, prophets, young students, and politicians in the making began to make a small mark as anticolonial nationalists. The new African leaders did not have armies at their disposal and could not form ad hoc armies as the precolonial political elite had done. Nevertheless, they had followers of a different kind—urban workers and poor farmers who joined them in a number of anticolonial protests.

Chapters 3 to 5 discuss this second phase. They provide evidence of various small-scale and spontaneous riots that challenged the colonial power and its agents at the local level. Court clerks, messengers, and warrant chiefs (in the case of the eastern areas) were the object of serious attacks. Those who joined in the riots were disappointed with the changes of the colonial era. A return to the past became the solution Nigerian leaders offered to many problems, and they advocated violence as one way to get rid of those in power in order to reclaim their lost past.

The two phases discussed above paved the way for a third phase (which is not covered in this book) that relates to violence and the struggle for power at a time when the British were disengaging in the 1950s. In this third phase, Nigerians began to fight not with the British but with each another, a theme that demands a book of its own. In the two phases covered here, one strategy the exiting colonial power used was to seek collaborators among Nigerians who would subvert resistance. Offering concrete promises of benefits from trade, Western education, and Christianity, the invaders were able to obtain the loyalty of a number of Nigerians who interpreted British imperialism from a narrow and self-interested point of view. More important, the British could use one ethnic group recruited into the British-established armies elsewhere, as when they used the Hausa against the Ijebu-Yoruba. Their assumption in doing this was that once the groups were disunited, they could use one group to destroy another. Just as the process of establishing colonial control divided Nigerian groups, so too the process of colonial disengagement turned one Nigerian group against another. The motives, however, were different in the two processes. In the colonial phase, the motive was to weaken and destroy local power centers. In the third phase, Nigerian groups and their representatives were fighting for political dominance. As the colonial power exited, specific groups could no longer be called "collaborators" with imperialist agents. The terminology shifted to that of "ethnic rivalries," with ethnic leaders disguising their ambitions in elevated language and rhetoric.

The wars of the late nineteenth and early twentieth centuries between British forces and several Nigerian groups, known as "small wars" or "low-intensity conflicts," were designed to conquer, to "pacify" restless groups, and to crush resistance. Other conflicts followed during the era of colonial administration (1900–1960) in response to policies on taxation, land, and politics. Chapter 7 shows how people organized themselves around certain specific interests. The outcome of the cases of resistance and violence reveals how fragile the colonial state really was. Nigerians were not fully committed to the colonial project and the government that represented it. The British had to measure and limit their use of violence to enable the government to function. The goal of British colonial violence was to maintain the fragile institutions of the colonized societies and ensure the survival of agricultural production and the extractions of minerals. Colonial officers pragmatically recognized the limitations of violence: if it was excessive and unrestrained, human and natural resources would be destroyed and it would be difficult to check radical nationalism. Resorting to a restrained use of coercion was not an act of magnanimity but a basic exercise in common sense. The colonial state had to maintain a balance in the use of power, a kind of paradox: it had to be strong to secure domination, but it had to be "weak" to ensure that it could govern. This framework of violence allows us to see both the power and limitations of the colonial state.

This is my third monograph on colonial Nigeria, following *Decolonization and Development Planning* and *Economic Reforms and Modernization*. As I have argued elsewhere, it is not true that the colonial era of Nigerian history has been studied to the point of saturation. Indeed, there is no era of Nigerian history that can be described as having generated enough studies. Definitive studies are rare on many aspects and subjects relating to Nigeria, and great works of synthesis are few and far between. Only a handful of studies of the use of violence exist, not even enough to generate a respectable historiographical essay. In the 1960s and 1970s, Nigerian scholars joined in the study of resistance, which was then fashionable. Resistance was an integral part of nationalist historiography, and a number of scholars, such as Obaro Ikime and Adiele Afigbo, made solid contributions on some communities in southeastern Nigeria.[10] The dominant theoretical thrust in all these studies is the celebration of Nigerian heroes who organized nationalist uprisings.

The various local studies have not been merged to provide any coherent picture for the country as a whole. This is the first book to attempt such a cohesion, although with regard to only one aspect of resistance—violence. There is surely a need for an overview of resistance as a comprehensive narrative that will bring out the issues of the roles of indigenous nations and power, ideologies, nationalism, and the cultural dimensions of protests. The goal is not to connect nineteenth-century episodes of resistance with anticolonial nationalism, a connection that has sparked some debate.[11] Rather, the goal is to show that at each phase of the colonial period, there were reasons for groups and individuals to respond violently. Of course, there were nonmartial responses, but the focus here is on responses defined as violent. Violence was used to play politics, as a preface or prelude to diplomacy and demands for changes. Without in any way inflating the importance of violence, I argue that activities associated with violence provide some of the dramatic elements in local history. The outcome of Nigerian violence is another matter; violent resistance failed to stop the British conquest. On some of the issues discussed here, available materials, published and unpublished, allow for some narratives and enable us to come to valuable conclusions. However, work on the 1940s and 1950s remains sparse, and the statements offered here should be seen as pointing the way to further research and detailed studies of violence during the era of decolonization.

This book does not include a catalogue of all the violent incidents. Even if such a list were desirable, it is unlikely that the records exist that would enable the historian to compile it. Instead, this book emphasizes the patterns that emerge for the two phases identified above in order to fully reveal the motives and methods involved. The events and violence of the colonial period have had a significant impact on the postcolonial state. Because post-independent Nigeria became more and more difficult to govern, attention will always be focused on issues of instability and violence. The very complexity of violence is shown in the reality that people could be safe from it in some aspects of their interactions with the state but vulnerable to it elsewhere. Thus, in some ways, this book will connect with my previous book on religious violence in modern Nigeria.[12] It is possible for a post-colonial government to underplay the importance and consequences of violent resistance in order to show that it is in control and that its subjects are happy. Scholars often present political instability in terms of leadership struggles and pay little attention to the reactions of ordinary people. And when the people revolt, attention may shift to studies of the police and army, the bodies that bring temporary peace. The nature and forms of violence and other forms of resistance require further documentation. We cannot ignore violence and other forms of protest, not just because we need to interest ourselves in social history but also because we need to better understand the forces of change and tradition, the alliances constructed by the underprivileged, and the nature of social classes and their interactions. What conditions and circumstances created violent protests? Who organized them and what were their motives? Why did they fail or succeed? This book provides answers to these and other questions. To facilitate an understanding of the book, readers unfamiliar with the outline of Nigerian history and its timeline may need to consult some basic works.[13]

ACKNOWLEDGMENTS

With most of my books, the idea to write the next one emerges in the process of writing the previous one. When I was completing a book on religious violence in Nigeria, two obvious gaps occurred to me—the linkage between colonialism and violence and that between ethnicity and violence. The idea of writing about both remained at the back of my mind for some years. As I came close to finishing another book on Nigeria, *Modernization and Economic Reforms,* I decided to return again to Nigeria's colonial past. This was good timing, in part because since the U.S.-led attack on Iraq and the unfolding consequences of that attack there has been greater interest in the study of empires. Scholars and amateur commentators on empires began to popularize the ideas of nationalism and resistance, which is always called insurgency in the Western media. Ideologies of domination and of revolt and resistance have attained a kind of epidemic attention, even if they are badly framed in the duality of what is called good and evil—domination becomes the "good," while the forces resisting external control are castigated as "evil." History begins to repeat itself, taking us back to the example of the era of British colonialism in Nigeria, when colonial violence was presented as "good" and anticolonial violence was presented as "evil." This duality is misleading and undermines analysis of the motives and outcomes of violence.

I have been privileged to be part of a community of scholars dedicated to the study of Nigeria. The members of the Association of Nigerian Studies are obsessed with Nigerian affairs, both in public and in private. Nigeria is not simply an academic subject to them, but the very reality of existence and the sole subject of their dreams. Discussions of Nigeria are a daily preoccupation on telephones and the Internet. I have been at the center of most of these discussions, pioneering an Internet discussion list called USA-Africa Dialogue and Yoruba Affairs. In many ways, my Internet activities slowed the pace of writing this book. What I lost in time, however, I gained in renewed energy and enthusiasm for the study of Nigeria. The challenges of studying Nigeria are enormous, far greater than the strictly career-oriented issues of methodology and sources. Just as my friends and colleagues draw me to present-day realities, I take them back in time. This book is another affirmation that the colonial past—the foundation of Nigeria's fragments of modernity and figments of post-coloniality—remains crucial.

The task that I have defined for myself is not always in accord with the American academic mainstream. I am permanently engaged with larger issues and broader questions that create relevance for academic monographs and works of synthesis. New and old knowledge has to be combined to create larger meanings in order to understand Nigeria and to present it to a diverse audience. There is a sense in which the pressure of the North American market is preventing a dialogue between authors and their African audience. Those of us who resist this pressure write a different kind of book that refuses to engage only with our North American audience, an audience whose primary focus is to pose the question of how new books relate to previous ones, in the process overlooking the resilience of particular problems and the fact that they have to be flogged—not to death, but to ensure renewal, regeneration, and the possibility of an alternative future. In their obsession with answering narrow, strictly intellectual questions, many academics have lost a sense of the responsibility of scholars to the people they study. My goal is to satisfy a diverse audience and to sustain my commitment to the relevance of scholarship to society in the subjects that I explore and in the way I shape the orientation and contents of my books. Thus, I engage the broader issues that deal with people's lives.

I have obtained help from various people in the process of writing this book. Without the dedication of archivists in Nigeria's three main national archives, at Ibadan, Enugu, and Kaduna, my books and essays on the colonial period would not have been possible. Arewa House, which holds important materials on Northern Nigeria, has also been a valuable resource for me. I have used the resources in all these archives far more than most other scholars of Nigeria. I will never tire of expressing my gratitude to the workers in the archives, from the cleaners to the most senior archivists. The staff keeps changing, but not the enthusiastic willingness to offer assistance. Those of us who use these archives must contribute to their maintenance by pressuring the federal government of Nigeria to pay attention to them and halt their current decline.

In looking for readers for the initial draft, I called on the members of the Nigerian Studies Association and my graduate students. I wish to provide a roster of those who gave the most valuable comments—Moses Ochonu of Vanderbilt University, Hakeem Tijani of Morgan State University in Baltimore, Jessica Achberger of the University of Texas at Austin, Jonathan Reynolds of Kentucky State University, Bayo Oyebade of Tennessee State University, and Julius Adekunle of Monmouth University—and close with a prayer: may the Nigerian people and their country have a better future. Finally, I thank Indiana University Press for its interest and Ms. Kate Babbitt for her various suggestions to make the final product more readable to a diverse audience.

NIGERIAN HISTORY

Major events covered in this book

Event	Date
Trade in palm oil grows	1840s
British annex Lagos	1851
Sir George Goldie establishes the United African Company (later Royal Niger Company)	1879
British sign treaties with chiefs in the Niger Delta to establish a "sphere of influence"	1884
Royal Niger Constabulary engages in over 100 military expeditions in the south and forces leaders to sign treaties	1886–1890
British establish the Oil Coast Protectorate (later Niger Coast Protectorate)	1891
British establish new system of government that includes collecting taxes, forced labor to build roads, incorporation of chiefs and kings into tax collection system, building of Native Courts and hiring of Nigerians as court clerks and messengers	1891–1912
Arochukwu resist the British, culminating in the Aro-British war of 1901–1902	1896–1902
British take Benin City after fierce resistance by King Ovonramwen	1897
British establish the West African Frontier Force	1898
Ekumeku resistance movement in Igboland	1898–1911
British form Northern Nigeria Protectorate	1900
British introduce Native Court system	1900
Lugard serves as high commissioner of Northern Nigeria; initiates system of indirect rule	1900–1906
British systematically attack northern emirates	1900–1906
Igbo groups in the south resist British rule	1901–1917

Event	Date
Fall of the Sokoto Caliphate in the north	1903
Native Revenue Proclamation	1906
Collective Punishment Ordinance	1909
Lugard serves as governor of two Nigerian protectorates	1912–1914
Lugard amalgamates Northern Nigeria and Southern Nigeria into Protectorate of Nigeria	1914
Collapse of the Egba United Government	1914
Lugard serves as governor general of amalgamated Nigeria	1914–1918
Violent resistance to colonial rule in Warri Province	1914–1916
Faith healer Garrick Sokarie Braide (Elijah II) leads religious revival, spreads message of black empowerment in the Niger Delta	1915–1916
Fierce resistance to taxation in the south forces British to postpone tax-collection system	1916–1926
Egba rebellion against taxation in the west	1918
Native Revenue Ordinance revised to cover southern provinces	1927
Anti-tax riots in Owerri Province in the southeast	1927–1928
Rural Igbo women of Owerri and Calabar provinces in the southeast conduct Women's Anti-Tax War	1929–1930
Nigerian Union of Teachers established	1931
Nigerian Railway Workers Union established	1932
Nigerian Union of Railwaymen (Federated) established	1939
Trade Disputes and Arbitration Ordinance and Workmen's Compensation Ordinance	1941
African Civil Service Technical Workers Union (ACSTWU) established	1941
Seventy trade unions register with the colonial government	1941–1942
Federated Trades Union of Nigeria (later Trades Union Congress) formed, a coalition of trade unions and Nigerian Youth Movement activists	1942
Nnamdi Azikiwe founds the National Council of Nigeria and the Cameroons	1944
General Strike of 1945	1945
Zikist Movement established	1946
Northern Elements Progressive Association established	1946
Zikist Movement promotes boycott against European goods and culture	1947
Burutu Workers Strike in the Niger Delta	1947
Nigerian National Federation of Labour formed	1948
Enugu Colliery Strike in the east	1949
Northern Peoples' Congress established	1950

COLONIALISM AND VIOLENCE IN
Nigeria

VIOLENCE AND COLONIAL CONQUEST

When the Europeans came to this division they did not come as friends.
—OWERRI DIVISIONAL UNION TO THE JONES COMMISSION, 1956

Whiteman war never finishes
Whiteman war is always big.
—KING KOKO OF NEMBE

Before gold and diamonds were discovered in South Africa in the 1880s, no region in Africa was more attractive to the European powers than Nigeria. Even when the possibility of greater profits opened up in South Africa, the British did not relent in their efforts to add Nigeria to their growing empire.[1] The trade in Nigerian palm oil and palm kernels was already well established, and enormous resources of peanuts and cocoa made colonial conquest a lucrative enterprise. There was the yet-to-be-fully-explored River Niger, which the British regarded as a principal route to the rich Nigerian hinterlands.

Colonization was achieved in Nigeria either by the use of war or by surrender because of the threat of war. The list of casualties is long: King Jaja of Opobo, for opposing the British advance into the interior market, was crushed and exiled in 1887; the Ijebu were attacked and defeated in 1892; King Nana Olomu of Itsekiri on the Benin River was attacked and removed from his fortified base at Ebrohimi in 1894; Oba Ovonramwen of Benin lost his throne and kingdom in 1897; Ologboshere, who wanted to regain Benin's independence, was defeated and executed in 1899; King Ibanichuka of Okrika was removed from power and exiled in 1898; and the Nupe and Ilorin were attacked and defeated in 1897. The loss of a war and the removal or death of a king translated into one major outcome: loss of independence and incorporation, by force, into an expanding British empire.

Modern Nigeria is, to a large extent, a product of violence. The condensed narrative that follows highlights the major cases.

THE SOUTHERN PUSH

In 1807, the way was paved for Britain's aggressive policy in West Africa with the abolition of the slave trade and the subsequent decision to establish a naval patrol to halt the activities of slave merchants. Treaties with other countries allowed British patrol to seize ships involved in the slave trade. The British identified a number of places on the West African coast that could serve as stations for their naval force. Fernando Po became one of the British naval stations, and liberated slaves were deposited at Freetown in Sierra Leone. This was a first major inroad, the policing of the sea that ultimately led to the control of the land. The first sign that the British planned to extend their control came in 1849 with the appointment of John Beecroft as consul at Fernando Po. Beecroft was given the task of monitoring British political and economic interests, especially the trade in palm products, which was replacing the trade in human beings. At this point, Beecroft was appointed as consul for Lagos and other parts of the West African coast. Later on, the British appointed another consul specifically for Lagos.

For the states along the coast, especially those in the Niger Delta, the abolition of the slave trade brought about a change in relations with Europeans. During the long era of the slave trade, the coastal states had offered protection to European merchants and ships that came to their waters. European firms had no forts along the Nigerian coastline, relying instead on kings and chiefs for trade and security. Trade was the bond: to the European merchants, the long trips brought considerable profit; to the Nigerian chiefs and kings, trade brought wealth, which translated into power and prestige. The abolition of slavery and the need to stop trade in human beings began to change the nature of political and economic relations.

When a British warship entered the Bonny River in 1836 to arrest four Spanish ships for carrying slaves, it signaled the change in relations. Bonny, together with other states in the Delta (Brass, Kalabari, Itsekiri, and Aboh), still regarded the slave trade as a source of wealth and these states continued to sell slaves to the European merchants who came to their shores until the 1860s. To protect Bonny's trade and exercise its sovereignty, Bonny authorities seized the British warship and a number of British traders. The British replied with firepower to release their ship and citizens. The episode marked the beginning of a new order, that of the use of violence to settle scores between an encroaching power motivated by specific commercial interests and an indigenous nation intent on self-preservation. Bonny thought that it could use its military to defend its sovereignty, and the British believed that they could use their might to impose a new political and economic order.

The 1836 incident also marked the beginning of the use of written treaties to renegotiate Euro-Nigerian relations. The British imposed a treaty that is usually described as an antislavery document on Bonny. It asked Bonny never to maltreat British citizens and to resolve conflicts through arbitration using a panel composed of Bonny representatives and white traders. Under the treaty, Bonny lacked the power to punish any British sailor, and this marked the beginning of the encroachment on its authority as a sovereign state. The British interfered in the politics of Bonny, assisting chiefs loyal to them against others and appointing those loyal to them as kings. The British signed similar antislavery treaties with Calabar in 1841 and Aboh in 1842 that provided justification for using military means when clauses of the treaties were violated.

The British began using violence on a large scale in 1851 when they annexed Lagos. The people of Lagos had probably seen a conflict on the horizon, but definitely not this outcome. Three years earlier, and without the knowledge of the inhabitants of Lagos, the British government had appointed a consul, John Beecroft, over Lagos and other parts of the extensive West African coastline. As if to deny its true intentions, the British government mentioned in the document that brought Beecroft to power that it had no aim of acquiring territory by purchase or conquest. This clause was crossed out in the draft document, although it survived subsequent revisions.[2]

The interests of British traders led to an aggressive push on the city. The British practices of inserting themselves into local politics and manipulating competing indigenous groups were some of the key strategies that gave them the success they sought in Lagos and elsewhere. A commercial elite in Lagos had consolidated itself in part on the basis of foreign trade, including the trade in slaves, and the British used the lingering trade in slaves as justification for their actions in the region. Conflicts and local politics in Lagos became partly shaped by the desire to either stop or continue the trade in slaves, although various personal ambitions and motives were also at stake. European representatives of established commercial interests in Lagos, who sought more goods and profits, pressured the British government to become engaged in local politics and supplied propaganda to the British to further their interests.[3]

An antislavery party led by the weak King Akitoye provided a means of intervention for the British, who claimed to have been invited by the king to intervene, allegedly to end the slave trade. Following two artillery battles and "the burning of a large portion of Lagos," the British established a consulate in 1851.[4] Akitoye became all but a puppet of the British consul, and he was unable to overpower his opponents, led by his formidable rival, Kosoko, who went into exile in Epe, where he successfully created a new power base and kingdom. Again capitalizing on the rivalries among the chiefs of Lagos, the British established a colony in 1861. A lull followed, during which the British limited themselves largely to the Lagos Colony, interfering only occasionally in the Niger Delta and maintaining a short-lived consulate in the hinterland city of Lokoja. For the rest of the 1860s and 1870s, the British gave the impression that they would not seek further territories.

However, European missionaries and traders began to demand British political intervention in many areas.[5] "If we remain passive," declared an agent in 1883, "we shall see our trade stifled, we shall find our traders furious, and we shall hardly escape grave complications with the French."[6] The agent was referring to France's move to make Porto Novo its protectorate in 1883. Thinking that the French would make other moves, the British chose to establish control on the Niger and Oil rivers. They also worried that the Germans, who in 1884 had signed some treaties in Cameroons, might pose an additional threat, although these fears seem to have been exaggerated.[7] Nevertheless, the British responded aggressively to incursions by other European nations on African territory. As a prelude to the Berlin Conference of 1885, the British consul in Fernando Po signed a number of treaties with the chiefs of the Niger Delta in 1884, which it later presented to other European powers as evidence of having established a "sphere of influence" in that area. In 1885, the British declared a protectorate over the central and eastern coast of Nigeria, which they defined as stretching from "a point on the shore of the Bight of Benin about 10 miles north-west of the Benin River to Rio del Rey on the Gulf of Guinea."[8]

From the palm oil exported from the area, a name emerged: the Oil Rivers Protectorate. Trade in palm produce gradually replaced the trade in slaves, and by the 1840s, all the states were involved in the palm produce trade. However, the trade in produce had social and political consequences that affected the nature of Euro-Nigerian relations. To start with, the trade in palm produce required a large number of laborers to produce oil and crack kernels. Labor was also required to transport palm produce from the hinterland to Lagos and the Delta states. The abolition of the transatlantic slave trade did not mean an end to domestic slavery, and the need for people to work as producers and carriers contributed to local slave-raiding and the extensive internal use of slaves. Missionaries and imperialists seeking territories to conquer used domestic slavery as a justification for intervention.

In the Delta, merchants needed to own large canoes in order to transport oil. As rivalries developed among the states and their traders, it became necessary for merchants to own a fleet of war canoes and provide soldiers to fight against rival merchants and to prevent piracy. Thus, war canoes had to accompany trade canoes. Large amounts of capital to procure slaves, oil, canoes, guns, and gunpowder were needed to participate in the trade. The use of slaves not only as producers but also as trading agents altered some aspects of social relations. A number of slaves were allowed to trade on their own and invest, an opportunity that gave them legal rights in some places, social justice in others, and considerable power at Opobo.

European merchants also arrived in large numbers, and the organization of the trade in palm produce generated many conflicts. To obtain the maximum supply, the Delta traders, who bought oil from thousands of small producers in the hinterland, received credit (known as "trust"), usually in imported items, from European merchants in return for a promise to deliver oil and kernels at a later date. When traders could not obtain a sufficient supply of produce, they had to fight both European merchants and local producers. There might also be disputes over the exchange of imports for palm oil, not to mention the disputes involved in negotiations over prices. Competition among the major traders, who all wanted to buy from a large number of small producers and transport oil, also led to small-scale wars and clashes between the supporters of rival merchants. It was in part to resolve some of these conflicts that the British traders pressured their government to appoint a consul. European traders also called for British involvement in local politics to ensure that chiefs and kings would not use their power to refuse to trade with the Europeans or block trade routes. While "trust" made capital available, a Nigerian merchant's access to this form of credit depended very much on his ability to prove his creditworthiness, and this might involve complicated rivalries with other traders. The Europeans who supplied the capital turned local rivalries to their advantage in order to get good deals. Established European merchants used "trust" to check the participation of new merchants and to control their Nigerian suppliers, which again led to many conflicts.

A trade kingdom emerged rather quickly in the Oil Rivers Protectorate, spearheaded by a trading company formed by an aggressive personality,

Sir George Goldie. In 1879, this astute merchant brought together a number of British firms in the United African Company, later renamed the National African Company. The company obtained several treaties with the chiefs in the area that provided documentary evidence that the British government turned to its advantage to make a case to other European nations that it "owned" the area. Between 1886 and 1899, the company, now known as the Royal Niger Company (RNC), received a charter from the British government to govern, at no cost to the government, a portion of the Oil Rivers Protectorate, defined generously as the area between the rivers Forcados and Nun, extending northward along and beyond the Niger and Benue. The charter empowered the RNC to govern, extend the territories under its control, and administer justice in ways that it defined. The RNC immediately used the charter to create commercial hegemony, as the RNC excluding both local and non-British firms from the profitable trade in palm oil and kernels. Its monopoly power enabled it to dictate prices as well as insist on the quality of products it wanted. Political dominance ensued, with the RNC behaving like a government, including signing treaties and fighting wars in areas close to the River Niger and its tributaries. The RNC acted swiftly to maintain its control, using force whenever necessary without hesitation.

In 1886, the company established the Royal Niger Constabulary, which was an army and a navy rather than a police force. It was the best-trained and best-equipped force in the Niger Delta area, with soldiers drawn from among Nigerians and officers from Britain. The constabulary became Nigeria's first professional army and operated for many years, paying Nigerians to work as soldiers and introducing new armaments and tactics in order to win its wars. From 1886 to 1900, the constabulary was involved in over 100 military expeditions, using large amounts of armaments to force groups and leaders to surrender and sign treaties.

The constabulary was a group of no-nonsense soldiers that chiefs and kings in the Niger Delta described as violators of people's rights and a nuisance to ordinary people. A man who stole small quantities of palm oil belonging to the company brought disaster not only to himself but to his entire village and its neighbors, and some men were taken hostage in these conflicts. The employees of the company might engage in ill treatment of the local population if their actions were treated as obstacles to profit-making,[9] and many people who took actions to protect their own trading interests were punished and complained of cruelty.[10] The soldiers received professional training and were constantly drilled and prepared for war. Their machine guns could quickly destroy the thatched roofs of houses. The goal of the company was more than clear: it would use force and violence to dominate commerce and establish political control.

One attack followed another. In 1888, the company attacked almost half of Asaba, the town where its political headquarters was situated. A year later, the town of Obosi, where the company's commercial headquarters was situated, suffered a similar fate. Other parts of the Niger area were subdued by force or the threat of violence by the constabulary. The people of Brass suffered a humiliating defeat in 1895. The RNC moved northward, waging wars against Ilorin and Nupe, to prevent other ambitious imperial interests from competing with it. The constabulary pounded the strong armies of Ilorin and Nupe with heavy artillery, and many lost their lives.[11]

British authorities built on the gains made by the RNC, using some of the company's strategies. In 1891, the British created the foundations of the government of the Oil Rivers Protectorate and located its capital in Calabar. Three years later, it renamed the protectorate the Niger Coast Protectorate. Its first consul general, Major Claude MacDonald, was given the task of running a government. He had an army, which was important for policing duties and expansion. He also had a staff and a budget derived from customs revenues. To create a visible permanent political network, vice-consuls were appointed and stationed at Bonny, Brass, Opobo, and Warri and on the Niger River. In the first few years, the consuls and vice-consuls had only small areas under their control, but they carefully mapped out military strategies, as they did for the naval and military buildup that led to the conquest of the Ebrohimi kingdom in 1894. The careers of officers rested in part on their ability to conquer additional areas or force the people of such areas to voluntarily surrender. Their job was to curtail any expansionist ambitions of Nigerian kingdoms and prevent kingdoms from negotiating treaties with German or French rivals of the RNC.[12]

In the 1890s, the power of the protectorate extended into its hinterland, to various groups and states in the Cross River, Ibibioland, and Igboland. Too much "shelling and burning" had to take place before many of areas could be subdued.[13] The RNC had to create excuses to justify the destruction. If kings or states were powerful, the RNC treated them as enemies standing in the way of European penetration. If an indigenous commercial class was organized, the RNC regarded it as an enemy opposed to free trade. One of the most dramatic examples of the RNC's efforts to expand its power by diplomacy and warfare involved the Aro.

By 1896, the network of colonial power had extended to the areas close to the southern boundaries of the Ibibio and Igbo. Many of the trading states in the Oil Rivers had been subdued, but an extension northward would clash with the activities and interests of the Aro. Both economic and political calculations underpinned the British diplomatic and military moves against the Aro.[14] To begin with, they condemned the Arochukwu in what became the eastern part of Nigeria as a slave-trading oligarchy that tyrannized other Igbo and Ibibio and other groups. They regarded the influence of the Arochukwu as damaging to European commercial and political interests. From the Aro point of view, the British constituted a threat for many reasons. First and foremost, the Aro needed to preserve the Long Juju, the oracle on which their power and economic survival depended. This oracle attracted hundreds of men and women to the Aro in search of solutions to myriad problems. The Aro turned the oracle to their advantage, using it to promote their commercial interests.

The Aro had profited from the slave trade. The British made known their opposition to the slave trade, even though their merchants were profiting from the palm products produced by the slaves, and the Aro understood that the encroaching British power would undermine the trade in slaves. The message of the missionaries would similarly undermine the Aro, as the missionaries were calling for changes to old customs and to institutions such as slavery. In addition, the Aro could lose control over access to and distribution of imported items. Some losses were already being recorded as Efik, Bonny, and Opobo traders moved to the interior and began to penetrate areas the Aro had formerly controlled. Other European traders were also flourishing in areas where the British had established political power, again taking away trade from the Aro.

The Aro took some steps to protect themselves and prevent aggressive moves against them. Through contacts with European traders and colonial officials, they made known their objections to the colonial encroachment. The Aro continued to maintain a grip on areas under their trading influence, warning the population there against giving support to the British. They even threatened some groups with war should they aid the British. By 1899 it was clear that diplomacy would not be enough to resolve the tension between the Aro and the British, and both sides anticipated a major war. In preparation for the war, the Aro built an alliance with some of their neighbors and attacked some groups for being pro-British. The British sent agents and spies to collect information on the power of the Aro oracle and the location of Aro forces.[15]

The British attack on the Arochukwu began on November 28, 1901, and lasted till December 24. Many villages were taken and retaken in the process.[16] The attack on the Arochukwu was well planned. Prior to it, four military stations were created, at Owerri, Oguta, Bende, and Akwete,[17] as if to launch the expedition not just from different directions but in ways that would be difficult for the Arochukwu and their supporters to understand.

With the defeat of the Arochukwu, the British forged ahead to establish power over the Igbo, but acts of resistance were not fully over. The British establish district headquarters, as in the case of Owerri, where administrators, military regiments, and a police force were stationed. The British requested land to build new offices and living quarters that was usually granted either free or for a nominal fee. By the time the British established a native court, the nucleus of administration and justice was in place. The courts signified the shift in power from the old kings and chiefs to the new colonial agents, the use of Nigerians to govern themselves according to colonial laws, the beginning of the actualization of the colonial objectives through new regulations, and the recognition of new spaces and new men as centers of power.

West of the Igbo was the Benin Empire. Long sustained by military power and trade, Benin struggled desperately to retain its independence as the British encroached on its territory. By the 1890s, Anglo-Benin relations had degenerated into conflicts. King Ovonramwen, who had come to the throne in 1888, was the last independent monarch of Benin, a victim of the Scramble for Africa.[18] The encounter between the British and Benin was one of the major epics in a series of violent events in the conquest of Nigeria.

Ovonramwen had begun his regime by consolidating his power. He removed from power those who were disloyal to him and forestalled hostility from neighboring towns and kingdoms. In addition, he retained the basis of the revenue of the Benin Empire, which was comprised of tribute from colonies, a monopoly on some products such as palm kernels, and a tax imposed on traders. The king closed markets and trade routes when the interests of his empire were threatened, a move that antagonized the European traders. As far as the British merchants and consuls were concerned, Benin constituted a challenge to the pursuit of colonial interests, and they portrayed him as a "savage" presiding over the "City of Skulls" or "City of Blood."

In the view of the British, Benin was a lucrative region that was rich in ivory, rubber, and palm products. European merchants interested in these products felt that the control of trade by the Benin king and chiefs was standing in their way. The invention of the pneumatic tire in the United Kingdom in 1887 added to the urgent need to control Benin, which was one of the richest areas of rubber resources in the region. Various consuls began to plan visits to Benin. In 1891, Vice-Consul Gallwey of the Benin River made preliminary visits to the periphery of the Benin Empire, traveling along the tributaries and creeks of the Benin River. In 1892, Gallwey decided to visit the city of Benin; this turned out to be a historic mission with major consequences. Gallwey's visit marked the beginning of the end of Benin. He interpreted a treaty with Ovonramwen as the *oba*'s acceptance of British power as well as the right of Europeans to trade in any part of the empire. In the eyes of the Benin monarchy, the treaty did not have the force of law and should not have any practical impact.

Nevertheless, pressure mounted on Gallwey to implement the treaty by limiting the power of the king and opening up his empire to trade and rubber extraction. By 1897, the pressure to attack Benin had become more widespread, and a new vice-consul, James Philips, was willing not only to listen but to act. Benin was under strain in this situation; the politics and diplomacy of dealing with the British had divided the Bini chiefs and war leaders, with one party thinking that a war against the British should be pursued and the other preaching collaboration. The terrified king resorted to elaborate rituals and sacrifices as well as the execution of opponents, which created further divisions and resentments. Benin was in turmoil because palace diviners and charm makers had predicted that a great disaster was imminent. A further prediction associated this impending trouble with European encroachment.[19]

In the first week of January 1897, a series of events led to violent conflict. Philips was eager to prove his mettle, and he decided to go to Benin to ask the king to sign yet another treaty. Abandoning an initial plan to use a large army to accompany him to Benin, he chose instead to lead a smaller army of seven Europeans and about 200 local carriers. His mission was to spy on Benin and collect as much military and economic information as he could. Philips also reckoned that the mission would enhance his prestige, while successful pressure on Benin to open up its land to trade would advance his career.

As Philips approached Benin, the king asked him to delay his entry to the capital city because of an ongoing festival, but Philips refused. The lingering division among the Benin chiefs now became more serious, with some advising peace and others war. The pro-war chiefs attacked Philips and his forces, reckoning that a preemptive move was needed to protect Benin's commercial and political interests. They killed almost the entire party, including Philips.

The British decided on immediate revenge, using the attack on Philips as the long-awaited excuse to impose colonial rule. In February 1897, a

1,500-strong army marched on Benin, where it fought for two weeks. The capital fell on February 17 and with it Benin's power and control over trade and colonies. When a rocket landed on the king's palace, the king quickly went into exile with a number of chiefs and a large group of people. The empire had crumbled. Trophy hunters looted the city, stealing close to 2,500 bronzes, which were carried to Europe where they were sold to private collectors and museums.

Oba Ovonramwen went into self-imposed exile, hiding for six months. When the king reentered Benin on August 6, 1897, he submitted himself to the British authorities. The king and his chiefs were tried for the attack on Philips. Six Benin chiefs were found guilty: three were executed and the other three committed suicide. The king, too, was found guilty, but he was deposed rather than killed. On September 13, he was deported and exiled to Calabar, where he died sixteen years later. Benin became integrated into the British Empire, first as part of the Niger Coast Protectorate and later as part of Southern Nigeria. European merchants entered the region to benefit from trade and the region's oil and rubber resources.[20]

The British conquest of the Yoruba in the southwest relied on the use of Lagos to control its hinterland. The penetration was slow, originally involving British intervention in local politics and the complicated Yoruba internal wars of the nineteenth century. To protect trade, Governor Molony of Lagos successfully brokered a peace agreement in 1886 to end the Sixteen Years' War between the Ibadan Empire and its numerous enemies.[21] Other treaties followed that sought trade advantages but became part of the justification to create colonies. The French and the British used treaties to create a western frontier for the Yoruba that divided the Yoruba population between two countries.[22]

Treaties were not enough to force all the Yoruba groups into an emerging British colony. Some had to be visited with violence. The first victims were the Ijebu, who occupied a gateway to the extensive Yoruba hinterland. For years, they had exploited their advantage by serving as middlemen in the lucrative trade between the coastal market of Lagos and the production centers in Yorubaland. The Ijebu controlled their markets, limiting others to two market zones located on the edges of the city boundaries. While other cities such as Ibadan, Lagos, and Abeokuta welcomed European missionaries and allowed their Yoruba agents to work with them, the Ijebu rejected the missionaries as well as other foreigners. The Ijebu used established religious traditions to protect themselves against others, and they refused to accept conditions of subordination.

For years, the strategy of the Ijebu in dealing with their enemies was to block trade routes and cut off supply lines. In fighting the British, the Ijebu chose a different strategy, concentrating on the defense of their capital city of Ijebu-Ode.[23] The British attacked Ijebu-Ode in May 1892, probably calculating that negotiation would not work with a people whom they had characterized as "arrogant." Rather, they opted to use an army comprised of a combination of soldiers drawn from various places (they were known as the West Indian and Gold Coast troops and the Hausa and Ibadan troops). The mission of the army, which was led by a few British officers, was to subdue the Ijebu. The Ijebu were prepared and had mounted a large army equipped with guns. The Ijebu army was much larger than that of their enemy, and the battles were intense.[24]

The Ijebu lost hundreds of men and the British defeated their capital. While they had guns, they did not have the most efficient artillery pieces and machine guns. Their tactic of standing up to shoot (instead of staying prone) allowed the enemy to see them and shoot at a group of them with greater ease.

The consequences of the defeat were far reaching for the Ijebu and other Yoruba groups. The Ijebu war prevented other smaller wars; groups that regarded themselves as less powerful than the Ijebu realized that submission was a wise option, and those who saw their power as equal to that of the Ijebu were afraid of a war with the British. Powers in hinterland areas such as Ibadan were afraid that they lacked adequate resources with which to fight.

When the war was over, the Ijebu quickly reconciled themselves not just to imperial conquest but also to foreign culture. As if accepting the failure of their ancient gods and religions, thousands of them turned to Islam and Christianity, seeking new answers to age-old problems. As the missionaries brought Western education, the Ijebu had no hesitation in accepting it.[25]

In a triumphalist mood, Governor Carter of Lagos traveled to various parts of Yorubaland, signing treaties with Abeokuta and Oyo and later on with Ibadan. In 1895, the British bombarded Oyo, whose destruction was characterized by some contemporaries as "indescribable."[26] Fatigued by a series of lingering and devastating wars, a number of Yoruba cities and groups were eager for peace. The Yoruba groups opposed to the Ijebu, such as the Oyo and Ibadan, were happy with the successful military expedition against the Ijebu. Samuel Johnson, the leading chronicler of that era, saw the defeat of the Ijebu as an opportunity to spread the Christian gospel, expand trade, and bring peace to the region. "The taking of Ijebu Ode," Johnson wrote, sent a shock of surprise and alarm throughout the whole land. The people felt instinctively that a new era was about to dawn on them. A new and foreign power had entered into the arena of active politics in the country, and everyone was exercised in mind as to how the country would be affected by it.[27]

Where prolonged wars and the enslavement that came with them had created instability, British intervention looked like an act of liberation. Many Yoruba had looked forward to peace so that they could farm, trade, travel, and pursue other businesses that the wars had prevented. This explains why the spread of British power in many parts of Yorubaland was so peaceful. By 1900 most of the region was under British rule.

THE NORTHERN PUSH

In the north, the British fought several emirates. The RNC had paved the way with its attacks on Bida and Ilorin. For many years, the RNC had been active in the Niger and Benue areas, trading with the people and signing treaties with kings. There were disagreements over the treaties—the RNC claimed that the treaties gave it political rights to a number of emirates, while the kings maintained that they had agreed only to commercial interactions. The British government accepted the interpretation of the RNC and used the treaties at the Berlin Conference of 1884–1885 to press other European powers to recognize its claim to parts of what later became northern Nigeria. The British revoked the charter of the RNC in 1899 and proclaimed a protectorate in the north in the following year. Force was needed to maintain the power of the protectorate and extend its territorial control.

In 1898, the British established the West African Frontier Force (WAFF) with headquarters at Lokoja. The goal was clear: the WAFF would be used to conquer and control the peoples and nations located in the region around the Niger-Benue confluence and beyond. Two years later, Captain (later Lord) Frederick D. Lugard became the first high commissioner of the newly created Protectorate of Northern Nigeria, which took over the existing possessions of the RNC. Lugard used force to subdue the population; he believed that people would be likely to cooperate after they had been crushed and humiliated. On January 1, 1900, Lugard hoisted the British flag at Lokoja, declaring a British protectorate with himself as the first colonial officer to head the new colonial government. His staff was small, and he relied on an army of 3,000 African troops and 200 European officers. Lugard had a fanatical bent to his mission, if not to his personal character:

he damned the consequences of his violent actions and did not wait for orders from the Colonial Office before launching attacks on the emirates.

The British had not consulted with the kings and chiefs in the north before they proclaimed the protectorate, and they needed to use force to make the colonial government a reality. No king or chief would quickly surrender or allow his freedom and independence to be easily forfeited. Indeed, when the rulers had been courted by various powers in the 1880s and 1890s, they had refused to sign treaties that undermined their power. In one bitter exchange between the caliph at Sokoto and British agents, the king and religious leader said that Muslims could not accept cohabiting with unbelievers. It was clear that the British would need to resort to war to subdue the people and their rulers. While the Sokoto Caliphate was not about to give up easily, it faced many obstacles. To start with, its military capabilities had major weaknesses, including insufficient military supplies. The caliphate leaders recognized the need to modernize their armies, and they tried to obtain artillery pieces and train soldiers to use them. But they were unable to obtain firearms because the traditional sources of supply in North Africa were closed and the British occupation in the south blocked access from that direction.[28] There was an even more serious problem: the grip of the caliph on the component political units within the caliphate was weakened. There were crises at various locations, some involving civil war, as in the case of Kano Emirate. A number of other crises related to the emergence of radical preachers who, in the tradition of Uthman dan Fodio, the founder of the caliphate, criticized the existing political and social order.

Between 1900 and 1906, the colonial army attacked the emirates of Bida, Yola, Kontagora, Kano, Bauchi, Sokoto, Borno, Zaria, and Katsina. In these and other places, the leaders and their followers fought to protect their states and their religion. Marching northward from Lokoja, the British were able to conquer such key emirates as Yola, Bauchi, and Kontagora in 1901 and 1902 following stiff resistance. A year later, the powerful Kano Emirate also fell. The emir of Kano left the city before the attack, warning that Muslims were helpless to confront the "dogs" that had surrounded them. He called for leaders to move to another location.[29] The emirates fell one after the other. They failed to unite their forces, and their old tactics of cavalry charges and defending walled cities could not prevent the devastation wrought by heavy artillery and machine guns. In addition, Kano soldiers who had modern guns did not shoot well, suggesting poor training.

The British still needed the biggest prize of all: the seat of the caliphate based at Sokoto. The capital had failed to use its enormous power as the center of a caliphate to mobilize a large army, in part because of the great size of the caliphate. It also failed to provide the leadership that might have enabled many of its emirates to form a combined army. The Sokoto leadership was not ignorant of the motives of the British, and it was familiar with the resistance wars in some of its emirates and the wars between the French and the Tukulor west of Sokoto. Lugard had also indicated to the Sokoto leadership that he would use all the force necessary to overthrow the Sokoto caliphate. When Kano fell, some of the advisers to the caliph saw it as a sign that it would be difficult to fight the colonial forces, and they called for a peaceful resolution of the conflict. Some others called for the abandonment of Sokoto as a form of *hijra* (withdrawal) to prepare for war. Those who called for resistance carried the day, and Sokoto leaders prepared for war by praying and preparing charms. They decided to meet the enemy outside the city wall to prevent the disaster that had befallen Kano when it fell to the British. The attack came on March 15, 1903. The invading forces of twenty-five European commanders, five noncommissioned officers, almost 700 African riflemen, about 600 African carriers were well prepared and well armed. They used Maxim guns and 75-mm cannon to break down the city walls.

As the conquering army appeared, panic set in. A contemporary observer reported that on sighting the colonial forces, "hordes of horsemen and footmen armed with swords, spears, old guns and bows and arrows appeared, charging the square over and over again, only to be mown down by machine gun and carbine fire."[30] The battle lasted less than two hours, and the surviving inhabitants deserted the city. The caliphate's army was no match for the power of the colonial army. Attahiru I, the caliph, fled toward the east, portraying his flight as a *hijra,* a religious flight sanctioned by Islam to prepare for a greater battle. Meanwhile, the British moved in and appointed a new caliph, Attahiru II, while some Sokoto theologians began to argue that one could reconcile with conquerors and unbelievers as long as one did not trust them. But the jubilant Lugard was shocked to discover that the fleeing caliph was not without support.

The conquering army pursued Attahiru I. His goals were unclear to them. Some believed he was not even ready for war, only preparing to head to Mecca. Others thought his plan was simply to relocate to found a new kingdom. Yet others believed he wanted to choose a more favorable location from which to fight. Whatever he did troubled the British. His moves became harder to interpret. His followers included not only many titled officers and senior chiefs but also thousands of ordinary people. Slaves and poor farmers, herders, and artisans were among the countless number of emigrants, a circumstance so frightening to the British that they characterized it as "madness."[31] The British had presented the invasion as one way to liberate the poor from the oppression of the kings and chiefs, and they were shocked that Attahiru I would generate such support and loyalty, even at the time of his downfall. As the embattled caliph traveled, people along the way donated horses and food to indicate their support and loyalty.

The colonial army pursued the fallen king for five months. It reached the fleeing caliph at Burmi, close to the boundaries of Borno to the northeast. The British lost the first battle there, but Attahiru I was not eager to capitalize on his gains. He asked only that he be allowed to keep traveling to the east as a solitary pilgrim without companions. "I am simply running away," the caliph pleaded.[32] The British felt, however, the weak caliph could still be dangerous. They ignored his pleas, and a better-organized colonial army arrived to besiege Burmi. The resistance was vigorous, but it ended after a seven-hour battle. The colonial army broke down the city gates, took the city by storm, and killed almost 1,000 soldiers defending the caliph. Attahiru I was counted among the dead. The caliph's son, Mai Wurno, continued with the flight, eventually ending it in the Sudan.

WEAPONS AND ARMIES

British economic and political interests created the violent confrontations that led to the colonization of Nigeria. The goal of conquest was to inaugurate imperial control and rule. The RNC had indicated that colonial domination would be accompanied by exploitation and violence, including the excessive use of power and violence to pursue narrow economic objectives and the transfer of wealth outside of Nigeria. The advancement of commercial interests began as early as the mid-nineteenth century, when the British sent troops and gunboats to the lower Niger. Later on, economic interests broadened into the larger interests of imperialism, which had to be established by force.

British violence occurred in two stages. The first stage used force to conquer or the threat of force to obtain voluntary surrender. Force involved terrorizing kings and their subjects. These wars marked the end of the independence of indigenous nations and groups. In the second stage, the British colonized the people through territorial governance. This involved the physical presence of police and the army. The British regarded the use of force as legitimate, and Lugard interpreted military success as a justification for imposing political authority.

Whenever necessary, the British regarded their need to impose imperial rule as a sufficient justification for the use of violence. However, as chapter 2 indicates, the superior force of the British did not mean that groups voluntarily surrendered. The initial interactions with the British were violent for many groups and states. In Central Nigeria, the arrival of the Europeans was associated with terrorism. Houses and farms were destroyed, people were killed, and there was chaos in many areas.[33]

The British collected knowledge about people and places before they launched their attacks. As incomplete or inadequate as the knowledge was, it was useful for winning wars that conquered various groups and their leaders. This knowledge came from a variety of sources, including British-financed "exploratory" expeditions, missionaries, and traders. Bruce Vandervort has listed the major advantages that came with the knowledge that Europeans had acquired in the course of their previous experience as colonizers:

(i) They had developed relevant diplomatic and fighting skills in two centuries of contact with the forest Indians of North America and the various peoples encountered in Asia.

(ii) These same experiences had also taught them how to recruit, train and employ local levies.

(iii) Europeans had plentiful experience of informal warfare, both as a result of bush fighting in their colonial possessions and their wars with each other in Europe.

(iv) Europeans had developed a logistics capability that enabled them to mount expeditions and gather supplies from the far corners of their domains and bring them to bear with fairly precise and often devastating effect.

(v) Europeans had reached a level of expertise in combined operations that enabled them to supply their troops and outflank their enemies by the use of river and coastal shipping.[34]

One of the most decisive factors in the success of the British was superior technology. The wars in the Niger Delta showed how naval vessels could be used to carry soldiers and supplies and even to shell villages along the coast and rivers. In addition, the British had better access to modern weapons, notably the machine guns and magazine rifles they supplied to their soldiers in adequate quantities. Many of the Nigerian groups also had access to guns, but not in numbers equivalent to those of their enemies. The invading forces had shrapnel shells, Maxim guns, and rockets, and the dane guns and single-shot rifles of many of their opponents were no match.

While a soldier fighting for the British might have a magazine rifle that could reach beyond 1,000 yards, his Nigerian counterpart could be carrying a single-shot breechloader or even the less efficient musket. A large number of Nigerian soldiers actually used bows and arrows and machetes. Nigerian groups had powerful armies, but military technology had changed. An army based on cavalry could be defeated by an army using machine guns. Early machine guns such as Maxim guns, Nordenfelts, Gardner guns, and Gatling guns, which discharged bullets at about eleven per second, were far superior to dane guns. Knowledge of machine guns did spread, but they were difficult to obtain. The powerful emirates in the north obtained some modern weapons through trade with the Nupe in the 1880s, but this access route was blocked by the RNC in about 1888. The European powers made it more difficult for Nigerians to obtain modern weapons. The RNC, the Niger Coast Protectorate, and the Lagos government banned the importation of modern guns in the 1890s, when the Nigerian groups needed them the most.

Wealthy astute Nigerian leaders (such as Jaja of Opobo) acquired modern weapons and actually built up impressive armories, but they did not have enough soldiers who had been trained to use the new weapons. There is truth to the observations of British officials that Nigerian soldiers with modern guns were not always good at using them. Observers of the Anglo-Ijebu war remarked that marksmanship was mediocre among many Ijebu soldiers. Similarly, in the British encounters with the armies of the emirates, a good number of the emirate soldiers had problems using rifles. The emir of Kano resorted to using spies to see how the British trained their forces in the use of arms, but this was a rather slow way of transmitting knowledge. These observations were repeated in connection with many other military engagements, and it calls for some kind of explanation, even if only a tentative one. It is clear that where ad hoc armies had to be raised to fight the invading forces, adequate training could not have been given to the soldiers. Even where there were standing armies, training in marksmanship was limited in order to conserve available ammunition. It would have been hard for Jaja to allow his soldiers to use his stored ammunition for target practice.

Any review of the resources available to the armies will reach one conclusion: the invading forces had more resources than the Nigerian groups. Europe's superior technology was not in doubt and was a major factor in Europe's penetration of Africa and Asia.[35] By the 1880s, the Europeans were able to communicate using submarine cables. The use of steamboats gave the British many advantages: they could move more personnel and supplies and they were strong enough to withstand fire, rocks, parasites, and small-scale military attacks. Guns were improved upon almost every year, making them ever more deadly. The armies of the Nigerian groups had no answer to the superior technology: six Maxim guns and seven artillery pieces defeated the massive army of the Nupe in 1897, while two artillery pieces and four Maxims defeated the powerful emirate of Ilorin in the same year. While the Nupe and Ilorin had cavalry forces and able horsemen, they lacked the strategy to deal with the guns and the better-disciplined enemy troops.[36]

What European armies needed the most was not the superior guns but the soldiers to use them. They turned to Africans to work for them, and this became another decisive factor in their success. For a variety of reasons, the British and other European powers did not go to Africa with large armies. There was a concern about tropical diseases and the tropical weather that could lead to serious illness and death. Europeans needed their soldiers in other places, especially in an unstable Europe where conflicts eventually led to the First World War, and Britain already had large armies in India and South Africa. European powers also calculated that their African enemies could not field large armies against them.

The wars involved tactics, strategies, and impacts. To British officers and ambitious soldiers, the colonial wars opened great opportunities to rise in the service, become celebrities at home, and administer large areas and numbers of colonial subjects. To the majority of the British army personnel, service in Nigeria and other areas afforded a golden opportunity. Successful wars could bring promotions and decorations. Frederick Lugard became a hero and was granted a peerage as a general who was able to win wars and administer the huge northern part of Nigeria. Lugard was not alone, and many others enjoyed their own glory and rewards for being able to subdue Africans and turn them into obedient colonial subjects. British commanders and administrators used the wars to bolster their careers and contribute to the glory of politicians and their country. The conquest of Benin and the pursuit of the caliph of Sokoto were "dramatic episodes" that the armies involved were eager to talk about with relish and that politicians and generals used to inspire patriotism and justify imperialism. The wars popularized the propaganda of a superior British force, and even energized Africans who served in the colonial armies. Wars that were won with superior arms were interpreted not only as successful for that reason but as evidence of the moral and racial superiority of Europeans over Africans.

The military strategy the British used to conquer Nigeria changed over time. The Nigerian groups did not see the totality of the plan, but there was a method to the series of so-called little wars that boosted the idea of imperialism in Britain. In the early part of the nineteenth century, the British used military squadrons and gunboats along the coast to create pressure in Lagos and the Niger Delta areas. The problem was that the gunboats were effective only in a smallish area.[37] Those involved were essentially British personnel, who could be deployed only for brief periods because of malaria and their unfamiliarity with the terrain. The ships were able to land soldiers only in navigable stretches of the rivers, which limited the effectiveness of the ground troops, since they could not move too far away from their ships in case they needed to retreat or regroup. With a small number of soldiers spread too thin, these squadrons were not very effective. In later years, the British began to use gunboats that could cover a larger stretch of land and were able to attack and destroy towns close to the rivers. While this made the conquest of Lagos and some Niger Delta states possible, it also had its problems: the people affected could relocate to a place beyond the reach of the gunboats, they could evacuate before an attack, they could rebuild after they had been shelled, and their leaders could resist an invading army with guns and gunpowder.

Conquering the hinterland and maintaining British power called for a different military strategy, one that involved the use of Africans. There were Africans available to serve, men who the British recruited in one region and moved to another to fight. In some cases, internal conflicts had created a number of displaced people who needed new jobs. When Lagos was attacked in 1851, the attack was carried out by the Royal Navy and about 650 soldiers supplied by King Akitoye, the Yoruba king. The British moved West Indian troops from Sierra Leone to Nigeria; two companies of the Third West India Regiment were stationed in Lagos in the 1860s.[38] The consul in Lagos used the West India Regiment to protect British interests and to resolve one local war or another in the 1860s. These regiment not only policed conquered areas, they also kept an eye on frontier zones still under indigenous control. Not only were Nigerians available to be recruited, but they were cheaper and less susceptible to tropical diseases. By the end of the nineteenth century, the armies the British used to subdue the Sokoto Caliphate had become better organized, more efficient, and more ruthless.

In 1862, the British established the first military unit in Lagos, which the press referred to as the Hausa militia or "Glover's Hausas." This was given the official title of the Lagos Constabulary, which was split in 1895 into a civil police unit and a military unit. Recruits were drawn from runaway domestic slaves and others who went to a liberated people's depot that antislavery groups had created in Lagos with the support of the consul. The British eventually created other military units with trained soldiers commanded by officers assigned by the War Office in London. Equipped with artillery, the men were prepared to conquer new areas, fight Nigerian chiefs and kings, and protect colonial governments. By 1898, the Lagos Constabulary had grown to 500 soldiers. The Royal Niger Company's own force had grown to 1,000 soldiers by 1896.[39] The Niger Coast Protectorate created a unit of 400 men in 1892. Until 1885, the British strategy was to limit its political influence to areas reachable by its constabulary. After 1885, a constabulary could conquer an area, but its inability to station a military unit there and police the people might enable the area to regain its autonomy, as happened among some Igbo groups. To increase their colonial territory, the British needed to enlarge their army and spend more money on armaments. In 1897, the WAFF absorbed many of the previous constabularies.[40]

The creation and operation of the WAFF provide important insights on the operations of the colonial force and its relationship to colonial subjects. The recruitment strategy was one of divide and rule. Frederick Lugard, the first commissioner and commander of the WAFF, concentrated on recruiting Hausa and Yoruba. The preference for Hausa soldiers was based on the belief that they had soldierly qualities and were used to horses. There were other reasons as well, notably the large number of runaway domestic slaves among the Hausa groups and the need to use them to subdue people of other ethnic groups. The Hausa soldiers knew little about the big plan—they simply followed instructions to raid, shoot, kill, and arrest. Africans were used to conquering Africans, even from their own groups and states.

The expedition against the Arochukwu consisted of seventy-four Europeans and 3,464 African carriers and soldiers. In defeating the strong army of the Nupe, the colonial forces had only thirty-two European officers who commanded 1,000 rank-and-file Africans. Yoruba soldiers were in the army that invaded Ijebu-Ode; the Hausa fought the Hausa at Burmi; and Aro slave dealers led colonial forces along the trade routes controlled by the Arochukwu. Whenever casualties were mentioned, whether on the Nigerian or the colonial side, they were not Europeans but Africans. The total number of Europeans who died in the conquest of Nigeria has been put at only around twenty.[41]

The role of Nigerians in the conquest was not limited to fighting for the British. Indeed, a large group of Nigerians made it possible for the army to function. There were the so-called friendlies—scouts, agents, and spies—

who collected information and performed other tasks to facilitate the use of violence. Usually larger in number than the soldiers, sometimes at a ratio of four "friendlies" to one soldier, they were recruited for shorter assignments and disbanded after a war. The "friendlies" performed a variety of unpalatable tasks such as destroying or consuming the crops of the people being attacked, forcing those in retreat to surrender, mounting a siege, and conducting spy missions.

Then there were the carriers, again Nigerians, whose services were indispensable in transporting food, medical supplies, artillery pieces, arms, and ammunition. To move an army of 100 soldiers, the British needed about 300 carriers. A machine gun and its belt required nine men to carry it, and about forty-five men were needed to drag one twelve-pound Whitworth gun from one location to another.[42] Where artillery had to be used, the real challenge was carrying the big guns, which could weigh over 200 pounds each, excluding the cradle and the trail. A 75-mm gun could require thirty-two carriers to move it.[43] Without the "friendlies" and carriers, the wars would have been limited to the vicinity of the sea and the areas along the River Niger reachable by the gunboats. Noncombatant carriers, who were usually larger in number than the combatants, protected the lives and health of British soldiers by minimizing their activities in roles regarded as too tiring, risky, or unhealthy.

Wars of conquest could be brutal. Houses, storehouses, farms, and farmlands were destroyed when deemed necessary. Full-scale wars produced casualties and brutalities, as in the case of Benin. Military defeats brought humiliation and shame. The powerful caliph of Sokoto, Attahiru I, not only abandoned his capital but was pursued and killed. The emir of Bauchi and a number of his chiefs were deposed and sent into exile. When the emir of Kontagora was sent into exile, he was held in chains like a common criminal. At Satiru in 1906, the WAFF treated its Nigerian enemies with enormous callousness: poorly armed people were attacked with magazine rifles, and about 2,000 of them were killed; the British burned the village of Satiru to the ground and a British officer pronounced that it should never be rebuilt; and prisoners of war were executed and their heads were put on spikes for public display.[44] Hundreds of people abandoned their villages to take refuge in hidden farms. The signs that a colonial army was advancing sent the people in many Igbo villages packing, the men driving their children and wives to hideouts in the forest.

The conquering soldiers might go wild, seizing livestock and foodstuffs and heaping insults on anyone with whom they came into contact. Cases of excesses on the part of the agents of the government made their way into the official records. These included the use of force to compel people to carry loads and construct roads, flogging, and the seizure of people as hostages to ensure compliance with the law.

Successful imperialist wars provided visible evidence that the British used to coerce others into submission. When the powerful emirs of the Sokoto Caliphate and the king of Benin fell so easily, many realized the futility of fighting and simply accepted the treaties imposed on them. Psychological warfare was conducted as colonial agents spread talk about the power of their guns and the strength of their regiments in dealing with stubborn kings and chiefs and their poor soldiers.

In most of Nigeria, as well as over the entire African continent, kings and states did not confront the situation with a unified political strategy. It was abundantly clear that most rulers overlooked the big picture, regarding the invaders as just another player in the never-ending struggles for power that had consumed them for over a century. Age-old rivalries among some states were based on competing political and economic interests, and some rejoiced when the British defeated their enemies. For instance, the Yoruba were so divided that not many sympathized with or assisted the Ijebu in 1892. For many years, the principal Yoruba groups had engaged in prolonged wars that had sapped the energies of their warriors and tried the patience of their people. When the Ijebu were standing up against the British, powerful parties such as Ibadan and Abeokuta concentrated on gaining access to the coast to obtain imported items, including guns and gunpowder. In the Niger Delta, the various groups and merchants regarded each other as trade competitors. A group or merchant could create a temporary alliance with European merchants to gain some short-term advantages, but this process ultimately weakened all groups and merchants. The apparently highly centralized Sokoto Caliphate was unable to create a centralized army to fight the British forces. When important chiefs suggested alliances, as in the case of the Nupe and Kontagora, they often fell through. The various emirates regarded themselves as independent political units with the power to conduct their own diplomacy and wars, and the non-Muslim groups did not feel any commitment to defend Sokoto's interests. The British recruited political agents, the official term for spies and messengers, from among the people of the Delta, and they were used to collect intelligence and to pressure many local chiefs and merchants to accept British rule.

Collaboration with the British was not limited to the activities of Nigerians who served in the colonial armies. Political and trade rivals betrayed one another, as in the case of the wars in the Niger Delta, where one group joined the invaders against another. A weaker group would seek the help of the British to settle political scores with more powerful neighbors. Even political differences within a state could damage it severely and prevent strong resistance. Benin was a case in point, where the chiefs and warriors were divided. Similar rivalries weakened Ilorin and Nupe, where one chief fought one another for dominance. And it is clear that the long wars among the Yoruba had weakened them severely.

An emerging African-educated elite also played a role in spreading the ideology of colonialism. While one group among them was opposed to colonialism, some supported it because they believed that it would bring progress to them and others. Educated Nigerians were also calculating the benefits that would come with colonial rule in terms of access to jobs and wages and, later, access to political influence.

While the use of violence could be seen in direct military attacks, it also manifested itself in other ways. A racially derived mental arrogance led the British to use violent ideas and words to characterize Nigerians. While Goldie was exploiting the labor of farmers for their products and cheating them on prices, he did not disguise his dislike for them, describing them as "natives, whose light and intermittent labours the most earnest negrophile" could use in order to lighten the burden of "the toiling artisans of Great Britain."[45] The open expression of triumphalism that followed a victory could be a public demonstration of superiority to show the people that their allegedly powerful chiefs and kings could be humiliated and reduced to nothing. For example, when the British forces entered Ijebu-Ode, they found the town deserted; the miserable king was left with only two staff members, and his chiefs were trembling. As an eyewitness reported, the king thanked the commander of the British army "for teaching a sharp lesson to those disobedient young fellows whom he had warned, and warned in vain, not to venture to fight the white man."[46] The jubilant commander replied that he was doing his job and made the king a dignified state prisoner to mark the beginning of the imposition of colonial rule.

In general, the British presented the conquest and the violence associated with it as benevolent acts designed by members of a superior race to aid backward peoples. They described wars of conquest as "punitive expeditions," and they called their responses to various acts of resistance by Nigerians "pacifications." The invaders justified the use of violence on the grounds that the people were opposed to "civilization," and they accused their leaders of promoting the slave trade and other primitive practices. British colonial secretary Joseph Chamberlain declared in 1895 that the only way to end "primitive practices" was to wage war.[47] Officers in the field resorted to the same methods, basing wars on allegations of primitivity, slave-raiding, and the warlike character of the people. The real motive was the colonial conquest of Nigeria. Morality and violence were reconciled in the service of the empire. However, success did not come that easily, as chapter 2 reveals.

RESISTANCE BY VIOLENCE

VIOLENCE AND THE ESTABLISHMENT OF COLONIAL AUTHORITY

Maintaining law and order was the top priority of the colonial government. Very early in the life of the administration, it established various guidelines to deal with law and order; these were revised as the government accumulated experience and dealt with cases of violence. Where individuals who caused "trouble" could be identified, they were arrested and punished. Where a group was involved or a person was sheltered by a village or town, the Collective Punishment Ordinance of 1909 empowered colonial officers to punish a group, a village, or a whole town for the "transgressions" of a member. The policy that the central government in Lagos kept repeating to its officers in all the districts and provinces was consistent:

> On approaching recalcitrant villagers, every attempt should be made to get in touch with the inhabitants and ascertain their grievances. Should the elders and chiefs come in to state their grievances they will be informed that their grievances will be considered but in any case they will be called upon to pay compensation for the damage done, punished accordingly under collective punishments ordinance. Should the elders and chiefs not come in, the village will be occupied and steps taken to make them come in. . . . On approaching a village the first condition will be that the mob be withdrawn to their respective villages. If the people come in peaceably steps will be taken to prevent them being subjected to violence.[1]

The officers were told to use soft language when it would work and tougher words and monetary punishments to silence people who resisted. Yet the colonial authorities did not follow their own policies. The levies and taxes the government imposed for creating disturbances could be arbitrary and often included individuals who had little or nothing to do with an incident. In light of the fact that the official policy was to use maximum force only as a last resort, why did colonial officers consistently eschew negotiation and compromise and turn to violence so quickly? At every level, the colonial authorities were always so obsessed with upholding their prestige and authority that they were quite happy to administer quick and brutal force when discussion and negotiations might have worked. In addition, the consistent failure of a number of leading officers to check, censure, or punish violations by their own rank and file is remarkable.

Two colonial officers illustrate how violence was a central principal of the colonial administration—Harold Morday Douglas, who worked at the lower level and in the early years of colonial rule, from 1897 to 1920, and Lord Frederick Lugard, who served at the head of the entire colonial administration between 1912 and 1918 at a most critical era, when the foundation of many of the colonial institutions was established. Felix Ekechi has shown how Douglas, who worked in eastern Nigeria, disproved the idea that was so prevalent in colonial writings that British officers were friendly and looked after the interests of their colonial subjects.[2] Douglas ruled like a despotic king; he maximized the use of raids and wars and felt that the exercise of colonial power should be based on coercion. He claimed to have subdued at least 135 villages and towns. His goal was also to produce unquestioned respect for the white man and he believed that violence was necessary if this goal was to be achieved.[3] The more the people protested, the more violent Douglas's responses became. His authoritarian style took violence for granted in his words, in his management style, and in his use of maximum police or military force when deemed necessary. Surviving oral traditions present Douglas as "extraordinarily autocratic, peculiarly difficult to deal with, and extremely overbearing."[4] He is regarded as the worst DO ever to serve in the region, and the people believed that the best way to deal with him was through violence. His actions provoked protest, wars, and deep anticolonial feelings.[5]

Douglas began his administrative career in 1894 as an acting vice-consul in the Canary Islands. He was based at Las Palmas until 1897, when he was transferred to Nigeria as acting district commissioner of Calabar.[6] This was the time of the wars of conquest, and Douglas "acted with energy" in these wars, so much so that his superiors nominated him for a medal. He was appointed in 1902 as the district commissioner of Owerri.

Douglas was involved in some of the wars to force the Igbo, whose determination to resist was fierce, to accept British rule. In some areas, the

Igbos' violent encounter with the British have been characterized as wars between the Igbo and Douglas, indicating the extent to which he was associated with violence and brutality. To Douglas, Igbo who were stubborn and rebellious threatened the prestige of the white man and should be dealt with in a way that would teach others a valuable lesson.

After the conquest, Douglas governed with harsh measures. He forced the Igbo to build roads and houses for colonial officers. Communities that refused to serve were punished, individuals who expressed their grievances were warned, and chiefs were told to surrender rebellious men to the government. It is worth reiterating that roads, which were subsequently linked to railways, were the major forms of infrastructure needed to move goods from Nigeria to Western markets. Within a short period of time, Douglas had created a network of dirt roads that linked Owerri with various hamlets, villages, and towns. He has been credited in the region as the architect of modern roads and was praised by the governor and missionaries alike for a stunning performance. He was rated by the governor as the best road builder in the entire Protectorate of Southern Nigeria; the roads he had built made it possible for the police and army to move more rapidly. They also made it feasible to build rest houses for British officers in various locations. In short, the roads Douglas had built created conditions that would accelerate economic production. The governor was not interested in the human cost of forced labor and badly underpaid workers.

Douglas swiftly punished people who refused to provide labor. When Chief Nwogu of the Ngor area in the east, who was all too eager to comply with the order, was allegedly murdered by his rebellious people in January 1905, Douglas immediately ordered the arrest of all the suspects. When no one could be accused or arrested, Douglas decided to use the Collective Punishment Ordinance. Douglas chose to attack the Norie, who lived not far away from Ngor, in April 1905 just to prove a point: the people must not disobey his orders. This incited a major resistance war, as the Norie actually prepared to fight, built alliances, and lost many lives.[7] The victorious Douglas earned praises and a medal for quashing a major rebellion in spite of his maximum use of force and the massive destruction of houses, farms, and crops. Official records gloated about his "prompt and severe punishment" of the Norie and the example that would bring other Igbo groups to their senses.[8]

Ekechi has given an example of the punishment Douglas meted out to another group, the Eziama, in March 1904 for their refusal to make roads or obey instructions Douglas had issued. The people were attacked, all their houses were destroyed, and the chiefs were ordered to force their subjects to construct roads. While the chiefs conveyed the message, many people refused to cooperate. For two months, a constable was stationed among them, but they still refused to yield. As a punitive measure, Douglas seized the Eziama chiefs, calculating that this would force their people to comply with his directive. The fear that the chiefs and elders would die in prison, as some did in other cases, forced the Eziama to yield to this blackmail, and they finally agreed to make roads and participate in the native courts. A year later, Douglas found himself fighting with yet another group, the Ahiara, who refused to negotiate with him, blocked the roads, and decided to collect tolls from traders passing through their area. That war lasted until April 1906, another tale of destruction, brutality, and death.

Douglas also directed his violence at individuals he regarded as obstacles. He ordered low-paid Nigerian workers in the colonial service, young men, and chiefs to be flogged, even in public. Individuals were flogged in the marketplace as well. A clergyman with the Church Missionary Society, seeing some of the atrocities, reported to his superiors and pleaded with Douglas to stop his "unbearable manners."[9] This was in 1905. In later years, he beat a government interpreter, a Nigerian, to a state of unconsciousness; and punished several others in violent ways.

The methods Douglas adopted were not without consequences. To be sure, he achieved his aim of colonial subjugation. Coercion also produced the labor to build the roads and colonial buildings. The previously stubborn people of Ngor were praised in 1917 for their cooperation in supplying fit and able men and for meeting all their quotas without creating trouble for the government.[10] However, Douglas's methods generated bad feelings toward him and many other officers and bitterness about the colonial system. In the area where Douglas pioneered his repressive habits resentment ran deep, and cases of anticolonial resistance, which were often expressed in violent ways, were reported in the 1920s and 1930s.[11] Where violent resistance failed, words could replace guns in the expression of anticolonial resentment, as attested to by the curses and insults that are abundant in oral traditions. The Nigerian agents in the colonial services might receive direct verbal insults, while Europeans who had nothing to do with the colonial service might be greeted with suspicion.[12]

Frederick Lugard was looking for a staff with many of the characteristics of Douglas. Men such as Douglas, Lugard maintained, were gentlemen of high moral standards. "There is no danger," Lugard asserted with confidence, "of such men falling prey to that subtle moral deterioration which the exercise of power over inferior races produces in men of a different type and which finds expression in cruelty."[13] Douglas, however, complained that high-ranking officers such as Lugard did not care much about him and failed to promote him or increase his salary. Douglas had to leave Nigeria in 1920 after writing a petition against his senior officers; he was sent to Southern Rhodesia, where he died in 1926. Lugard would also have endorsed this kind of ending: officers should be obedient to the cause and their superior officers. Yet Lugard himself achieved much by ignoring London; he made several major decisions before informing the Colonial Office.

Lugard served as the first high commissioner of Northern Nigeria from 1900 to 1906 and as the country's governor-general from 1912 to 1918, during which period, in 1914, he amalgamated Northern and Southern Nigeria into a single Colony and Protectorate of Nigeria. He was ruthless in the conquest of what became Northern Nigeria, he was fanatical in pursuit of the principles of indirect rule, and his views on the establishment of dominant colonial power were emphatic. He wrote two manuals that guided the work of later colonial officers—*Political Memoranda: Revisions to the Instructions to Political Officers on Subjects Chiefly Political and Administrative, 1913–1918* (1919) and *The Dual Mandate in British Tropical Africa* (1922). Lugard's views prevailed over alternative views about indirect rule and the ways that colonial officers should exercise power. Indeed, he was harsh in his criticisms of those who departed from his views.[14]

Lugard believed in small wars. He was a trained soldier, and he wasted little or no time in moving against many emirates in the north. He believed that for his small wars to succeed, he had to ignore the Colonial Office in London. In his opinion, the Colonial Office was timid, too concerned with public opinion in Britain, and too sensitive to the larger international politics of Europe. Lugard refused to wait for too long before fighting, and he disliked instructions on how to end rebellions against his authority. Before the Colonial Office could decide on the course of action to take with respect to a rebellion or the use of violence, he would move in his army. Numerous times he announced the conclusion of the war and the signing of a peace treaty to his superiors in London before he had consulted with his superiors about such actions.

Lugard's small wars were successful. Only a small portion of land along the rivers Niger and Benue was under the control of the Royal Niger Company when Lugard assumed power as the high commissioner of Northern Nigeria in 1900. The policy of the Colonial Office in London was still fluid when he moved in the direction of wars. Traders in the region had argued that a gradual penetration of what became Northern Nigeria was possible. Lugard disliked the traders and dismissed their views. Presenting the possibility that the French would encroach on British territory as one reason and the need to terminate the slave trade as the other, he decided to use force against the emirates of Kano, Sokoto, and Katsina between 1902 and 1903. Lugard removed the kings who lost the wars and replaced them with new men, usually rivals of the old. He presented the deposed emirs to the Colonial Office in London as crude, cruel, and corrupt. For a brief time, Lugard contemplated changing entire dynasties, until the fear of a possible peasant rebellion dissuaded him from such a scheme.

He also distinguished himself as an administrator, working long hours to establish new rules and standards of behavior. Lugard behaved like a king with absolute power—he refused to delegate authority. He worked with only a small staff in the central secretariat; and his most trusted ally in the Lagos secretariat was his younger brother. The staff members who received praise and rewards were those who did not question Lugard and who implemented his policies. Even while on vacation in England, he put a measure in place to run affairs as if he were still around. He discouraged his subordinates from discussing Nigeria with the Colonial Office, even when they were on leave, and he attempted to muzzle the fledgling media. Lugard nominated members to an Executive Council, which enacted laws that were drafted by him. He engaged in long disputes with the Colonial Office, which wanted to vet these laws. He was disrespectful to superiors who did not agree with him, and his subordinates were afraid of him.

Lugard felt that the purpose of violence and authoritarianism was the opportunity to civilize Africans. Without his force and violence, slavery, alcoholism, and other vices would not disappear, or so he thought. He exuded the attitude that he was not worried about riots because he had the police and army to use at his pleasure. In Lugard's view, the government should not be slow in taking punitive measures when necessary. "I do not regret the loss of life among the aggressors," wrote Lugard in 1915, "for these people hold life so cheap that the only way to prevent a recurrence of the outbreak is to make them understand that it will be severely dealt with."[15]

While violence created Northern Nigeria, the politics of indirect rule consolidated the colonial administration there. Lugard turned to the Fulani emirs as a way of governing at a reduced cost, managing with a small staff and using established indigenous political institutions in order to avoid organized rebellions against alien rule. Lugard was astute in his definition of indirect rule. While others before and after him defined indirect rule to mean reliance on African institutions to govern Africans, Lugard defined it as his own rule through the agency of local chiefs. Not antagonistic to Islam but not devoted to it either, he made no effort to learn Hausa. He wanted the emirs in power, but he did not respect them or necessarily find them worthy political leaders. As long as the emirs established a chain of authority between him and their subjects, with him as the leader, they were doing their job. He used the emirs as powerful authorities to collect taxes and run other important errands for the colonial administration.

As Lugard extended his ideas of indirect rule to the south, he began a process that altered the basis of traditional power and generated conflicts and riots in a number of areas. His memoranda called for granting power to the chiefs and kings as long as the administration ran smoothly. Yet the chiefs and kings could be dictatorial and corrupt and ruthless in the collection of taxes. In the south, Lugard gave the kings and chiefs more power in a chain of authority that ended with himself as the ultimate ruler. Smaller provinces emerged, and the residency system meant that powerful residents were better able to monitor local politics and call in the police at short notice. Because the kings wanted to satisfy the residents, many clashed with fellow chiefs or with their people.

Both Douglas at the lower level and Lugard at the apex believed that they were laying the foundations for the creation of a permanent British empire in Nigeria. Their actions and policies did not envision a future in which Nigeria would be controlled by Nigerians. Lugard saw himself as the king of Nigeria; Douglas saw himself as the king of his district. A chain of command emerged in which the chiefs and people were under Douglas, who was in turn under Lugard. The autocracy in the north suited Lugard, facilitating his efforts to turn it into a system of government by indirect rule between 1900 and 1906. The principal cause of many conflicts and riots involved the adjustment to indirect rule and the distribution of power and opportunities that came with it. He sold the idea to the Colonial Office that indirect rule should be introduced in the south, too. As soon as he succeeded in amalgamating the south and north in 1914, he began the process of administrative reforms in the south. Lugard embarked upon the process of reforming the court system in the south and creating native authorities, both of which led to resistance, especially in the east. He also planned to send future chiefs to Western schools and use the proceeds from direct taxation as the basis of native treasuries, two ideas that also provoked hostile reactions.

RESPONDING TO VIOLENCE: NIGERIAN RESISTANCE

Many Nigerian groups understood the aims of British imperialism and struggled to resist with wars and by other means. The majority of rulers knew that the British conquest would bring about a loss of power for them.

The superior firepower and technology of the invading armies did not prevent various groups from using dane guns, rifles, and flintlocks to fight for their freedom and independence. Ad hoc Nigerian armies sprang up that used spears, bows and arrows, and even machetes against British armies that were using the much more powerful Maxim and Gatling guns. When resistance collapsed quickly, it was not because of a lack of will or manpower; inferior technology led to rapid defeat. Some have suggested that Africans should not have embarked upon resistance in the first instance, since they could never have won.[16] These scholars dismiss those who fought as "romantic reactionaries" who abandoned the profitable strategy of negotiating with the British in favor of wars that they were bound to lose. Resistance wars impacted positively on the development of political consciousness and nationalism. Some of the leaders who participated, such as Koko, the *amanyanabo* (king) of Nembe, have become legends whose names are invoked to encourage patriotism among their people. To dismiss the wars of resistance is to fall into a big trap: that of the failure to understand the complexity of and role of violence in Anglo-Nigerian relations. The activities of Africans, including their resistance, shaped some of the actions of the British.[17]

What for the British were wars of conquest were wars of resistance for Nigerians. When Nigerian groups were attacked, they had to respond, as the Ijebu did in 1892. A Nigerian state had no option but to fight when colonial invaders began to take actions (without negotiation or discussion) whose consequences would have undermined the state's economy or politics. Organizing a resistance war involved mobilizing thousands of people and creating a basis of unity. A number of Nigerian groups (as in the case of the Igbo) and leaders (as in the case of Koko) resorted to preemptive wars, attacking those about to impose control on them in the hope of stopping the process. Many rejected the option of negotiation, refusing to sign treaties meant to end their sovereignty and ignoring the diplomatic option that would lead to their subjugation. Instead of diplomacy, they took to warfare. In other cases, chiefs and groups began with the diplomatic option, as in the case of Oyo and the emirates in the north, thinking that cordial but prolonged verbal exchanges would keep the British away. When they realized the futility of diplomacy, they resorted to warfare. Where a long period of Euro-Nigerian tension had preceded the conquest, as in areas where the Royal Niger Company was entrenched, a lack of trust and a fear of the danger imperialism posed energized political leaders. The epic conflicts, such as the wars in Benin and Burmi, are well recorded in the colonial records, but their impact was not necessarily more far-reaching than that

of the smaller wars. Many conflicts, including numerous Anglo-Igbo encounters, were not of epic proportions, but their memory is now ingrained
in local histories. Some resistance efforts were organized to defend trade,
as in the struggle of the states in the Niger Delta to retain their role as
middlemen in the commerce in palm produce.

By and large, the resistance wars were based on the methods Africans
used to organize armies and wars before 1885. Various groups were accustomed to war, such as the Yoruba, who had spent the greater part of the
nineteenth century fighting one another. Their armies were composed of
infantry and cavalry (where horses were available or could be imported)
with a core of officers and large numbers of rank-and-file soldiers. Although
training and experience varied from place to place, the wars of resistance
demonstrated continuity with previous wars. The chiefs and kings could
raise armies when needed, commanded either by the chiefs and kings themselves or by war leaders who represented the states. It was not uncommon
to see "citizen armies" comprised of volunteers who rose to defend their
towns and people. Usually, adult males who served in citizen armies did
so without remuneration and returned to their regular occupations when
wars were over. The small number of professional soldiers that existed in
many places were associated with cavalry or the use of modern guns. Common soldiers expected guns, gunpowder, and horses to come from political leaders. Since horses were usually expensive to buy and maintain, they
tended to be associated with status. In the Niger Delta, where rivalries for
trade were intense and chiefs had long needed war canoes to protect trade,
armaments included traditional spears, lances, bows and arrows, and firearms. Many groups who engaged in violent resistance knew the value of
cavalry and muskets and worked to solve the problems of obtaining supplies. Brave soldiers in the Middle Belt put a high value on fighting with
spears on horseback, although their confrontations with opponents using
guns were difficult.

In what follows, case studies of resistance are provided, and the chapter closes with a broad commentary on the nature of violent resistance in
Nigeria. Areas where cases of violence were intense included Benin and the
Niger Delta (for example, the confrontations with Jaja of Opobo and Nana
of the Itsekiri kingdom) and various towns and villages among the Igbo.

RESISTANCE IN THE SOUTHEAST: THE IGBO AND THE EKUMEKU

The long River Niger divides the Igbo into eastern and western populations,
with the largest population concentration in the east. On both sides of the

river, the numerous Igbo groups engaged in various wars with the British between 1901 and 1917. Unlike the Yoruba and the Hausa, the Igbo were largely rurally based and were organized under village governments rather than highly centralized authorities. Their encounters with the British involved many small-scale wars with villages and chiefs. One of the best studied has been the Ekumeku wars, which involved three Western Igbo groups: the Aniocha, the Owa, and the Kwale. In what was known as the War of the Silent Ones (Ekumeku), the three groups organized guerrilla warfare, resisting even more strongly than was expected of such large-scale empires as Ibadan and Sokoto. Indeed, as powerful as the Ibadan Empire was during the nineteenth century, it did not engage in a single war with the British. The much larger Sokoto Caliphate did not even mobilize a respectable challenge, and the caliph did not send troops to support resistance in emirates such as Bauchi, Yola, and Kontagora where resistance wars occurred.[18] With the Igbo, it was different, as British expeditions against them were constant; a British officer involved in the conquest of Kano and Sokoto described the Igbo as the "most troublesome" group.[19] It was not uncommon for some groups to desert their villages, telling the British to destroy the villages if they wanted to and hiding on farms and in ravines until the soldiers dispersed.[20]

The British encounter with the Western Igbo began in the 1880s with the activities of the Royal Niger Company, which established a trading company at Asaba after signing a treaty with the town's chiefs. As with other areas with which it came into contact, the company not only wanted to advance its interest in trade but also sought political dominance by exercising the rights of a legitimate government over the people. Using Asaba as its base, the company began to extend its economic and political power to other Igbo groups in the region west of the Niger.

The Ekumeku began during the 1890s. The goal was to rid the area of external domination over people and trade by the RNC and by missionaries. The Ekumeku movement, which began as a league of radical and anti-European young men drawn from various villages, sought to turn a secretive organization into an underground movement to fight Europeans and their local agents. The group's activities were hard to document, but its mission was to strike fear and terror in the enemy. To both local people and Europeans, the Ekumeku became known as "the uncontrollable," "the whirlwind," and "the devastating," terms that all suggest the efficiency of the underground movement.

The movement was led by political leaders who appointed war leaders. Various arms of the Ekumeku also served as secret societies that executed war plans. Indeed, many of the Ekumeku's members had formerly belonged to secret societies that had served as ad hoc police forces for their various communities. Although individual cities and kings organized separate resistance wars, the Ekumeku was a combined effort of many towns and villages, a move that Don C. Ohadike describes as "a radical departure from traditional Igbo military traditions."[21] The Ekumeku used the ability of various towns and villages to come together to overcome the limitations of small political units and armies. The movement lacked a unified structure and did not have an overall commander or military hierarchies. Rather, the towns and villages that were members contributed forces to engage in specific battles. The soldiers of each village or town worked as a unit under their own commander. Various male clubs and occupational associations of hunters, charm makers, and others were loosely combined into a temporary army to fight for a well-defined goal.[22]

The absence of a central authority does not seem to have weakened the Ekumeku. Its political and military leaders met in secret locations to discuss the targets of attacks and agree on war plans and attack dates. They sent delegations to warn, to kill, to threaten traitors, and to deliver messages. The people cooperated and agreed with the leaders' decisions out of fear of the movement. The leaders operated in secrecy, kept quiet, and maintained firm solidarity. They dispersed after an event or battle in a way that made it difficult to blame a single person for a collective action.

The Ekumeku were excellent proponents of guerrilla warfare. They disguised their movements through secrecy and deliberate silence. Because they used the forest for protection, it was difficult to trace their locations until the noise from their guns revealed them. Before 1898, when they joined in collective battle, the strategy was to support a town or village that was in trouble or under threat of British invasion. The Ekumeku made it difficult for the RNC to expand and limited its activities to its base at Asaba. In 1898, the RNC decided that only a war could remove the obstacle in its way. Since the Ekumeku were hard to defeat, the RNC opted for a peaceful negotiation. The peace settlement between the RNC and the Ekumeku lasted for two years, by which time the company had lost its charter.

When the Ekumeku began to take a united position, they chose Igbuzo, close to the town of Asaba, where the pro-imperialist RNC and missionary activities were concentrated. In 1898, they launched a surprise attack on the RNC, forcing company employees and missionaries to run to Asaba. Other raids by the Ekumeku rid the area around Asaba of European control, but they did not defeat the fortified town where the RNC's army and headquarters were located. As the Ekumeku movement spread, it became a serious threat to the colonial government. The Protectorate of Southern Nigeria, which replaced the RNC in the task of administering Asaba and its hinterland, faced difficulties in dealing with the Ekumeku. The Ekumeku not only attacked the Europeans but even those among the Igbo who worked for the protectorate. Many of the steps the protectorate took angered the people of the area, and support for the Ekumeku grew. For example, British officials asked the chiefs of many villages and towns to carry out unpleasant tasks, and the establishment of native courts took away power from the elders. As the interests of priests, elders, and chiefs were threatened, the Ekumeku gained in popularity, and more young men were eager to identify with the Ekumeku to prove their bravery.

In contrast to places where the British could attack identifiable chiefs or kings, it was much harder to deal with the Ekumeku, whose members operated in secrecy. The RNC and the protectorate acted only when they suspected individuals might be members of the movement. Colonial political officers did not know who to deal with, who to punish, or who to reward so they could negotiate with or destroy the Ekumeku, which destroyed the property of those sympathetic to the colonial governments and attacked mission houses. Either because they were afraid of retribution from the Ekumeku or because they were members of the movement, many important elders avoided colonial political officers as much as possible and refused to honor invitations from them.

When a rumor became widespread in 1902 that the Ekumeku were about to launch an attack, the British launched a preemptive strike, arresting many local political leaders and destroying a number of villages and towns suspected of belonging or being sympathetic to the Ekumeku. Two years later, the movement reorganized itself, defending each town rather than using the guerrilla warfare that the movement had perfected. A confrontation between the colonial army and the Ekumeku at Ubulu-Uku in 1902 led to the fall of the town to the British after a three-day siege. About 300 Ekumeku prisoners were taken. Of this number, 200 were taken to the southern town of Calabar, where some committed suicide and many died of disease. Only five survived. In the view of the British, the Ekumeku was finished. But the movement rose again in 1909, mobilizing at Ogwashi-Uku, where its members twice repulsed British forces. The leaders were engaged in confrontation for about three months. Two years later, the British staged another preemptive attack, arresting many Ekumeku leaders who were accused of being subversive. After reviewing their various activities, Ohadike concludes that the Ekumeku was effective:

The discipline instilled in its members, the tenacity of its military wing, the speed with which its activities spread to the various towns, its logistics, its scientific methods of preparing for defense and attack, and its hit-and-run tactics were innovations that were not equaled anywhere else in Nigeria.[23]

Elsewhere, other Igbo groups resisted the British during the same period and later. Between 1902 and 1905, the Ezza in northeastern Igbo territory took to violence to fight the British, although they used conventional tactics of alliance formation and war. When the British had established their colonial authority over Afikpo in 1902, they had moved next to the Ezza to the north. The warlike Ezza were right in their calculation that the British would extend their power over them, using forces based at Afikpo and Obubra Hill. The Ezza were quick to reject discussions with British officers in 1900 and 1901, fully aware that they would be asked to sign a treaty that would surrender their independence. The British pursued a failed policy of diplomacy from 1902 to 1904, then they made a move, sending troops to the Ezza territory in 1905. The Ezza quickly responded by ambushing the troops and killing some of their escorts. The Ezza told the messenger the British sent to them after the ambush that they had never been conquered and would not accept any alien control. Between heaven and earth, said the chiefs representing Ezza, there was only one force in the middle: that of the Ezza. As if to press home the message of their courage, they told the messenger that they were aware of the conquest of the Aro and some other groups, but they were not worried or frightened. The bottom line, as the Ezza told the British, was that they preferred war to negotiation.

A war was imminent. Learning from the defeat of other groups, the Ezza realized the futility of fighting alone. With shrewd diplomacy and the threat of force, the Ezza formed an alliance with a number of villages and groups to the south to prevent them from joining the British. Colonial authorities retreated once again to diplomacy. The political officer in charge of the Cross River Division sent a messenger to the Ezza authorities to arrange a peace meeting, asking them for a list of their grievances. When the colonial agent arrived, not only was he rebuffed but he was asked to deliver angry and threatening words to his masters. The colonial agent was told that he would be the last one to visit them: the heads of subsequent messengers would be chopped off and sent back by relay through villages and towns friendly to the British to the political officer who had sent them. The war began on March 25, 1905, and lasted till May 16. The Ezza did not launch a preemptive attack; instead, they waited for the colonial troops to fight them on their own territory and terrain. Their machetes were no match, however, for the guns of the colonial army. They lost, but not without fighting hard and later engaging in other forms of resistance.[24]

Similarly, the Afikpo group of villages opted for war. Originally, the Afikpo chose a strategy of diplomacy and collaboration. They had been badly shaken by the fall of the Aro in 1901–1902, and on their own initiative they sent an emissary to the nearest colonial political officer in 1902, promising loyalty and cooperation. They did not even object when colonial authorities requested a piece of their land for their administrative office. However, in the last months of 1902, the Afikpo decided to resist. They rejected negotiations with the agents of the colonial government and asked the government not to station an administrative post and troops among them. They ambushed colonial agents who passed through their territories and attacked neighbors who were friendly with the British. The colonial authorities found it difficult to communicate with the Afikpo because no one would deliver messages to them and their neighbors refused to help by taking messages. The Afikpo spent a considerable amount of time preparing for war. When they were eventually attacked on December 28, they fought with courage and determination but were defeated.[25]

TRADE AND CONFLICTS IN THE NIGER DELTA

The Niger Delta produced famous men who combined commercial and political power. When the British encroachment began to undermine their economic and political interests, they fought to protect them. Men such as Jaja of Opobo, Nana Olomu of the Itsekiri, and Koko of Nembe are now commonly regarded as "patriots," even though self-interest underpinned their agenda. These leaders understood the goals of the RNC and the British, and they rejected the idea that colonization would promote civilization and free trade. With a consular authority established in the Delta, the way was opened for European traders and others to penetrate into the hinterland. British traders were able to establish many trading factories, and by the 1860s they had pushed further inland, as far as Lokoja, Aboh, and Onitsha.

Trade led to a series of conflicts, which in turn energized Delta leaders to fight for their autonomy. In the 1850s and early 1860s, when trade disputes occurred between the British and the Itsekiri, the consuls either imposed fines or bombarded the Itsekiri when they were accused of violations. In spite of the superior power of the British, the Itsekiri continued to resist, and they banned trade in 1868, 1879, and 1886 in order to negotiate favorable prices. Aboh, which was located further north and had chosen Brass as its trading ally in the Delta, faced greater difficulties with European traders. From Brass, Aboh obtained guns and gunpowder in exchange for slaves and palm produce collected from its neighbors. In 1857, it welcomed the establishment of a European factory, calculating that its middleman position would be enhanced. Within a short time, the European traders began to undercut Aboh by establishing trading stations at Onitsha and Lokoja and trading in other places to divert more trade and profit to themselves. Fearing that the European monopoly over trade would destroy them, the people of Aboh looted the European trading factory in 1862 and forced a British gunboat to retreat. As it turned out, this was the last success of Aboh. Sir George Goldie moved in in 1882 and strengthened his power by buying up other companies. When Aboh resisted by attacking Goldie's trading station that same year, the RNC bombarded the city with many gunboats in retaliation and hundreds of Aboh people lost their lives. Goldie established a monopoly over trade and cut Aboh off from its major markets. Four years later, Aboh had to sign a treaty of protection, thus losing both its economic and its political power within a short period.[26]

Elsewhere in the Niger Delta, the story was the same: trade generated conflict and resistance. For some twenty years preceding 1884, European traders, European missionaries, the Royal Navy, and the consul all combined to establish a presence and power base that the British used to their advantage. The people of the Niger Delta who resisted were coerced and bombarded into submission. After 1884, the British government began to convert the previous gains to greater advantage, further encroaching upon the power and territories of the various affected groups. Various so-called protection treaties were signed in 1884–1885 to prevent the Delta states from entering into relations with European countries other than Britain. These treaties allowed missionaries to spread the Gospel and British traders to trade anywhere. While the kings and chiefs agreed to sign the treaties, in part because they wanted to continue to trade and in part because they wanted to avoid being bombarded, they realized the harm that would be done to their independence. Some refused to accept some conditions in the treaty, as in the case of Jaja of Opobo and Nana of Itsekiri, who objected to the "free trade" the Europeans demanded. In protest, some chiefs asked for clarification of the meanings of the treaties they had previously signed, and all believed that their independence would not be lost with these written treaties.

The most prominent leaders of the resistance were Jaja of Opobo, Nana of the Itsekiri, and Koko of Nembe. Jaja was both a successful trader and a political leader who established the new kingdom of Opobo. His wealth depended very much on his role as a middleman; he bought palm oil from the Igbo hinterland in exchange for European imports. Jaja grew wealthy and powerful by setting prices and directly exporting oil to Britain. The Anglo-Jaja treaty of 1873 recognized Jaja's extensive influence, but some British traders understood that he could be manipulated to gain access to the market. By 1887, European traders were filing complaints against Jaja that accused him of exercising too much control over trade. Consul Harry Johnson sided with the European traders and decided to remove Jaja because he stood in the way of imperial interests and British commerce. Johnson invited Jaja to a meeting aboard a British man-of-war. He promised Jaja that he would be safe and said that he could leave for home immediately after the meeting. At the meeting, Jaja was given two options: he could either accept exile in Accra, where he would be tried, or he could allow his town to be bombarded. To save his people from being killed and his town from being destroyed, Jaja accepted the option of being tried. Although he was not a British subject, he was tried for creating obstacles to commerce, found guilty, and deported to the West Indies, where he died in 1891. With Jaja's fall, the resistance of Opobo to the British ended.

Nana Olomu, a prominent trader and powerful "governor" of the area known as the Benin River, was a leader of the Itsekiri, a farming and trading nation located northwest of the Niger Delta.[27] In August and September 1894, the British military and naval forces confronted Nana's forces. The British accused Nana of supporting the slave trade, establishing authoritarian control over trade, and threatening the Itsekiri's neighbors. Nana rejected all of these accusations and saw the British as the greater threat to trade and the politics of the Niger Delta.

Nana had inherited wealth and trading experience from his father, and many of his political and economic strategies were based on his inheritance and his understanding of local and international practices. Born in 1852 during a time of turbulent politics, Nana became a master of political instability. When the king (*olu*) of Itsekiri died in 1848, the struggles for succession were so bitter that a long interregnum followed. Power based on the privilege of birth shifted to power based on the acquisition of wealth. To succeed, one must engage in trade, and in Nana's era, trade was based on palm oil and palm kernels. Profitable participation in the trade involved negotiations with local producers and traders, on the one hand, and with European firms and traders, on the other. Nana and his rival merchants had to acquire war canoes to transport oil and an army to protect the oil, canoes, and money from pirates and enemies. Europeans who advanced credit to them wanted oil as agreed upon while also desiring to increase their profit margins by buying directly from the hinterland.

Nana, who grew wealthy on the oil trade, used his profits to acquire a large number of slaves, war canoes, and armaments. With large quantities of dane guns and blunderbusses, hundreds of kegs of gunpowder, thousands of soldiers, and a fleet of trade canoes, Nana was not only the most wealthy Itsekiri but also the most powerful. He became the governor of the Benin River in 1884, a powerful position that involved collecting customs duties, fixing oil prices, and ensuring peace and the collection of debts. Controlling Nigerian traders was always more easy than controlling European merchants—his only weapon was to shut down trade. Two of Nana's predecessors had been removed because of controversy with European traders. When Nana came to power, the politics of trade in the region were added to the politics of the Scramble for Africa, complicating the situation.

Nana agreed to a treaty in 1884 that made Itsekiriland part of a British protectorate, although he refused to agree to a free trade clause that would have allowed citizens of all countries to trade anywhere they wanted. Such a policy would have undercut the middleman positions of Delta chiefs and merchants. When Nana banned trade in 1886 in order to assert his political authority with European merchants, the British consul forced him to lift the prohibition. A long period of hostility began, with Nana refusing to take orders from the consul to leave his town to attend meetings with him. Nana's success as a wealthy merchant was a source of irritation to the consul, who feared that Nana might use his enormous wealth against the interests of the British. The consul accused Nana of attempting to establish a monopoly, using excessive force to collect debts, and keeping too many slaves. In September 1894, the British attacked his town of Ebrohimi. Nana mounted a vigorous resistance, but he lost in the end. He escaped to Lagos, but he miscalculated by reporting himself to the British governor, who arrested and prosecuted him. Nana was found guilty of the accusations mentioned above and deported to Calabar and later to Accra. He was allowed to return to Nigeria in 1906, and he died in 1916.[28]

Thanks to the studies conducted by E. J. Alagoa, we know a great deal about Koko of Nembe.[29] Like others who fought the British, Koko challenged the authority the British established over groups without their permission or consent. At the high point of his success, Koko attacked the RNC depot and headquarters at Akasa on January 29, 1895. He also engaged in resistance against the army of the Niger Coast Protectorate, which had far-reaching consequences for the kingdom of Nembe over which he presided.

Nigeria had become divided into three: the Colony and Protectorate of Lagos, the Oil Rivers Protectorate (renamed in 1893 the Niger Coast

Protectorate), and the Niger Territories, which were under the control of the RNC. Each of the three colonial governments believed it had the power to use its army against indigenous nations in the quest to extend the frontiers of empire. The government of the Niger Coast Protectorate regarded Koko's kingdom as under its control, although his markets were located in areas controlled by the RNC. Koko had to deal with two authorities who had little or no respect for him.

As with other conflicts in the Niger Delta area, control of trade was at the root of all the problems.[30] A number of trading states that flourished in the nineteenth century, such as Bonny, Nembe, Opobo, Calabar, Okrika, and Kalabari, had agreed to cooperate in ending the previous commerce in slaves and had shifted to the new "legitimate" trade in palm oil and palm kernels. In addition, their chiefs had signed treaties that they believed would lead to the expansion of trade. The Nembe chiefs agreed in 1834 to end the slave trade and agreed in 1865 to the conditions for "legitimate" commerce on the Brass River. They agreed to protect traders from exactions and to assist in debt collection; in exchange, European traders would pay *comey* (fees) to the king of Nembe.

Thus, the chiefs turned treaties and trade to their advantage in order to grow wealthy. Acting as middlemen, they collected credit from foreign merchants, then bought palm products from the hinterland and delivered them to Europeans, making huge profits. The Nembe king and chiefs added these profits to the *comey* they collected. Things went smoothly until 1879, when the merchant Goldie established what became the National African Company and immediately set out to control the trade on the Nun River. His goal was to prevent the Nembe and other traders (including Europeans) from reaching the hinterland markets. The British consul promised to help the Nembe in their conflict with Goldie's company and persuaded them to sign a treaty of "protection" in 1884 and again in 1885.

If the Nembe were expecting the consul to call the RNC to order, they were disappointed. The treaty had no effect in checking Goldie's goal of establishing a monopoly on trade. The Nembe assumed that the principal duty of the consul was to resolve this kind of dispute between parties involved in trade and to ensure that the Court of Equity set up to arbitrate with regard trade disputes ran with efficiency and fairness. But when Goldie's company received its royal charter in 1886, becoming the powerful Royal Niger Company, it became difficult for the consul and the Court of Equity to ask the company to settle conflicts with chiefs and kings, and its trading tactics and belief in the use of force became a real threat to the Nembe and other kingdoms in the area. And the RNC's complete control of the market and the production centers Nembe had previously had access to meant economic ruin to the chiefs and the king.

When Koko became the king of Nembe in 1889, he was a young man who saw the problems of maintaining the middleman position that had sustained the wealth of Nembe chiefs and merchants. He had served as an apprentice with his uncle, who was also involved in the negotiations with the RNC. Those who selected the young man to become king were probably looking for a war leader to resolve the crisis with the RNC and reverse their declining economic fortunes. On ascending the throne, Koko renounced Christianity, indicating his alliance with established traditional forces, and began to build his army from members of his mother's lineage, where he felt a greater sense of security. Between 1889 and 1895, the revenues of the king and chiefs declined rapidly. The RNC even cut the sources of food supplies to Nembe, creating a widespread economic decline and dissatisfaction in the kingdom.

After nothing changed when Koko protested to the consul about the trading practices of the RNC, he began to plan for war in 1894. He succeeded in building a large army of about 1,500. With the support of a few other towns, Koko attacked Akasa early in 1895. The secrecy with which he did this was by itself an act of genius. Even the soldiers involved did not know the intended target until a few days before the attack. In the surprise attack, Koko and his forces destroyed the company's premises and warehouse and killed a number of African staff members.

A counterattack came later when the RNC and the Niger Coast Protectorate attacked Nembe and destroyed parts of the city. Koko was a stubborn fighter, and many of his chiefs had to appeal to him to leave Nembe in order to avoid its destruction. Self-imposed exile enhanced Koko's credibility as a fighter and a leader, and he refused to meet with the representatives of the British and the company. Among his people, he acquired the nickname of the "restless shark," and even his death in 1898, probably from suicide, did not diminish his status as a hero. Attacking Akassa, refusing to negotiate, and preferring exile to capture were all impressive behaviors to his people and neighbors. So fearful were the British that they stationed large forces in the Delta to prevent any similar resistance.

Koko was not the only victim: the conflicts caused a series of disruptions to the general populace. The war also marked the beginning of the end of the RNC. The complaints against the company by other European traders who felt cheated by its trading practices and by local merchants who sought more profits became louder, and a royal commission had to be established to investigate charges of monopoly power. The company's charter was revoked, and the British government reconstituted the region into the Protectorate of Southern Nigeria.

NORTHERN NIGERIA

The RNC initiated the use of violence to conquer the north, and Lord Lugard believed in this strategy as well. Although many Yoruba towns had been cowed by the fall of Ijebu, it was not so in the north where, with the notable exception of Zaria, many emirates and groups chose to fight. To many Islamic leaders, the invading forces were "infidels," agents of evil who had to be resisted with all the violent means possible. Lugard's attacks on the Nupe and Ilorin in order to expand colonial power to the north met with violent resistance. In 1897, the Nupe mobilized over 25,000 infantrymen and cavalrymen to meet the forces of the RNC. However, the Nupe's cavalry charges did not work well against an army with rifles, artillery, and guns.[31]

The emirates prepared for war. In the capital city of Kano, preparations began when the city heard hints of war in May 1902. Kano had previously procured large quantities of arms through the connections it had formed in North Africa during the long-established trans-Saharan trade. In preparation for the conflict, Kano and other towns in the emirate repaired and strengthened walls. Kano added at least thirteen strong gates to its walls, which were eleven miles in perimeter and over thirty feet high and forty feet thick. A moat was constructed around Kano, adding to an impressive defensive system. Slits were made in the walls so marksmen could shoot at the enemy from within the city. Lugard, who was in charge of the attack on Kano, also took additional measures to ensure victory. To prevent additional armies from infiltrating into Kano from the caliphate's capital at Sokoto, he stationed a British army at Argungu. When the two large armies engaged in battle on February 3, 1903, about 300 Kano soldiers lost their lives. Other smaller battles followed in which reorganized remnants of Kano forces launched unsuccessful counterattacks.[32]

In the northeast, where the Borno Empire was established, a political interloper, Rabih Fadlallah, was able to take advantage of diplomatic complications among the British, the French, and Germans. Between 1893 and 1895, he took control of parts of the eastern Sudan and Borno, killing Shehu (king) Hashimi in the process. Rabih's career began in the Sudan, where he served under Zubeir Pasha, a businessman and slave dealer. Forced to flee westward by an Egyptian attack, Rabih began his own wars of conquest in 1893, overthrowing the authorities in Baghirmi, Dar-Kuti, and Wadai. Presenting himself as a savior, Rabih teamed up with another religious leader, Hayat B. Said, to attack Borno in 1893. They sacked the capital, Kukawa and they pursued and killed *shehu*. Rabih ruled as king from 1893 to 1900. Members of the displaced royal family scattered in different directions. One faction teamed up with the French who were in the Lake Chad region and collaborated to appoint a new *shehu*. This faction attacked and killed Rabih in April 1900. His son, who succeeded him, had to compete with the *shehu* installed by the French, and both kings sought the support of European powers and engaged in military confrontation with each other. In 1901, Lugard sent an expedition to Borno to search for a candidate to install as *shehu* and check the growing influence of the French, a process that ended in the colonization of this empire.[33]

PATTERNS OF RESISTANCE AND VIOLENCE

When the cases of violent resistance in Nigeria are analyzed, they reveal a number of features about the military and spiritual capabilities of leaders and the attitude of the common soldiers. Contrary to some opinions, the groups fighting the British and their agents understood many of the implications of the colonial invasions. Some groups may have underestimated the strength of their enemies or exaggerated their own capabilities. Others were unable to fully grasp the amount of resources they needed to mobilize to repulse and defeat the invaders. Some leaders made feeble attempts to forge alliances to create a bigger force. Oral traditions relating to the period are clear about the prevalence of violence, small wars, and the spirit of rebellion. Indeed, where people fought for long periods, it was an indication that they were clear about their motives. The last war did not end until 1918, when the British subjugated the Ikwo, an Igbo group in the Abakaliki Division.

Even before the invasion began, some political leaders understood what the consequences would be. A visitor from North Africa warned political leaders in what became Northern Nigeria that Europeans visiting their courts were enemies who would "eat up the whole country," adding with confidence and insight that "these are the words of truth."[34] The chiefs and kings were probably not waiting for the foreigner to tell them this "truth." The king of Nupe was warned by representatives from other places that he should distrust the British and regard them as dangerous intruders. The powerful Al-Kanemi of Borno told his counterpart and former rival at Sokoto what the king of Nupe had heard, narrating the history of how the British had taken over India "by first going there by ones and twos, until they got strong enough to seize the whole country."[35] While the British presented their treaties with Nigerian rulers as documents of friendship, not all the Nigerian rulers were deceived. In the Niger Delta and some other places, a number of chiefs rightly saw the treaties as attempts to take over their land and control their commerce. As early as 1841, the king of Calabar told British visitors that their coming would end up spoiling his country, as had happened in the West Indies.[36] In the 1880s and 1890s, a number of leading traders and chiefs in the Niger Delta were hostile to the presence of European firms and the high-handed administration of the RNC. The hope for the future, as some expressed it in the late 1880s, was that European traders and others would leave the area.[37] Chiefs and kings contested the Europeans' interpretations of the treaties they had signed with the agents of imperialism that allegedly gave away their sovereignty in exchange for trade relations. Because many leaders were originally focused on commercial exchanges, they did not regard the treaties as documents that signed away their freedom and sovereignty.

Just as the chiefs misunderstood the treaties, so also many British officers chose to mischaracterize the motives for resistance. Rather than connecting the wars and attacks to noble political goals, the British portrayed them as examples of anarchy and terrorism, thus attempting to delegitimize wars and indigenous leadership. They described the Ekumeku, for instance, as senseless killers. When the Ekumeku fought, the British assumed that they did so because they lacked the capacity to create institutions to resolve conflicts and created native courts for them. This further angered the Ekumeku. When the Ekumeku attacked the native courts, the British believed that they did so because the courts lacked efficient supervision. They sent political officers to travel around and explain the activities of the government to the grassroots. No improvement resulted, and the British resorted to using violence to suppress violence.

Resistance was largely embarked on to defend the sovereignty of a state and the power of its kings and chiefs. Confrontation was one of the carefully considered modes of resistance, involving violence expressed as wars, raiding expeditions, and guerrilla tactics. Prior to 1885, kings and chiefs had established armies that were able to control the land, ensuring the integrity of their states. The Europeans who came before 1885, whatever their reasons, recognized the established political authorities and limited their interactions to small areas along the coast. Trade policies recognized the rights of chiefs and kings, many of whom became merchants and profited from their power. After 1885, when the Europeans moved to control the land through violence and treaties, the chiefs and kings clearly understood what this meant for their power and privileges. The "masters of the sea," as the Europeans were known in some areas, were about to become the masters of the land as well.

Some cases of resistance however, were embarked on to protect trade interests, as in the examples of Jaja, Nana, and the chiefs of Aboh and Brass. The states used all sorts of methods to retain control of trade. Like other Nigerians, the Ekumeku realized that the colonial forces had a technological advantage over them. The challenge was how to minimize the damage. The Ekumeku took to guerrilla warfare, which relied on a limited use of weapons in surprise attacks on concentrated targets. Controlling the pace of war could be another way of overcoming limitations, as we see in the case of Sokoto, where the caliph wanted to relocate to seek a tactical advantage. Yet another way to overcome the difficulty was to procure equipment of similar capability to that of the Europeans, but this was difficult.

Both common soldiers and their leaders were motivated by established beliefs in magic and war rituals. While their spears and old guns were inferior to the weapons of the conquerors, many believed that they had magic capable of protecting them from death and injuries. Nigeria had no equivalent of the Maji Maji in Tangayika (now Tanzania), where a charismatic prophet, Kinjikitile Ngwale, produced the sacred water that thousands believed they could drink to withstand enemy fire.[38] A number of indigenous medicine men played the role of political leaders in creating anticolonial movements in other parts of East and Central Africa. The connections between indigenous religions and resistance were manifested in Nigeria as well, although they served as psychological motivation rather than as a source of political movements. The embattled *oba* of Benin resorted to extensive human sacrifice in the hope that the gods would be sufficiently appeased to ward off the danger of British conquest.[39] A large number of people in Benin and other armies used charms for good luck and to escape various injuries.[40] Many individuals buried potent charms in the hope that invading armies would step on them and perish, as if the charms had the same power as land mines.

In Islamic areas, religion played a multiplicity of roles. Many Islamic leaders saw the British invasion as an attack on Islam. Documents of the period written by Islamic scholars capture their pain and anguish. One observer described the encounter with the colonial army as "the terrible trouble."[41] "The Christians have brought war on us," he continued, while narrating his story of escape and giving assurances that he would "hide from the severity of the earth's dampness, until it dries." He would not follow "unbelievers even if my towns are captured." In Sokoto, the caliph

turned what could be regarded as capitulation into an advantage sanctioned by religion by presenting his 1903 flight as a *hijra*, a voluntary withdrawal from infidels before they staged an attack. Established as a practice
by the Prophet Mohammad in the seventh century, *hijra* as emigration was
a form of resistance utilized to avoid being governed by "pagans." A senior
chief of Kano advised all Muslims to emigrate.[42] Prayers were intense:
"Help lies with Allah alone, and if He makes easy for us this matter, He is
all powerful."[43]

Leadership was crucial. In numerous cases, political leaders chose to
die rather than surrender. These leaders demonstrated great courage as
they led troops armed with spears and bows and arrows into battle with a
colonial force armed with machine guns. A few military leaders mobilized
a large number of common soldiers to fight to prevent loss of sovereignty.
Armies were easily formed, and some of them were large and well coordinated. The evidence is clear that these leaders put considerable thought
into their war strategies. A key element was obtaining, storing, and distributing firearms to warriors and soldiers at the appropriate time. In large
states like the emirates, a command structure was already in place and
the emirs put their military officers in charge of war strategies and tactics.
Here, as in many other places, the war commanders were professional soldiers trained in the use of firearms and other armaments.

While it is true that adult males dominated the armies of resistance,
women also played significant roles in managing supplies, maintaining
the agricultural basis of society, serving as spies, and performing other
tasks. Some armies were accompanied by women who prepared food and
cared for the sick. Without the activities of women, the logistical problems
would have multiplied: it was women who prepared the dried beef, bean
and corn cake, and snacks that soldiers carried.

Charms and magic energized the fighting forces, making it possible for
leaders' statements to be believable. The Ekumeku leadership relied on the
members of secret cults and societies to cement their unity and promote
trust. It was very common for chiefs and kings to consult oracles about the
outcome of encounters with Europeans or ask the gods how to prevent
Europeans from coming or how to get rid of them.[44] Where a religious
leader led the resistance, as in the case of Mallam Jibril, a 70-year-old Muslim preacher, the movement was energized by an appeal to Allah. Using a
small army of about 600 men armed with bows and arrows and spears,
Jibril was able to muster a rather stiff resistance.[45]

Soldiers believed that charms and elaborate rituals could halt advancing
armies or prevent them from winning. They strongly believed that gods

and powerful charms could stop an enemy from arriving or even change the course of the action. The Benin monarchy performed human sacrifices, but in vain. The Ijebu did the same thing, offering in sacrifice livestock, a woman, and a man. In addition, "charms of imprecation for which they were famous were uttered over the creek that the vessels might founder and the expedition might end in failure."[46] Many towns and villages buried charms at various locations as well. Some British officers actually believed that the charms had some efficacy, as in the case of a district officer who was terrified by a ghost and a snake.[47]

Where wars could not be prevented, war leaders and common soldiers obtained charms to make them invincible or bulletproof their bodies. Medicine that had been used for previous wars was applied to the new wars: such instances included a request for bees and snakes to attack invading soldiers, making them blind. When disasters befell a colonial officer or an agent, even a Nigerian, there were those who attributed these events to the charms used against them. The leaders in some areas that European merchants and missionaries avoided claimed that such disasters occurred because of the use of powerful charms buried in the ground to scare them away once they stepped on the resistant area's soil.

While there is no evidence that the charms worked, the use of charms and other magical methods of resistance produced two possible outcomes. The first, as we found in the case of the Ekumeku, was that secret societies and charms could bring villages and their leaders together. Members of these resistant groups would swear an oath to unite in the face of the enemy, as in the case of the villages in the Bende Division in 1902, where many men swore to "oppose the whiteman, kill all his messengers and drive him out of the country."[48] The second outcome was the ability of an oracle to motivate people to hate the enemy and fight to defend their people and their cultures. A priest could promise the people that the charm he offered was potent and that they should disregard the government and its commands.[49]

In eastern Nigeria, the evidence is both clear and abundant that oracles instigated resistance, providing a powerful example of the relationship between religion and violence. As elsewhere, oracles were part of the religious complex, patronized by people partly to solve problems and partly to enable them to understand the future. Elders and chiefs might represent an entire village or community to consult oracles in order to understand the nature of the tragic events befalling them and find out how to seek prevention or cure. In some cases, hundreds of people visited an oracle to seek the power to resist. So prevalent were the visits to oracles between 1909 and 1911 that a British officer became afraid of the possibility of rebellion.[50] Violent incidents were widespread in a number of districts where people who were emboldened by the power of an oracle attacked chiefs loyal to the colonial government.

Several groups, such as the groups that had fought to avoid incorporation into the Sokoto Caliphate or Benin Empire, were already familiar with the need to resist. It is clear that previous skills in war and diplomacy were applied to the new engagements with the British, although not always successfully. Some groups already had a war strategy in place and could deal with emergencies and supply lines, and many of them had an established fighting or military tradition. Where a group had a history of success, as with many in the Middle Belt or the warlike Ezza in the east, its members based their expectation of success on past achievements. Where a group had recorded failures in previous wars with neighbors, its members worked from the experience of failure and might choose charms instead of guns as means to resist or manage a surrender.

Military strategy was very important. The emirates of the Sokoto Caliphate and the Ijebu adopted a strategy that was familiar to them: open field battles and cavalry charges. This strategy appears to have been ineffective, as the British forces were able to see the enemy formations. Strategies that involved getting too close to the enemy proved to be disastrous for Nigerians; when the enemies were within shooting range, the invaders could use their Maxim guns to easily destroy them. The Ekumeku strategy of guerrilla warfare was more effective. Guerrilla tactics, ambushes, and hand-to-hand combat were some of the favored tactics, although not all proved successful. War tactics could be spontaneous, as oral traditions of war commanders and brave soldiers indicate.

Resistance could be brutally suppressed, as in the experiences of the Ekumeku and Ijebu. The British used their superior force not only to obtain a surrender but also to destroy forests and villages when they deemed it necessary. This is what happened in Ijebu. The terrified Ijebu soldiers fled in panic, abandoning their central command and returning to their homes. Similarly, the expeditions against Igbo villages brought panic and fear to many people, like the Owerri, who refused to embark on armed confrontations. In some places, the people interpreted the strange appearance of white men and the loud sounds of Maxim guns to mean that the end of the world was near.

Not all groups resorted to armed confrontations, and resistance by other means should not be ignored as irrelevant. Some groups chose to surrender when they realized the futility of wars, while others believed in diplomacy and forming alliances. Oral and documentary evidence report cases of flight and migration; some of these cases are presented in colonial records as acts of cowardice. This is clearly an incorrect interpretation, as flight could be a demonstration of faith and strength. Where some emirs abandoned their capitals, the interpretation was based on Islam, which sanctioned such moves as a means to avoid accepting the authority of nonbelievers. The decision to use violence as a form of resistance could also be tied to the method of colonial conquest. Where treaties and negotiations led to voluntary surrender, violence was avoided. In some places where missionaries were active, as among the Yoruba, the advantages brought by trade and Christianity made accommodation with Western agencies more peaceful and desirable to those in power.

Even then, what the people originally intended to be nonviolent actions could degenerate into violence. Such was the experience of the Muslims in the north who made a transition from wars to eschatological protest. A frightened leader, the Sarkin Kano, wrote to his colleagues around 1900 that "these dogs have surrounded us and threaten to overcome us" and advocated a mass migration away from Hausaland to another country.[51] Some fled "to hide from the severity of the earth's dampness."[52] Others advocated staying behind to maintain their traditions.[53] Islamic leaders who were no doubt shocked by the conquest of course wanted to resist, but many accepted the limitations of war. Many preachers and leaders began to interpret the conquest as a sign of the beginning of an end that would lead to a new era based on peace and justice. This belief found expression in the ideology of Mahdism, a view that a leader, the Mahdi, known in Islam as the "Rightly Guided One," would emerge toward the "last days" and reform the world with order and justice. The violence and conquest that sent the caliph of Sokoto into exile and ultimately to his grave as well as the fall of many emirates to the British gave this already established ideology the force it needed to gain popularity. From Ijebu-Ode in the south to Nupe in the Middle Belt and to various locations among the humiliated emirates (Bauchi, Jebba, Yelwa, and Kontagora), Islamic leaders emerged who proclaimed themselves the Mahdi or predicting the emergence of the Mahdi. The Mahdist leader at Nupe wanted a movement to drive away the British; his counterpart at Kontagora predicted the arrival of powerful guns, about 70,000 of them, that would be distributed to fight the British.

Arguably the most successful of the Mahdist movements occurred in 1906 at Satiru, about fifteen miles from Sokoto.[54] The rebellion also spread to Hadejia. In both places, the ideology of eschatology and resistance violence became merged. The Satiru uprising invited an immediate response, but the colonial army suffered a defeat at the hands of resisters who relied on spears, machetes, clubs, and bows and arrows. The colonial army regrouped, determined to use greater force. The religious leader of the Satiru uprising called on the caliph for help. Not only was he ignored, but the caliph and his chiefs chose to support the British, even providing soldiers to fight against the people of Satiru. The caliph and his chiefs were on the payroll of the colonial administration, and many of them had been asked to swear an oath of allegiance on the Quran to the new government. In addition to their calculations of self-interest, the caliph and his chiefs may also have regarded the Satiru rebellion as likely to be crushed by the colonial government.

A larger colonial army moved on Satiru and Hadejia. Satiru village was completely destroyed. Although the people were fierce and courageous in battle, their spears and cutlasses failed them. Both at Satiru and Hadejia, the colonial army went on a killing spree. The army treated those who were captured as common criminals and imposed all sorts of punishment on them. Senior colonial administrators closed their eyes as soldiers and those with some kind of authority embarked on revenge.

The importance of resistance should not be underestimated. Resistance enabled the leaders and their followers to defend their sovereignty and express their nationalism. Not a few resisted because of their fear of the changes that might come with the imposition of colonial rule. It is true that resistance failed to stop the colonial conquest, but the process helped to create a distance between the colonizers and their subjects in ways that later fostered nationalism. The wars gave rise to a perception that the colonizers were not saviors, as they had portrayed themselves in their friendly statements, but exploiters and destroyers.

Nigerians who resisted saw the political agents who represented the conquerors not as friends but rather as overbearing leaders who would use command and violence to attain their objectives. They felt that colonial soldiers (Nigerians who were drafted into colonial forces) were threatening, brutal, crude, and rude. Allegations of rape and wife-snatching were made against them, not to mention petty thefts such as stealing from market women and poor farmers. In many places, the terrorism associated with soldiers created a great deal of fear when the people saw them: people either avoided them or were forced into hiding. The tension that characterized the relationship between the colonial army and police and the public continued for the entire colonial era and continues even now. Soldiers (and the police in many cases) were not regarded as representatives of a friendly agency that was protecting the people.

The resistance efforts collapsed in almost all cases, but not for lack of endurance, courage, or effort. As the British administration set about establishing its control, it realized that its work would not be without problems, some of which were violent in nature. Chapter 3 examines how violence shaped the colonial order.

3

VIOLENCE AND COLONIAL
CONSOLIDATION

During the first two decades of the twentieth century, the British often complained that various groups and individuals were hostile to colonial authorities and their Nigerian agents. They characterized resistance as "barbaric" acts of violence by "primitive" people who lacked any idea of what they would gain once they were civilized. Many colonial officers filed reports that stressed how difficult it was to manage some areas, but they would close their grim statements with confident assertions that things were under control.

However, all was not well in Nigeria, and the realization of this trickled back to Britain. Following major violent anticolonial protests during the First World War, *West Africa,* a weekly magazine based in London, remarked that Nigeria was in crisis:

> Today Nigeria has a black mark upon its record; like Ireland, part of South Africa and part of Quebec, it is one of those portions of the Empire which have added to the anxieties of Great Britain by having civil disorder within their boundaries. Unlike the other three places named it is a country whose people are not at all sufficiently developed as to be able to govern themselves.[1]

Leading colonial officers in Nigeria probably would have dismissed the first part of this statement as an exaggeration, since many consistently maintained that they were in control. They might have complained that they did not want to spread their soldiers and police too thin, but they would have added that they were not afraid of dealing with revolts.[2] However, they would have agreed with the second part of the statement; they refused to allow riots and other forms of protest to prevent them from developing measures designed to ensure that the British would dominate Nigeria forever.

After World War I, the economy was not doing well, and many who had expected colonial rule to bring progress were feeling disappointed. During this period, the colonial government took wide-ranging measures to change the politics and economy of Nigeria, such as constructing roads and railways and distributing coin and paper currencies. It introduced taxation, generating problems in some areas, as will be shown in chapter 4. In addition, its policy of recruiting males for the military created tensions.[3] As a result, the task of consolidating colonialism also included responding with resistance and rebellion. Like the violent resistance the forced imposition of colonial rule had provoked in the first decade of the twentieth century, the administrative changes of the second decade, notably the creation of administrative units and the imposition of a system of indirect rule, instigated many rebellions. The government's reaction to rebellion was consistent: a resort to punitive expeditions to enhance the prestige of the government.

A World War I–era encounter with the Egba of Abeokuta, who had been granted a semiautonomous government in 1893, illustrates how the British used violence to capitalize on political dissension and expand their control in Nigeria. An 1893 treaty had granted the Egba an "independent" political unit, the Egba United Government. The British expected the government to run on so-called modern lines in alliance with the *alake* (king) of Abeokuta, although a colonial officer had the right of supervision. As the turmoil of the First World War engulfed the Egba and their capital city of Abeokuta, the Egba United Government encountered multiple tensions. There were two fundamental fault lines in Egba politics: loyalty to lineages and communal identities and disagreement on how to move the society forward in ways that some groups defined as "progressive." These fault lines produced the violence of the war years. Much of the conflict and violence was between chiefs, and the focus of criticisms and insurgency by the local people was the Egba United Government (notably Adegboyega Edun, its secretary from 1902 to 1918) and the *alake*.

The first fault line was based on lineage and communal identities. The city of Abeokuta grew during the nineteenth century as an amalgam of previously autonomous settlements, all driven to the same location in 1830 by the political turbulence of the era that led to the fall of the Oyo Empire and a series of Yoruba wars. Thus, Abeokuta contained four sharply defined identities—the Owu, Gbagura, the Egba-Alake, and the Oke-Ona—each constituted into semiautonomous governments, each with its own king, *olowu*, *agura*, *alake*, and *oshile* respectively. Each had its own quarter, and the *alake* was treated as senior because the Egba-Alake had a numerical advantage over the others. These groups and their leaders regarded themselves as competitors with a stake in markets and city affairs.

Egberongbe, a Muslim leader, provided the leadership for a second identity group of disgruntled Muslims. In a highly contentious contest, he had competed for the exalted position of *alake* (king) of Abeokuta and lost. Rallying Muslims to himself and his cause in 1914, he became a bitter enemy of the *alake* and opposed most existing arrangements, which he regarded as unjust.

Women constituted a third identity group. They had been active in Egba politics since the nineteenth century, even participating in wars in certain roles. The *iyalode*, the head of the women's group, could be fiercely independent. The politics of the city had divided the women into factions. Subuola, one of the daughters of Egberongbe, led the more combative faction and sought to align the women with the interests of Muslims. The *iyalode* was pro-*alake*.

The second fault line was based on education and visions of modernization. The educated elite often were the rivals of the traditional elite in the contest for power. Church ministers and prominent members of their congregations constituted a bloc known as the "church party," which regarded itself as modern. The members of this bloc relied on both the Bible and English secularism for their ideology and developed their own notions of what modernity meant for the Egba. The articulate leaders used members of different churches to spread their ideas. Their reach extended to Egba villages and towns with schools and churches as well as to other educated Egba living in Lagos and Ibadan. A British account portrayed them as influential, wealthy, and aggressive.[4] The members of the church party wanted power and influence in Egba politics. They tried to undermine the Egba government by telling the traditional chiefs that because they did not have a Western education, they and their people were being cheated by the government and the British. The church party disliked Edun, the secretary of the Egba United Government, and worked hard to seek his downfall.

Similarly, the church party recognized that without destroying the Ogboni, a male secret society and a power bloc that had been constituted as the basis of traditional power in the nineteenth century, it could not advance its own agenda. The Ogboni performed multiple roles as a judicial, religious, and civic organization of influential men. Noted for networking and settling disputes, its influence penetrated all the major sectors of society. It sought to extend its power into the twentieth century by controlling the Egba United Government. The Ogboni and the church party were bound to clash, and members of the church party verbally assaulted it whenever the opportunity offered itself.

These various interest groups focused their attacks on the *alake*, the Egba United Government, and colonial leaders. Egba was ruled at the local level by section heads, each of which governed his section and its villages outside the city. In the view of the section heads, the Egba constitution did not make the *alake* paramount; it only made him "first among equals." As the *alake* acquired more power, the section heads became resentful. In 1914, Edun recommended that revenues be collected on "modern lines," which would mean abolishing the tolls from which many chiefs had profited. Members of the Ogboni, who relied on judicial fees and gifts—the main income for many of them—also worried that this reorganization of the local treasury would undercut them.

The crisis that led to the loss of Egba's independence and the abrogation of the treaty of 1893, which had recognized it as an autonomous state, began in late July of 1914. Historian Akinjide Osuntokun identifies this crisis as "the first sign [to British colonizers] that something was wrong in Nigeria" during the war years.[5] At the end of July 1914, the Egba United Government ordered the arrest of a 90-year-old Ijemo section head, Sobiyi Ponlade, for refusing to order the people under his control to participate in a forced unpaid labor program to construct and repair roads in his area.[6] Ponlade had refused in part to demonstrate that the *alake* and the Egba United Government could not give instructions to his people and to him as a section head. Threatened by a challenge to its power, the Egba government reacted in a way that brought identity politics to a conflict situation. When it tried to arrest Ponlade in his village, the old man resisted and the police used force and bruised him. Ponlade was dragged to the court, which was controlled by those who had arrested him. Edun and British commissioner P. V. Young publicly humiliated him: they put him in a prostrate position for many hours in the sun, thoroughly beat him, and tied him to a tree all night.[7] (Young later attributed his cruelty to goodwill: Ponlade had threatened to commit suicide, he said, and tying him to a tree was a way to prevent it. He added that there was no "lock-up" facility and that he could not trust the local guards not to release Ponlade.)[8] He and his cousin, Odebiyi, were convicted of assaulting a police officer and were ordered to pay a fine of £2 each or go to jail for two years. In a separate charge, Ponlade was convicted of violating the Road Construction Ordinance and fined. An angry and humiliated Ponlade chose to go to jail.

As the news of Ponlade's ill treatment and arrest spread, it energized all the factions and forces opposed to the Egba government, including the pro-Christian party based in Lagos. When Ponlade died in prison after a few days, no one believed the verdict of the postmortem arranged by the government that he died of natural causes. Instead, anger and the energy to oppose the *alake* and the Egba government grew. The Ijemo protested, calling for the dismissal of Edun. The *alake* miscalculated by trying to bribe the Ogboni to side with him against the Ijemo; instead, the Ogboni asked him to fire Edun or be dethroned.[9] The *alake* then put his faith in the colonial government and its army. He asked British Commissioner Young to arrest the Ogboni chiefs from Ijemo, including the high-ranking *oluwo* chief. The British warned the *alake* that colonial intervention would jeopardize the autonomy of the Egba, but his own throne was now at stake and he was eager for help from the British.

On August 5, 1914, widespread riots broke out in the city and its villages. The *alake* and his authorities were unable to end the riots for three days. Afraid that the violence would spread to the villages and smaller towns, the *alake* turned to colonial officers to end the crisis. Lugard immediately realized that intervention raised the possibility that the British could terminate the 1893 treaty and take over Abeokuta completely. Such a takeover would end the Egba government's ability to collect fees on goods that passed through its territory, including goods freighted by the railway.[10] In other words, the coffers of the colonial government in Lagos would be enriched by a complete takeover. Lugard moved quickly, asking his officer at Abeokuta to insist that the Egba renounce the 1893 treaty and place themselves fully under the British. Young assumed full control of the city, and colonial troops moved in on August 6, 1914. Osuntokun notes that August 5 marked the end of the Egba's independence. He quotes an important memo that Lugard sent to his officer:

It is obvious that if the head of state says publicly that he is compelled to appeal for the assistance of armed forces of the colonial government, the state can no longer be deemed capable of standing alone as an independent state. It is also obvious that the existence of such a state in the middle of the British western provinces becomes a source of danger to government. Again the colonial government cannot be called upon from time to time to support the authority of a native ruler unless the government has had full opportunity of investigating the cause of the disturbances endeavouring by its own authority to secure peace without the loss of life. This it can only do if the state is under its control. Finally it is imperative that a stop should be put to the possibility of riots breaking out and troops being required, at a time when England is at war or troops are needed elsewhere. If it is true that advantage was taken by the malcontents to provoke hostilities purposely at such a time, measures must be adopted to render such action in future impossible.[11]

The colonial government chose to use maximum force to end the riots and gave Commissioner D. E. Wilson the task of putting down the rebellion. On August 8, 1914, he went to Ijemo quarters (part of Abeokuta) to arrest about twenty people as a threat and a warning to others. The commissioner gave the *oluwo* the impression that he would be coming to attend a peace meeting. When Wilson arrived at Ijemo with his army, he met about 1,500 unarmed people who were waiting to talk. Instead, Wilson instructed them to hand over all their chiefs. No one obeyed his command. Wilson later claimed in his report that one of the crowd attempted to kill him and a British officer shot him. As Osuntokun tells the story, "the shooting was the signal for a general fusillade upon a panic-stricken and unarmed crowd."[12] Within a few minutes, the *oluwo*, two of the *oluwo*'s wives, six chiefs, and twenty-seven other people had been murdered in cold blood, although Lugard later presented this to the Colonial Office as an act of self-defense.[13] Wilson ordered his troops to enter the *oluwo*'s compound, where they used machine guns to shoot the *oluwo*'s wives and a young boy in their rooms. This massacre was followed by a callous approach to the burial of the dead: the British asked prisoners to collect the bodies in a single trench. (For the *oluwo*, one of the major rewards of being an Ogboni member was the elaborate burial rites.)

As the crowd was dispersed by force, the residents of the city headed out of the city to the villages and farms. After the city was deserted, the colonial troops went on a rampage, destroying houses and property at random. Commissioner Young defended the army, claiming that he had been instructed by the *alake* to use force in order to teach the people to be obedient to the king. The army blamed two members of the Christian party, Anthony Green, a former president of the Egba Mixed Court, and Soyemi Alder of Lagos, for instigating the Ijemo riot. It arrested and thoroughly beat both of them and destroyed their homes. Commissioner Young accused the two men and other educated people of seeking power at any cost. The chief justice was happy to impose a one-year jail sentence on Green and Alder, castigating them in harsh words for "nursing private and personal grievances against the Egba administration and particularly the government secretary." He added that "they made use of the unfortunate incident which caused such profound discontent and dissatisfaction among the Ijemo section as a lever to obtain their own objects, chief among which was the dismissal and disgrace of the government secretary."[14] Such blame was intentional, a careful device to protect the *alake*, Edun, the commissioner, and the troops. The two convicted men represented just one viewpoint in the debates and struggles to negotiate the future of the Egba and the character of the Egba's modernity with the colonial government. By trying to protect their power, the *alake* and Edun fell prey to the ingenious designs of the British to terminate Egba's independence.

In September 1914, P. V. Young, the commissioner and secretary to the Nigerian government, convened an emergency meeting at the *alake*'s palace to conclude a new treaty with the Egba United Government to terminate the independence of Abeokuta and its dependencies. Because of the "Ijemo incident" and the use of violence, the Egba became part of modern Nigeria, while its previously assertive and autonomous Egba United Government became a local government under the control of a British political officer.[15] When the Church Missionary Society and the Anti-Slavery and Aborigines Protection Society pressured the colonial government to investigate what became known as the Ijemo massacre, the government grudgingly agreed but refused to publish the report.[16]

The Ijemo case illustrates the importance of focusing on violence as a political strategy. How and why were colonial forces and colonial administrators able to attack, maim, and injure people; destroy property; and humiliate local leaders? Why did British authorities in London not condemn these actions or apologize for them? The colonial authorities allowed little room for negotiation and consultation. What did this show about the nature and practice of the British system of indirect rule? How did the other Egba and Yoruba people react to this sharp and brutal administration of a lesson in European imperialism? With fear, sullenness, surrender, or submission? Could it be that the eventual surrender of the people was in part based on the fear of the coercive power of the colonial state?

Rather than provide additional illustrations, which in many cases are similar to those given above, this chapter sets out to identify the patterns of violent resistance as well as the institutions and agencies the colonial state established to bring things under control. The analysis offers an answer to some of the questions posed above. As many of the institutions emerged, it became clear that they were being set up primarily to maintain peace and order. The people had to be tamed, many officers believed, and could not be allowed to display verbal and physical aggression. I start with patterns and forms of violence drawn from various cases, then I look at the attitudes of the officers who had to deal with each crisis and the nature of the colonial institutions the British set up to solve the problems.

FORMS AND PATTERNS

Several efforts to consolidate colonial rule and administer colonial subjects created conditions for protests and violence, which Nigerians expressed as revolts, verbal and written petitions, strikes, migrations, and other anti-colonial statements and actions. We see examples in pockets of resistance in eastern Nigeria, rampant protests during the First World War, the formation of radical political associations, schisms within churches and the establishment of indigenous churches, and resistance to the introduction of taxation. Where colonial rule had not been firmly established, the people believed that it was still possible to escape domination, as in the example of some remote areas in the Middle Belt or various cases of rebellion in the east in 1914 and 1915. The most difficult period was the first twenty years of the consolidation of colonial rule, when the newly colonized subjects and rulers were still unsure about the agenda and policies of the colonial government. The British, too, were uncertain about their strategies and policies, although their overall goals were clear.

For the colonial government, the most difficult years were those of the First World War. The global violence of the war produced local violence in Nigeria. Rioting and rebellion broke out in many places, especially in the south. The government reacted very violently to many of these incidents. There were various reasons for the intensity of the riots and the drastic reaction of the government. The people had many grievances that some believed could be resolved through violence and protest. Wartime conditions and the war economy added to the existing problems: the sale of palm produce slowed and trade was disrupted in some areas, leading to inflation and scarcity. On top of all this, recruitment campaigns were conducted in a way that alienated some groups who had to part with their able-bodied men.

Another reason for wartime rebellion was that the colonial government was weakened by the war; it had to divert resources to the war effort and it was badly understaffed. Some areas seized the opportunity to fight while the British were unable to govern effectively. Some groups believed that the British were about to depart in areas where the army and police were withdrawn to perform services elsewhere. As the rumor of the imminent departure of the British circulated, hope was rekindled in those who wanted to organize anticolonial resistance. One interpretation of events was the possibility that the Germans would win the war and British officers would withdraw from certain areas and duties. The colonial government believed that the best way to kill the rumor that the British were about to withdraw was to use violence against communities that believed and acted on the rumor by organizing rebellions. Heavy punishment, argued one officer, would impress "upon the natives that in so thinking they were labouring under a delusion and that government is in a position to quell a local disturbance."[17]

The government's reaction to revolts was immediate; authorities gave the police and army permission to act decisively and ruthlessly. The British believed that punitive expeditions that brought heavy casualties to rebel forces were necessary to maintain the colonial order. Because the riots were scattered in various parts of the country, the strategy was to use maximum violence to suppress an outbreak as quickly as possible so that the soldiers and police could be rushed elsewhere. As the treatment of the rebellious Igbo shows, the colonial authorities did not see the use of maximum force and heavy casualties as immoral but as a sign of strength. Many officers argued that if a rebellious group experienced serious damage to property and numerous deaths, its members would not repeat their protest.

A series of violent escalations of trouble in the eastern and central provinces in 1914 was indirectly related to the war. These were primarily related to trade and secondarily to changes in the administration of local areas. Before the war, German traders had penetrated this part of the country, competing vigorously with the British and others. They had gained a good reputation among Nigerians as traders in palm oil and kernels. Indeed, the people had become dependent on German goods, which they considered to be superior to the goods of others. When the war broke out, the British colonialists saw the Germans as enemies and began to accuse them of using trade to foment trouble. Early in 1914, when the world war broke out, they temporarily banned German traders, creating hardships among Nigerian producers and suppliers. At a time when people were already unhappy with administrative changes, the measures the British took to limit German participation in trade created trouble.

The crisis started in the Kwale District of Warri Province in the south. In November 1914, the people revolted, as if they had been bitter for too long and needed to placate their spirits with blood. They killed messengers and court clerks, who were prime targets for two reasons.[18] First, although the clerks and messengers were Nigerians, they were regarded as symbols of colonial oppression. Second, and more important, the clerks and messengers had converted their jobs into political and economic capital. They used their positions to extract bribes and gifts from people, especially those in trouble with the law. Before the war, district officers had presided over the courts or supervised the agents who presided. When wartime exigencies led to the withdrawal of district officers from the native courts, clerks and messengers had used the opportunity to engage in corrupt practices that alienated the people.

As others heard about the Kwale incident, the violence began to spread westward, and the Urhobo and Ika Ibo people joined in killing the colonial agents. A mob tried to destroy the premises of John Holt and Company and other English firms. The outbreak then acquired an ethnic dimension, a preface to a larger-scale interethnic crisis that could not have been antici-pated. The Kwale, Urhobo, and Ika Ibo began murdering Hausa and Yoruba traders in the area. They declared a war on "aliens," who they defined as those who exploited the local people economically. As the violence inten-sified, the government had to bring in the army. Senior army officers expressed panic and had to mobilize troops from other troublesome areas to quell the growing rebellion. The use of maximum force was authorized, a violent approach that put an end to the rebellion. Verbal threats followed, and a senior government officer, F. S. James, traveled to the areas involved to warn the chiefs, kings, and elders that the government would deal with troublemakers.

The British placed the blame for this series of riots, known officially as the Kwale rising, on the Germans. "The most sinister feature underlying all these revolts," declared a police officer, "is the repeated statements one hears proving that in many cases the towns have been intrigued into dis-affection either by German agents immediately or at least by dissemina-tion of lies by strangers from other parts of the province as to the effect of the war upon the position of the government in the colony."[19] The fact that the Germans had been allowed to resume their trading, concluded the official report on the crisis, led the Kwale, Urhobo, and others to believe that the British would soon leave Nigeria and that the local people would be able to profit more from trade. "The native mind," declared James, "can-not grasp how we English can be at war with Germany and yet German subjects are allowed to compete against their English rivals."[20] Other colo-nial officers alleged that German traders encouraged the Kwale to fight or that they told Nigerians that Germany would win the First World War and the British would be forced to leave Nigeria. British traders fueled antago-nism toward German traders was by pressuring the colonial government to send the Germans out of Nigeria. Local people preferred the German traders, in part because of their more generous use of credit and their more respectful system of debt recovery. But even if German traders could have triggered anti-British resentment, this would not explain why the rioters killed Yoruba and Hausa traders and colonial agents. A feeling of power-lessness, the fear of losing trade, and the despotism of local agents were some of the reasons that provoked the widespread rebellion. The spread of the rebellion to other areas, notably in the southeastern provinces, strongly suggests that the British exaggerated the role of the Germans in instigating the riots.

Violence spread through other parts of Warri Province from 1914 to 1916. Riots also occurred in Udi, Afikpo, Owerri, and Okigwe districts. In Udi District, the riots owed much to a strong belief among the local people that the hundreds of railway workers in the area would dispossess them of their land and thus deny them access to their major means of livelihood and survival. The rioters killed innocent artisans working on the railway from Port Harcourt to the Udi colliery, themselves victims of the colonial economy. The rebels drove policemen out of their district and from October 1914 to February 1915 successfully withstood the forces sent to suppress them. Without an army ready to move—the closest regiment was in the Cameroons as part of the war against the Germans—the colonial officers asked for a volunteer army of Europeans to join the police force. A massacre that killed about 252 of the Udi rebels followed and finally brought the rebellion to an end in February 1915. Violent protests continued in other parts of Owerri Province for another six months and sporadic protests continued on a small scale for another year. Where the government was active in recruiting carriers for the army, sometimes by forcing chiefs to look for people, the resentment was deep.

We do not need to look too far or too deep to understand the reasons for violent attempts to stave off or undermine colonization in Nigeria. The colonial political system disempowered the majority of the people. The Native Court system the British had introduced in 1900 had transformed indigenous political and judicial institutions. Where kings were given more power than before, as in the case of the *alaafin* of Oyo and the emirs in the north, or where new chiefs were granted "paramount power" over their people, the colonial system not only destroyed the established distribution of power but also disturbed the age-old balance of power. Where power had been diffuse, involving elders, priests, women, age grades, and secret societies (as among the Igbo), the native courts and the appointment of paramount chiefs concentrated power in a few hands, thus marginalizing many groups. This created the conditions for political disintegration. The chiefs and kings with power, who were now agents of the colonial system, and even ordinary messengers began to use their power in corrupt ways. Autocracy replaced republicanism in some areas, while many kings and chiefs became autocrats working as agents of the colonial state. The power of a number of kings, such as the *alaafin* of Oyo and the emirs in the north, was enhanced to a level far above the traditional requirements and privileges of their titles.[21] This was the beginning of the social disintegration that provoked protests and violence.

If the people were troubled by the behavior and activities of their own chiefs and kings, they were even more troubled by the British officers. Many of the pioneer officers were described as hard, overbearing, and cruel. Some were military officers in search of glory and promotion and some were civilian administrators in search of fame and career advancement. Irrespective of where the British officers found themselves, they were the first evidence that an indigenous nation had lost its independence, that kings and chiefs now had supervisors giving them instructions and commands. While they were still at a higher level than their subjects, kings and chiefs experienced a loss in personal dignity. Those unwilling to cooperate with the new officers might be humiliated and insulted; some arrogant officers slapped local chiefs when they did not comply with orders. One of the most notorious pioneer officers was Harold Morday Douglas, a high-handed and tempestuous man who acquired a negative reputation in eastern Nigeria; he flogged chiefs and ridiculed them in public and intimidated ordinary people.[22] Douglas was so overbearing that he became a subject of discussion in the press and local churches, while the governor had to reprimand him. Douglas probably was an extreme example of a colonial administrator. However, the goal for all of them was the same: colonial subjects had to respect the new colonial institutions and obey the officers appointed to run them. Respect had to be visible and symbolic: in the ways that officers were addressed and greeted and the speed at which their instructions were to be carried out. Policies, even bad policies regarding forced labor and taxation, had to be obeyed. Traditional chiefs had to accept the new political system, which could impose tasks upon them or remove them and confirm the appointment of new chiefs. A new set of laws was gradually enacted, and these, too, had to be obeyed.

The Kwale rising revealed yet another dimension of the process of political disempowerment. Court messengers and clerks appointed by the British were not just carrying out the administrative tasks assigned to them but were also playing the role of chiefs in areas that were not traditionally used to the idea of kingship. These new bureaucrats, who were not even Kwale men, behaved as if they had the right to replace elders and community leaders. With the colonial army and police behind them, the clerks and agents acted in ways that antagonized or alienated the people. When the people were pushed to the wall, they directed their initial attack against the clerks and agents. The goal was not just to kill the agents and clerks but to change the political system altogether. To those involved in the violence, getting rid of the agents and clerks was like getting rid of those who had put them in power, and participants in the attacks spoke and behaved as if the era of the British would end in 1914.[23]

The political background was racist, and this inevitably contributed to tension. "The African may condone individual cruelty or injustice," warned one British officer in 1929, "he may put up with what appears to him oppressive laws and taxation, for he is good-hearted and bears no malice, but racial prejudice hurts his sensitivities, rancours in his heart, and becomes the root source of all sedition. Therefore let us eradicate the evil from amongst ourselves. It avails us nothing."[24] The officer assumed that racism could be divorced from colonial practices and violence, when it was embedded in them. Only racist arrogance could permit British officers to insult people and flog them. British colonizers linked racism and violence in one ideology that they used to attain the specific objectives of political domination and economic exploitation. Indeed, officers admitted that flogging and using violent words were endemic, but some attributed that to sadism, loneliness, and personal weaknesses. Individual officers did have their own styles and idiosyncrasies, but it is a fact that most officers had only contempt for Africans. "The only way to correct black people was to flog them," pronounced the chief justice of Nigeria in 1908.[25] This statement reflected a widespread belief among colonial officers. The premise was that Africans could not develop their land and resources to generate progress, that it was the task of "civilized people" to do it for them, and that doing it for them entailed the use of violence in word and deed. Many officers regarded Africans as children who had to be lectured and flogged to get the best out of them and enable them to mature quickly. This combination turned the exercise of power into an activity organized along color lines: white domination, black subjects.

The use of force was necessary to back up the colonial political system. Military power had to be visible to prevent the people from challenging the chiefs, kings, and colonial agents the British had put into place. A military presence was also necessary to prevent challenges to the police. Force was also required to spread the authority of the colonial state beyond its original centers. The common practice was to establish headquarters in a town that could be dominated. The outlying villages and towns were then incorporated in what were known as wars of "pacification." Military operations, described as "patrols," were conducted to display the presence of military might. In eastern Nigeria, military operations lasted until the period of the First World War in which British soldiers attacked villages, destroyed oracles, and forced local leaders to accept the new colonial authority.[26]

Nigerian resentment and hostility translated into protests. Some protests were expressed as refusing to obey official orders, failing to cooperate when labor was needed, avoiding government officials as much as possible, refusing to take legal matters before the native courts, failing to carry loads for colonial officers, or not showing up for road construction. Until about 1920, many older nations and their leaders hoped that the past could be reborn and the independence they had lost to the conquest could be re-created. This helps explain the attacks on the agents of the new order, the closure of roads, and the exercise of power by collecting tolls from traders passing through the area in a way that threatened the free trade the colonial government was promoting.

Violent protest was not uncommon. Public property was destroyed. Some of those who worked for the colonial administration were killed by those who felt a sense of outrage and injustice. In several instances, colonial agents were beaten up or insulted by members of the public who took the law into their own hands to exact revenge. In the early years of colonial rule, some local leaders ordered people not to cooperate with the government and to beat and drive away police and court messengers.[27]

Nigerians who used violence had multiple goals. Where violence was directed at major officers and establishments, it involved some belief that lost power could be regained, that the old chiefs and kings could return to power. It took some years for a number of groups and their leaders to accept that their sovereignty was lost for good. But there was also the belief that violence was necessary in order to negotiate with the new order, a use of force to seek accommodation. But individuals did not necessarily engage in violence on behalf of the traditional elite; they often did so to protest new policies or call for an end to the excesses of colonial officers.

Violence begets violence. The colonial government had its police and army and various laws and orders. Arrests, revenge, and other punishments were not uncommon. The British used military patrols to keep reminding the chiefs and kings that their power was gone. When the British were establishing the administration in the period 1885–1914, they attacked some areas for protesting against or assaulting the agents of the state. For example, when the people of Norie and Ngor in eastern Nigeria killed their chief for carrying out the orders of the government and assaulted another agent, the colonial army marched on them in 1905.[28] The war lasted over a week, bringing heavy casualties on both sides. The government troops used excessive force in order to raise the prestige of the colonial government among the Igbo.[29]

The colonial government justified its use of violence to enforce its decisions or punish individuals and groups who disobeyed instructions by its need to prevent chaos and the breakdown of law and order and the need to coerce colonial subjects into complying with new regulations. Colonial wars in the early years were fought to check resistance as well as punish the people for intransigence.

One well-documented case was the 1905 military expedition against the Ahiara, an Igbo group.[30] The Ahiara began their protest against policies that demanded their labor to build roads and serve as carriers, both of which took able-bodied men away from their regular jobs and families. The Ahiara showed their hostility to the colonial government by blocking their roads against the representatives of the government. Then in November 1905, Dr. Stewart, a medical officer working for the Southern Nigeria Expeditionary Force, was murdered. His death shocked the colonial establishment in Nigeria and Britain, where it was described in gory terms and as cannibalism: "His body was cut up into small pieces and distributed by way of fetish, with the idea that those eating a portion would be protected from harm by any white man and be released from his domination."[31] The government decided not only to investigate the murder but to unleash violence on the people for almost four months. A clear instruction to the district officer of the area asked him to exact the maximum punishment for the crime. A military expedition began on December 7, but when it met with stiff resistance, the colonial army responded with a surprise attack on Ahiara on December 13. Farms and houses were destroyed and the people abandoned the town, running away to the north. As the army pursued them, their hosts and neighbors were also forced to flee. The Igbo eventually lost and were forced to surrender about 17,000 guns, open all the roads for easy passage, and accept the leadership of a headman who was supportive of the colonial government.

The success of the expedition led to a display of power and arrogance. The government decided to show its force and presence; the divisional officer not only visited towns and villages but appointed chiefs (headmen) to govern them. The headmen were paid agents and political upstarts, and their loyalty was not to the people but to the government.[32] Unlike the rebellious elders, the new headmen had to carry out the government's instructions, especially those relating to labor recruitment and road construction. The British also established native courts to interpret the laws in ways that were favorable to the government.

Many attacks were directed at Nigerians who worked for the colonial service and native authorities; such attacks took place over the entire period of colonial history. A clear pattern emerged: an angry person or group would insult or physically attack an agent, the police would be informed, and punishment would follow. A few examples from a wide span of time should suffice. In January 1930, a group of villagers at Mbiafun Ikot Abassi in Ikot Ekpene District (Calabar Province) prevented a court messenger from the Ikono Native Court from issuing a summons to one of them. Villagers assaulted and wounded the messenger and his agent.[33] As soon as the colonial officer in charge heard of this, he sent a platoon of the Third Battalion Nigerian Regiment to the village. The force was too large for such a small offense, and the point was clear: the villagers had invited a war by attacking the agent. The officer also imposed a fine of 1 shilling 9 pence per adult male, a heavy burden for a poor community. A military officer assembled the chiefs and elders of the village on January 31 and reprimanded them for "their deliberate mass obstruction of the course of justice, necessitating the bringing of soldiers to their village" and were told of the new fine.[34]

To the community, it was one tragedy piled on another: one of them had been wrongly accused of an offense; an army had been sent to them, a case of killing an ant with a gun; and now they had to pay compulsory fines. But the district officer (DO) was not ready to lay the issue to rest: the village chiefs were ordered to look for the man that the court clerk originally wanted to arrest, all the ringleaders that had assaulted the clerk and his agent, and a man who had refused to pay tax. When the news reached the village, many chose to flee, fearing the indiscriminate arrest of innocent people. The DO insisted that the chiefs look for the accused, even if it meant combing the countryside. The chiefs, perhaps playing politics, reported back that they had found no one. The Nigerian agents of the government went to the village, threatening to confiscate the chiefs' yams and livestock. However, when they reached the village they found neither people nor food, suggesting that many people probably viewed their relocation as long term or even permanent. A Nigerian agent provided an update on the event in a way that revealed the excesses of the government:

The following morning I was sent out with nine other men under a Court Messenger to find yams. We were about to enter into a certain place where there was a yam stock, quite close to the camp, when I saw a certain man of Mbiafun Ikot Abassi, called Akpan Iyang, with a gun, about as far as that tree away (indicates a distance of about 25 yards). He said "Is it against me only that the white man comes?" He called to his companions "It is only Mbiabong carriers, without the white man; let us come out." They were threatening, and we ran away. There were about eight men with him with matchet and sticks. So we ran back to camp and reported, and the D.O. went out with some soldiers. When we got there with the D.O. the men had run away, and the D.O. ordered the place where the men had opposed us to be burnt.[35]

The British strategy of seizing the people's yams was a way of forcing them to surrender, as they would be denied food and seed yams for the next season. In addition, the government needed the yams to feed the soldiers it had brought and to "[liquidate] any fine that might be inflicted."[36] Weeks later, when some villagers began to return, the DO insisted that they produce the "offenders" among them. He asked the adult male population of 230 to pay a fine of 21 pounds within a few days and forced them to supply rations for his troops and carriers, laborers to build a road and bridge to the village, and a rest house for government officials. As far as the DO was concerned, the episode closed with a happy ending:

It is not desirable to reduce the village to a condition of poverty, but to bring its extremely backward and primitive inhabitants more into harmony with present conditions. This result I hope will be attained now that a rest house has been built there and a road constructed to join up the village with the road system of the Division.

This DO justified his use of violence and his draconian measures as a way to create "harmony with present conditions." The "rest house" became a place from which British officers could keep an eye on the poor villagers, who were very angry and resentful. Since troops had been used, a report had to be sent to the governor in Lagos. In summarizing the matter, the secretary of the Southern Provinces expressed his belief that the people of Mbiafun Ikot Abassi had capitalized on the "general atmosphere of unrest," and while he admitted that there was no evidence to confirm the incidents reported by the colonial staff, "there was a general attitude in the town of defiance of authority as represented by the Native Court and its emissaries and . . . the introduction of troops was essential."[37]

Where powerful oracles had energized the people, the government responded with violence, destroying the oracles and their priests. In parts of the east, some oracles, such as the powerful Ogbonorie oracle at Ezumoha in Okigwe Division, had served as meeting points for a large group of people who believed that the oracles protected the lives of innocents, destroyed evil people, and could aid them against the British. A punitive expedition by the colonial army directed at destroying the Ogbunorie oracle in 1910 proved to be far more difficult than the British anticipated. While the number of opponents was no larger than had been expected, many villages were already deserted by the time the army arrived. The army attacked the areas surrounding the oracle for over a month, destroying many houses and killing many people. It also destroyed the oracle itself, together with the objects associated with the shrine, such as trees, skulls, and crocodiles.[38]

While some Nigerians used traditional religion as a way to express resistance, other used the new religion of Christianity to the same end. In the Niger Delta in 1916, the threat to the government came from the least expected quarter: the religious-cum-political movement led by Garrick Sokari Braide, a member of the Church Missionary Society (CMS) in the town of New Calabar. Braide began his resistance in a conservative religious mode and various CMS leaders saw him as a gentle and passionate individual. But his belief systems and actions frightened the British.

His message took on a radical tone when he began to see himself as a sort of prophet. Renaming himself as Elijah II, he spread the belief that blacks would soon acquire power from whites. He was a tireless worker and missionary, able to preach to and convert thousands. His faith healing practices, based on the Bible and some traditional practices, attracted many people and his fame spread very rapidly. There were nonreligious elements to Braide's appeal. During the First World War, the economic downturn, especially in the palm oil business, made Braide's message resonate among the poor.

To the colonial government, Braide's message was nothing short of subversion. Attracting considerable attention in 1916, a time of insecurity and rumors of the fragility of the colonial system, his message and his personality were inimical to the activities of the government. He was accused of damaging trade, preventing trade in valuable ivories, and instigating rebellion. His opposition to alcohol was seen as an attack on the lucrative liquor trade. European traders eager for profit saw him as an enemy who could destroy their opportunities and markets. Colonial officers began to believe that Braide's message was dangerous. Even some Nigerians believed that Braide might use his popularity and teachings to lead others into "paths which are inimical to good government."[39] He was described as a "black Mahdist," a negative label that combined the idea of radical preaching with the concept of violence carried out with zeal. If he was not destroyed, many officers warned in fiery language, the fanatic would bring the empire either to its knees or to its end. Some members of the Nigerian elite agreed, seeing Braide as the leader of a cult who would destroy the emotions of "native minds," turning them into dangerous elements. Elijah should be crushed before he became too strong, warned the *African Mail* in 1916.[40]

Braide did not conceal his goal of linking religion and politics as he advocated the independence of the Niger Delta people. He believed that the Germans and the British would destroy themselves in the First World War, thus paving the way for blacks to emerge as leaders. Threatened colonial authorities charged Braide with collecting money on false pretenses, and in 1916, they arrested, tried, and jailed him. He died two years later. Although the colonial government continued to be suspicious of them, fringe and small churches proliferated in later years and contributed to the development of Nigerian nationalism.

AGENCIES OF CONTROL AND VIOLENCE

The judiciary, police, and prisons suffered many unexpected attacks. These attacks were not coordinated by specific interest groups but were made by individuals throughout the colonial period. The historiography of the period does not yet cover ordinary people and their engagement with the colonial order. While a separate study of the scattered nature of resistance will be necessary, a preliminary attempt is made here.

The police were created primarily to maintain order. Police forces continued to expand, and officers were recruited and police posts were established in all towns and cities. The link between the police and maintaining colonial order was clearly defined from the beginning of colonial rule.[41] The regulations enacted to facilitate the work of the police included laws dealing with the use of nongovernment vehicles for emergency purposes,[42] the arrest of suspicious people, and the immediate punishment of offenders in certain cases.

However, police, soldiers, and other colonial agents routinely went beyond the stipulated rules. They and the uniforms that came with them were symbols of terror. Since the police could "redefine" laws and regulations to suit their whims, the people were generally afraid of them. The involvement of the police in illegal violent acts is a negative comment on the nature of the colonial rule in Nigeria, a situation in which political officers were not always able to control the police and soldiers. When the people tired of these excesses, they composed insulting songs and jokes to ridicule the police and soldiers. There were countless cases in which police and soldiers stole goods from traders and hawkers. Sometimes this led to physical confrontations, as it did in October 1943 at the Aba market, where soldiers who refused to pay for expensive imported items they had helped themselves to such as velvets, silks, earthenware, and foodstuffs were attacked by angry traders.[43] A similar incident occurred in 1943 at Jattu market in Auchi Division, where a soldier tried to steal yams from the trader, "kicking the owner, a pregnant woman in the stomach, and hitting her husband in the mouth."[44] Not long after this, about 200 soldiers descended on the market to create trouble. Soldiers also drank at local bars without paying, thereby creating the conditions for public fights. The police abused the law, taking on the role of judges and whipping people. While elaborate regulations were set in place to punish soldiers and police, they were not always applied to the satisfaction of the public.

The police and soldiers clashed with each other in public to demonstrate their power and show their frustration. Although the law mandated that police arrest erring soldiers, such as those who assaulted market women, soldiers would always protest against such arrests. Some clashes between police and soldiers, called "affrays" in official documents, led to death and injuries. The government sanctioned the humiliation of public whipping of unruly soldiers and police as a warning to others.

Many attacks were directed against the police. In the colonial records, the police were always right; most attacks on them were recorded as happening in the course of duty. The reports portrayed the attackers as criminals, vagabonds, and dangerous elements who wanted to resist arrest. While there is truth to this presentation, there is another side. The official records hint at rebellion; in these incidents, people not only questioned the laws but challenged the authority of those who arrested them.

The aforementioned points can be illustrated with some evidence, albeit of a scattered nature, drawn from different parts of the country. On August 27, 1936, four police constables were attacked at Ntek Ibesit, a village in the Ikot Oboro Native Court Area of Abak District in Calabar Province. According to the police record, the four constables had gone to the house of prominent businessman Job Akpan Udo to execute a search warrant.[45] Udo had been accused by his enemies of being a "coiner," a counterfeiter. At the house of Udo and his brother, the police found a machine for counterfeiting coins as well as locally distilled gin, which was considered illegal. The police arrested, handcuffed, and detained Udo and his brother. The police remained in the village for some hours. When they decided to leave, "a crowd collected and assaulted them, releasing the prisoners

and taking away all the exhibits except 22 counterfeit coins and the bot-
tle of illicitly distilled liquor."[46] When the report reached the assistant district officer, he immediately authorized a noncommissioned officer and
twelve armed constables to go to the village. Presumably anticipating this,
the people had deserted the village before the government forces arrived.
For days, the police stayed in the area, combing villages and farms, until
they had arrested about forty-seven people, although they did not find
Udo or his brother. As in other cases, innocent persons were arrested for
crimes they did not commit. Interrogations followed, with the usual police
arrogance.

On February 2, 1938, at Uyo, also in Calabar Province, a small problem
involving a policeman turned into violence, as happened so often. A police
constable who was on motor traffic and point duty tried to arrest two men
who were involved in a collision. Both resisted arrest for reasons not stated
in the official records and were joined by other men in and around the market in hustling the policeman, who later alleged that he had been assaulted.
When word of this reached the Uyo Police Station, a corporal and twelve
policemen were immediately sent to the market. When they reached the
market, the police arrested twenty-six people. They accused sixteen of this
group of taking part in the incident and charged them with obstruction
and released the others. The official records fail to indicate how guilt was
determined and how the culprits were identified. That the public had a different interpretation of the case from that of the authorities became clear
on February 3, when many chiefs and people went to the DO to complain
of police violence. At a public meeting three days later, the native court was
packed full of people who complained about police brutality and "whole-
sale arrests of innocent stall holders."[47] Feeling in Uyo and its villages was
now running high, and many used the opportunity to criticize the police
and other government agents for arming themselves with whips and beating innocent people in the marketplace. Some elders met and decided to
stop everyone from attending the market until the issue had been investigated, which suggests that something was wrong with the way the police
had reported the incident to their officers and the DO.

To prevent widespread disorder, the DO launched his own investigation
and concluded that the policeman involved was responsible for the crisis,
that he had become involved in what should not have been of concern to
him, and that he had acted in "a most high-handed manner as a result of
which the obstruction and assault occurred." The DO also noted that the
corporal and the twelve policemen who arrived later had used unnecessary
violence in a high-handed manner. Having blamed the police, one would

have thought that the DO would now take the side of the people. As the colonial dictates suggest, however, the people to punish were not the police but the Uyo who had become involved, even as peacemakers:

> But the fact remains that the constable had arrested two individuals, that he was obstructed and assaulted and therefore a criminal case must lie against those responsible for the obstruction and assault. The action of the local chiefs in preventing people from attending Uyo market is mainly directed against the police and Government employees in Uyo station (who will find it difficult to buy foodstuffs), as a mark of their displeasure over the incident. This action is, I contend, not only an abuse of their position, but calculated to foment further unrest.[48]

The DO decided to post police on the roads leading to the market in order to prevent any incoming traders from being stopped by the chiefs, and he summoned a meeting of the chiefs to make them "see the error of their ways." In spite of these actions, "a certain state of tension" continued between the local people and government employees. The DO was pressed by his superiors to investigate the police, and he concluded in a report in April that "no unnecessary violence in connection with the disturbance has been proved against the police." Rather than improve upon relations between the public and the police, the government tried seventeen people for the criminal offence of assaulting, resisting, or willfully obstructing a police officer in the execution of his duty. Four were acquitted and the others received sentences of one year each; five of them also received twelve strokes of the whip. The chiefs and other elders of Uyo were enraged, and they encouraged all those sentenced to appeal. On appeal to the High Court, the convictions of seven of the accused were upheld. The people of Uyo resigned themselves to their fate, blaming the police and the DO for punishing innocent people.

There are few studies of Nigerian prisons, and the connection between anticolonial protests and the behavior of prisoners is yet to be made. As in the case of the police, the evidence of violence in prisons is scattered, and a few cases are presented here merely to indicate the nature of the protests and the way the government handled them. We do know that whether people were jailed for offenses they had committed or merely as a punishment for taking part in riots or attacking agents of the government, they continued to engage in violent protests in prisons. On May 16, 1933, eighty prisoners rioted at the Enugu prison and the police had to be called to suppress them. Although the police attributed the riots to the activities of a few "hardened criminals," an official enquiry by the resident of Onitsha suggested additional reasons. Some prisoners resented the police and prison staff. Some did not believe they should be in prison to start with. The majority involved in the Enugu case resented the way the prison wardens searched them for prohibited items. They also complained about bad food, cuts in rations as a punishment, and merciless beating by prison wardens.[49]

Violence was rampant in prisons. As far as the colonial authorities were concerned, the solution was to build more prisons in order to separate hardened criminals from those who had committed less serious offenses and to use staff members and officers who were able to cope with violent behavior. Authorities typically dismissed reviews of prisoner complaints and instead attempted to counter violence with greater discipline. The director of prisons in the southern provinces summarized the problem as he understood it in 1933:

> Convicts do not work sufficiently hard nor are their hours of work long enough. The recidivist is invariably lazy. If he was not, there would be hope of his not relapsing back into crime so frequently. In Nigeria he may be seen in the gangs as the cleanest convict and his one hope is that a rake is the heaviest tool he is called upon to wield. If he was compelled to work longer and the work was of a heavy nature I am convinced that he might think twice before risking further imprisonment. This would be especially so if he was taken in hand before he had served too many sentences.[50]

Thus, the reformative aspect of prison life was unimportant; prisoners were to be exploited for their labor. As prison conditions deteriorated, the behavior of prisoners became aggressive and they seized the opportunity to riot. Many were charged with rioting, conspiracy to riot, compulsion by assault, resisting public officers, and assault to others occasioning harm. Those found guilty had additional years added to their terms. There were many small-scale riots and violent acts in prisons, some to relieve pent-up grievances, some directed at prison staff, and a host of others related to prison conditions.[51] The police were usually drafted to use force to suppress riots, using tear gas and clubs and the threat that they would shoot to kill. Sometimes the police encountered organized violence from prisoners armed with stones, sticks, and machetes.[52] The police would eventually win and additional changes in prison policies would be made in order to deprive prisoners of the opportunity to create weapons.

Prisoners reacted violently to all these changes; many found secret locations in prison compounds to hide weapons, stones, coal, and wood fuel.

"Crimes of violence," an official label for various riotous acts, commonly appeared in the files of prisoners. This is a comment on the nature of the colonial state and its focus on maintaining law and order.

The use of force and of coercive instruments of state power to consolidate colonial regimes did not put an end to violent reactions. Some specific policies generated crises, and people reacted against demands for labor and products. A major cause of violence in Nigeria was the introduction of taxation, in part an aspect of indirect rule, to which we turn in chapter 4.

4

TAXATION AND
CONFLICTS

Violence and protests were part of the anti-tax resistance of the colonial era. Some cases of anti-tax violence took on the characteristics of what the official records called "wars" because of their intensity. Some were small-scale violent protests that required police action to end them or to prevent greater anti-tax violence in other places. Notable cases of anti-tax violence included the Iseyin-Okeiho riots of 1916, the Egba rebellion of 1918, the widespread riots in Owerri Province in 1927–1928, and the Women's War of 1929. Some of these revolts were caused by the novelty of taxation (especially in southern Nigeria), and some were caused by the incidence and rate of taxation. Anti-tax protests could also be part of broader anticolonial resistance, as in the examples just mentioned and in other forms of reaction to the imposition of taxation in other parts of Africa.[1] The chapter examines why taxation generated intense hostilities in some areas and discusses the nature and consequences of violent resistance to taxation. The women's anti-tax war of 1929 receives separate treatment in chapter 5 because of its uniqueness, scale, and consequences.

The collection of taxes brought the colonial government to the grass roots as part of the indirect rule system of local government.[2] Taxation was a demonstration of colonial power and domination, the extension of power to all the nooks and crannies of the country. The Native Revenue Proclamation enacted in Northern Nigeria in 1906 allowed local populations to be directly taxed. The British appointed emirs and gave them instructions on how to exercise power, collect revenues, and spend revenues. Part of the bargain that gave chiefs and kings the power to continue to govern their people was that they should use this power to collect taxes. To reward them for their services, chiefs and kings were allowed to keep part of the tax they collected as salaries.

Incorporating chiefs and kings into the colonial administration was part of the gradual creation of a native treasury system, which was later appended to indirect rule. The principle of the native treasury was simple: a local authority should generate the funds to govern itself so that any dependence on central authorities would be minimal. If a local authority was able to collect money, it could offer a "civilized administration," which the British defined as the ability to build roads and courthouses, pay its staff, and spend on security matters. The native treasury involved local chiefs in the direct collection of taxes; the goal was to teach them "to feel that they occupy a position of responsibility."[3] This position of responsibility was to get many of them into trouble, setting them against their people and costing them their lives. The positions of "power and trust" they occupied were no more than a device to turn the local power elite into subservient agents of the colonial government.

The first phase of this process of creating a new system of government lasted from 1891 until about 1912. Because wars of conquest were still ongoing during this period, the British considered the use of force to be part of routine government activities. When they captured villages and towns, they appointed men among them as "chiefs." While some of these chiefs were respected elders, some were mere upstarts and nonentities. When a man was appointed a chief, the British gave him a certificate, called a "warrant," thus assigning the title of "warrant chief" to him and legitimizing his power. Below the warrant chiefs was a category of "minor chiefs," or "headmen," who represented the government and the warrant chiefs in villages and wards. The warrant chiefs were new men: their power was not rooted in traditional institutions and they were not respected among their own people. When the government wanted another warrant chief, they could choose from among the headmen and minor chiefs, thus making them "warrant chiefs in waiting."

The British also instituted a native court system; each native court was comprised of all the warrant chiefs in a division or district. More of a native authority than a court, a native court had a staff of court clerks and messengers that was assisted by the police. As its name suggested, it performed judicial functions. In addition, it served as the seat of local government and had executive and bureaucratic power. There were also minor courts, native courts located in areas away from the district headquarters that were constituted for a period of three months each year under the leadership of a local chief. At the district headquarters, the native court was known as the native council, which had power over the minor courts. One of the goals of taxation was to create a stable source of funding for each local authority. It was from this fund that the chiefs and staff members were paid.

From the very beginning, the colonial government and the people perceived this political structure differently. In the eyes of the government, it was a great experiment in managing "primitive" people at little cost. The arrangement created distance between local people and the white officers who played the supervisory role and gave instructions, an advantage to the British officers because the people might well be angry with them. Distance was important to the British for another reason; they believed that a strategy of distancing was crucial to maintaining an image of white officers as powerful and superior to the colonial subjects. While this system worked to the advantage of the British, it was much resented by the local people. They saw warrant chiefs and the courts as symbols of oppression and exploitation. In the view of the majority of the population, the warrant chiefs had too much power; the clerks and messengers in government uniforms were also too powerful for the people to tolerate. They associated them with trouble: the clerks translated Igbo into English and vice versa, turning modest control of languages into maximum power, and the messengers took summonses, legal documents that brought bad news, to people's homes.

TAXATION AND ITS PROBLEMS

The introduction of a new form of taxation began in Northern Nigeria with the Native Revenue Proclamation, promulgated in 1906 as part of a set of measures designed to cover various aspects of local administration. Although the south could survive on indirect taxation based on customs duties collected from merchants who used southern ports for their import-export trade, the north did not have this advantage; it was landlocked and unable to generate much from indirect tax. That the new colony of Nigeria must generate the resources to govern itself was an established policy. Where to raise the money from and how were the important issues. The Native Revenue Proclamation laid the basis for tax collection in the country. In determining what an individual should pay, the British calculated the gross income of a village based on a crude determination of harvests, prices in produce markets, and the value of livestock. Colonial taxation was thus a revision of an established poll tax system that calculated the material assets of an area by levying taxes on its residents. In the new taxation system, the rich farmer and the poor farmer would pay the same amount, an unfair burden on the landless and those lacking the means to pay. Taxation was not just about raising revenues but also about finding a devious way to ensure that millions of poor farmers would be forced to produce and sell to obtain the cash they needed to pay the tax.

There was a basis in tradition for the new system, since the Islamic caliphate had built a successful revenue system partly on direct taxation. The colonial government made the economic and political gains clear to northern kings and chiefs: they were paid from the revenues they generated and they had some power to determine expenditures. At the same time, there was a deep history of hostility to taxation in the north. Indeed, one of the reasons for the jihad and the establishment of the caliphate by Uthman dan Fodio in the first two decades of the nineteenth century was excessive taxation on land and cattle that had created social discontent among the people. As the caliphate consolidated itself, however, it returned to the excesses of the past that its leaders had criticized. As the jihad spread to non-Islamic areas, it manifested its brutality in excessive taxation and the high-handedness of tax collectors. Political leaders established an army that forcefully collected levies and taxes. Tax collectors, who were known by different names in different places, were located in various parts of an emirate to collect grain, cash, and cattle. Protests were not uncommon—anti-tax riots were expressions of anticolonial resistance in many places, notably the southern parts of the caliphate. The communities such as the Akoko that voluntarily surrendered to the jihadist armies were asked to pay "peace taxes," a way of buying freedom with their money and products.[4] Taxes were also collected in slaves, which entailed small-scale raiding expeditions against weak neighbors. So deep was the memory of taxation and its excesses that the new form of taxation the British introduced met with instant hostility in various Islamic areas.

In spite of suggestions that taxation would be difficult to implement, Lugard was forceful in proposing and implementing the idea. "Without a tax," Lugard insisted, "there can be no Treasury and without a Treasury no real eventual measure of self rule."[5] Not only would the central government be free from the burden of funding the native authorities, but a percentage of the tax collected would also make its way back to the center, thus ensuring that Nigeria would be able to run on its own without any support from Britain. Lugard also connected taxation with able leadership and the ability of Nigerian leaders to manage affairs with efficiency:

The greatest value of a system of direct taxation is that it ensures the selection of the most capable and most influential men as the chiefs and advisers and invests them with authority and responsibility. Both in the assessment, collection and disposal of this revenue they become part of the Government of the country and incompetence or dishonesty is soon exposed. With the advent of competent and responsible native rulers, discipline and good order are introduced.[6]

Some who paid the taxes did not see any of these merits of taxation; they pointed to greedy tax collectors who abused their power and insulted the people. Even when it was obvious that abuses were a common part of tax collection and spending, especially in the north, Lugard was unshaken in his belief that taxation and the native treasury were necessary to produce good leaders and an efficient local government. The British also exaggerated the power the chiefs were supposed to exercise regarding taxes. Not all the chiefs had the opportunity to participate in discussions of how revenues were disbursed, and European colonial officers did not always give up their power to supervise budgets.

British authorities interpreted the power to collect taxes as a test of imperial success. Tax payment was "the keynote of the political situation," declared the lieutenant governor of the north in 1917. He added that "no native tribe, I am convinced, really appreciates that it is under control until the people pay taxes: so long as the people can evade taxes, they are under the impression that they have been able to resist conquest successfully."[7]

The problems with taxation escalated when it was extended to the south, especially in areas that lacked the elaborate collection system associated with the caliphate. Although the Yoruba and groups in Benin paid levies and tribute to chiefs and kings who had established successful central authorities over villages and cities,[8] the British badly miscalculated that these kings and chiefs in the south had powers similar to those of the Islamic caliphate in the north. This ignorance was very costly when they introduced direct taxation in native administrations in the south and east as the key component of administrative revenue during the First World War and into the mid-1920s.

Introducing taxation in the south did not progress as smoothly as it had in the north. Resistance to taxation was so strong there that it was almost a decade before the policy was fully implemented. During the First World War, when Lugard requested the permission of the Colonial Office to introduce the Native Revenue Ordinance in the south, he was warned that unrest could follow.[9] Nevertheless, he persisted and finally obtained permission to introduce taxation in areas where he thought there would be no disturbances, where the kings and chiefs would readily cooperate, and where the people were already accustomed to paying fees and levies to traditional authorities. Protests in the areas of the north bordering the south, where the people were paying taxes and complaining that their southern neighbors were not, provided an additional reason to impose taxation all over the country.

Lugard introduced his taxation policy among the Yoruba in 1916 and 1917. The people resisted immediately. Small protests and riots broke out in a number of provinces, culminating in the Adubi War of 1918. Many communities failed to pay taxes. In some areas, the anti-British sentiments of the war years found expression in anti-tax protests. "Every tribe was in a state of unrest," declared a political officer in the south in 1914. "Songs were sung against the Administration and the majority of the tribes were firmly convinced that our occupation of their country was coming to an end."[10] Officers toured many districts, accompanied by the police or soldiers, threatening to use force if people refused to pay their taxes. In areas such as Kabba Province, soldiers and police had to supervise tax collection, lending their forces of coercion to the power of the chiefs. It was two years in many areas before many decided to pay, although their resentment was not over.

In spite of the hostility to taxation among the Yoruba and Benin people, Lugard explored the possibility of introducing taxation in the eastern provinces. The residents of the region were unanimous in criticizing the extension of the policy to areas where the people did not have institutions of strong kingship and centralized authorities and where the idea of direct taxation was totally new. Thus, for many years, Warri Province and areas in east of the Niger were exempted from taxation.

The idea of collecting taxes in the southeast was thus postponed for some years. But by 1926, some officers were calling on the Colonial Office to extend the policy of taxation to every part of the country. In a major report of that year, W. G. A. Ormsby-Gore, the British under-secretary of state for the colonies, made a strong statement in support of taxation after touring the colonies:

> I cannot over-emphasize the importance of the part played by the existence of Native Treasuries with clearly defined sources of revenue. Without such treasuries, chieftaincies cannot be adequately maintained, and in the absence of such[,] part of the native chiefs will be encouraged. . . . It is a matter for early consideration whether direct taxation should not be introduced into the remaining provinces composing the Southern Provinces of Nigeria. . . . The absence of organised native administrations with local revenues in Southern Nigeria is one of the factors accounting for the less developed state of these Provinces compared with the rest of the country.[11]

The colonial authorities sent junior officers from the east to the north to see how the system worked in practice. The assumption was that indirect rule was working well and that the people were better governed under indirect rule than they had been before. Those in the east, argued a number of senior officers, could not be part of the new march of civilization without direct taxation. Neither could they be educated "in the art of self-government unless funds to establish Native Administrations were forthcoming in the shape of direct taxation."[12] The hands of British officials who were opposed to taxation were tied by a more persuasive argument for extending the same policy to the entire country. "It was a matter of equity," argued the government, "that when the far greater proportion of the people of Nigeria were paying direct tax the remainder should not be immune."[13]

In 1927, the British revised the Native Revenue Ordinance to cover the southeastern provinces. A year later, and without consulting the chiefs or their people, they introduced direct taxation there. It was immediately met with numerous small-scale protests. (The larger-scale Women's War of 1929 is analyzed separately in chapter 5.)

Across Nigeria, whether the riots were large or small, the causes were similar. First, the poor saw taxation as a burden; this group included the farmers who constituted the majority of the population and various others. In northern and central Nigeria, where kings had extracted too much in tax from poor farmers, there was a deep history of resentment against taxation. Fief holders in some places had been notorious for sending their private armies to forcefully collect taxes from poor peasants, seizing goods, livestock, and cash. It was easy to see the colonial government as another "fief holder" that was taking goods and cash by force. Both in the nineteenth century and in the colonial period, many wondered what governments did with the taxes they collected.

Second, the connection between taxation and good government was not always established. The collection of taxes and establishment of native treasuries did not automatically produce educated and enlightened chiefs. Instead, taxation was one of the reasons that people mistrusted all agents of the government. The people did not necessarily see the chiefs and native authorities as friends or allies in the development process. In the east, taxation made it harder for warrant chiefs to obtain the support of the people they were meant to govern. As Adiele Afigbo has noted, the warrant chiefs became extremely unpopular for imposing taxation on their own people, for collecting unjust taxes, and for abusing their offices.[14]

In the southeast, unlike the situation in the north and among the Yoruba and Benin in the south, it was not clear who had the power to collect taxes.

The government knew that the challenge in that region was how to collect taxes from those who regarded taxation as a burden or an injustice. Indirect rule had made possible the use of kings and chiefs, working with their staffs, as tax collectors in the north and the south. However, in the eastern part of the country, there were no chiefs and kings with power similar to those of the Yoruba *obas* and the northern emirs. In the early years of British rule in the east, warrant chiefs had replaced the titled men and elders who exercised authority over villages and towns. For a few years, the British appointed warrant chiefs after consultations with village elders. However, by the 1920s, the warrant chiefs had acquired power that did not come from their own people and constituted a bureaucracy instead of a traditional chieftaincy; they even promoted each other and filled vacancies among themselves.

The warrant chiefs redefined the concept of power at the local level, not just because of the nature of their appointment (by outsiders—that is, the British colonialists) but because of the way they exercised their power. While the elders in the pre-British days had acted as "democrats," recognizing that power had been delegated to them by the people, the warrant chiefs acted more like autocrats because power was granted to them by the British without the sanctions derived from local cultures. Warrant chiefs were neither the voices of the people nor the voices of gods; they were accountable only to the colonial officers who appointed them. In other words, the warrant chiefs were "rulers" rather than delegates to the village assembly of old. As the warrant chiefs concentrated power to themselves and exercised it in ways perceived to be both corrupt and excessive, they became intensely hated by the people. Many citizens described the combination of court messengers, court scribes, and warrant chiefs as "totally evil" and ruthless.[15] The British practice of using these three types of agents to collect tax from those who hated them was a major cause of violent protest.

The process of collecting taxes created additional problems. As people were never willing to pay, tax collectors acquired a negative image. The process discredited many chiefs because of their ruthlessness and brutality. Many junior agents involved in tax collecting behaved as if they had the power of the police to arrest and detain tax defaulters. Whether taxes were paid in products (as they were in many areas until 1920) or in cash (as they were for most of the colonial era), people complained that they were a considerable burden. Additional hostility emerged when the government increased tax rates when it calculated that the prosperity of the people had improved. When the government decided to increase taxes, a fact-finding team would itemize the average incomes of various occupations and the prices of goods. In order to spread the burden more fairly in a graduated capitation tax system, the government determined the assets of rich and poor farmers by the size of their lands and the type of crops they produced. (For example, palm and kola nut trees would mean higher taxes, since these products sold for better prices than yams and corn.) Farmers found it difficult to determine what they could realize after the harvest. As the chiefs were forced to announce the tax rate per adult, they became the enemies of their own people.

PRE-COLLECTION CRISES AND VIOLENCE

The story of the violence and protests associated with taxation can be divided roughly into two phases. In the first phase, and generally in the most serious cases, people resisted the attempt to impose taxation on them. In the second phase, after the government had used state power to enforce payment, the people resisted the collection of taxes and engaged in various complaints and forms of resistance against the agents who collected them. Direct taxation has always been a source of conflict between the government and the people, and direct taxes had to be abolished in various places after Nigeria became independent in 1960.

The first phase is better documented than the second in the official records. Anti-tax wars in this phase involved entire communities and the use of maximum force. In the second phase, many cases were largely undocumented because they involved individuals in acts of rebellion against the state. Spontaneous protests and riots followed the introduction of taxation in a number of areas. The Colonial Office and a number of local officers anticipated anti-tax riots during the First World War, but Lugard and his loyal associates dismissed these speculations. Lugard later blamed tax riots on the media and on educated southerners who did not wish his government well. However, investigations into the causes of the riots found no evidence of instigation by disgruntled members of the educated elite. Instead, the investigations found the causes of the riots to be resentment against taxation policies and against the changing role of chiefs in the new policy of indirect rule.

Where taxation was not part of the traditional economic system, its newness was a source of problems. Some wondered why aliens who came to their lands should ask them to pay taxes. Some were confused about the purposes of taxation. Among some Yoruba groups, the search for an appropriate name for taxation suggests the nature of the problem. Some called it *owo ipa* (a compulsory levy or money collected by force). To others, it was *owo opa* (a mandatory payment), a term linked to the fact that those in authority enforced the tax law, both in words and deeds. The most common name, *owo ori* (a per capita levy), referred to fixed rates per person. In many parts of the south, revenue was raised through the native courts and fines in the early years of colonization. The people were used to this kind of payment, but many resisted the direct taxation of later years because it was compulsory and because of the burdensome rate of taxation.

Two cases are presented here to illustrate the first phase: the Egba revolt of 1918, and the riots in Owerri Province in 1927–1928.

The Egba Revolt

Relations between the colonial government and the Egba capital of Abeokuta in the southwest had deteriorated long before 1918. There was a major violent outburst in 1914 over the use of forced labor and the boundaries of colonial power. While the Egba eagerly awaited the report of the commission set up to probe the causes of the 1914 revolt, another revolt broke out, this time a far larger protest against taxation. The imposition of direct taxation on adult males began on January 1, 1918; each adult was mandated to pay a minimum of five shillings. Many complained that the amount was too large, but they were ignored. Adegboyega Edun, the government secretary, insisted that it was impossible to reduce the amount in view of the needs of the city. During the war, the income of most people was reduced because of the depressed economy. Because those in the villages surrounding the city were also affected by the tax, they, too, complained that they did not produce enough to justify the amount being demanded.[16]

As the taxes were being imposed, the British were making far-reaching administrative changes, all in the name of bringing rapid "progress" to the people.[17] First, the power of the Ogboni chiefs, who for years had been in charge of judicial matters, was undermined in 1918 in favor of a new set of native court judges that was more loyal to Edun, the government secretary. When they lost their basis of power, the Ogboni chiefs began opposing the government and colonization. Egbaland was about to be divided into seven districts, each headed by a district head. Although their palaces were in Abeokuta, the new district heads were expected to leave the city and live in their districts. Because the chiefs had regarded themselves as *oba* (kings), this was a serious blow to their prestige. Other chiefs were afraid that they would eventually be affected by the reorganization of Egba into various districts under local chiefs. The aim of this restructuring was for the colonial government to facilitate the collection of taxes and to have local chiefs who would handle such collections and, if necessary, punish the citizens under their care who refused to comply.

By May 1918, people began to express discontent more openly. They sang abusive songs in public that criticized Edun, the British, and the tax collectors. Various "concerned individuals" drafted petitions expressing all sorts of complaints against the government. A. G. Boyle, the lieutenant governor of southern Nigeria, decided to tour the Egba area with Edun and the *alake* in order to restore normalcy. This was a trio many did not want to see. Boyle was greeted with insults and public hostility; in one instance, a dane gun was brandished to warn him that people were not afraid of him. Disappointed and angry, Boyle told the *alake* and Edun to end the crisis or he would call in the police to end it by force.[18]

Complaints and protests mounted, both in the villages and at Abeokuta. Serious cases of lawlessness were reported on a daily basis. The anti-tax agitations were multiplying, and various groups and communities united in their opposition to the government, pro-government chiefs, and colonial agents. By mid-May, the police had begun to alert administrators of an imminent danger that they might not be able to handle.[19]

In panic, the government decided to lower the tax rates. The announcement of the tax reduction was widely publicized, but it met with indifference. The people's anger was too deep. For years, they had endured the excesses of government officials, and they regarded the new policy on taxation as yet another way to exploit and cheat them. The coalition of antigovernment forces was so large that by the end of May, the central government in Lagos had to rush troops from Kaduna to Abeokuta and Wasimi, two emerging "war zones."[20]

Riots began on June 13, 1918.[21] The outburst had all the characteristics of a war, and it has been so described in contemporary oral and written sources. The people revived the precolonial armies as hundreds of men reached for their old weapons and charms. There was a strong belief that victory was assured, a belief that was bolstered by a general lack of respect for the colonial government. For four years, the government had been recruiting people to work for the army in wars outside Nigeria, campaigns that lasted longer than they had expected. If the government could be involved in "killing their sons," some reckoned, there was nothing wrong in mobilizing against it and the chiefs who supported it. There was also a strong perception that a large part of the money collected as tax was going into private pockets. The people believed that the *alake,* a number of chiefs, and Edun were enriching themselves at the expense of the people. Even Lugard described Edun as "unscrupulous" in acquiring wealth and land.[22]

Antigovernment armies were raised in the districts and were divided into three attack columns designed to capture Abeokuta. The armies were large, numbering about 30,000 people in all. While the government knew that the people were angry, it was taken by surprise by the sudden outburst and the large size of the antigovernment forces. In spite of their ad hoc nature, the armies were efficient and well organized. Even the police, who had warned of danger in mid-May, anticipated acts of violence in only one or two locations. The government believed that poor farmers and marginalized city dwellers were incapable of such a massive feat of organization. The resident of Egbaland insisted that the Western-educated elite based in Lagos had played a role in precipitating the crisis and in helping organize resources and armies. The power of the Lagos elite, he said, was such that "the people cannot understand that advice from so-called well wishers and supporters in Lagos may not always be unbiased or that their Lagos friends resent not being taken into confidence before schemes are embarked upon."[23] This statement was an exercise in denial of reality. It was true that many members of the elite had been opposed to taxation and the management of the Egba government, but there is no evidence that they participated in the war. It is even more difficult to verify the speculation by some colonial officers that the Egba fighters were assisted by soldiers the British had already trained in the Nigeria Regiment.[24]

The size of the armies is just one piece of evidence of the peoples' deep anger about taxation and other colonial policies. There was other compelling evidence. All the essentials of a peasant rebellion were evident. The war songs were opposed to the British, to the chiefs, and to Edun, the secretary to the government. The armies included a large number of poor farmers and members of the urban underclass. Volunteers also came from the neighboring country of Dahomey. (The Yoruba had been partitioned into Nigeria under the British and Dahomey under the French, but the two new national identities had yet to be consolidated. The boundaries were porous, and it was clear that the majority of the people had not accepted the new concept of citizenship being forcefully imposed upon them.) The Yoruba in Dahomey had been fighting the French government over colonial policies, especially forced recruitment into the army during the First World War. Various deserters had even set up a colony for refugees at the border town of Ijofin on the Nigerian side. Many of these refugees and others saw the war as an opportunity to liberate themselves and joined the Egba. A failed attempt by the insurgent movement to kill the governor of Dahomey in 1918 forced those who fled from the police and army but were still bent on revenge to find common cause with the anti-British Egba. To further complicate matters, many angry protesters in the neighboring Ijebu and Ibadan divisions also joined the ranks of the Egba armies.

Most parts of Egbaland were engulfed in the rebellion. As the armies moved from one village to another on their way to Abeokuta, they obtained the support of village heads and chiefs along the way. At Oba, eight miles from Abeokuta, the *osile* (the district head and a chief next in rank to the *alake*) lost his life after he refused an offer to lead the protest. Afraid for his life, his son joined the Egba armies to lead them to Abeokuta. As the armies moved toward Abeokuta, they set ablaze railway stations, destroyed rail lines, and damaged telegraph lines. They damaged or stole property valued at thousands of pounds. The police were powerless to deal with the attacking soldiers. At Abeokuta, all the Europeans abandoned their stores and homes to congregate at the residency, apparently fearing for their lives. The *alake* left his palace to take refuge in a Roman Catholic mission house.[25]

The situation could no longer be handled by local forces and the local administration. The central government in Lagos saw it as a war that required the services of a huge army. The attack on the rail lines and railroad stations could paralyze the south-north trade, a primary source of the nation's income. If the rebels attacked the water dams, they could flood many parts of the city. The outbreak had halted European commerce. The colonial headquarters in Lagos reacted with fury; its primary objective was being threatened. Abeokuta was too near Lagos to make it possible to quickly mobilize the army. Because the First World War was nearing its end, there was a surplus of soldiers ready to be used to quash the rebellion.

The British in Lagos raised a large army of almost 3,000 fully equipped soldiers drawn from various sources: the Nigerian Regiment in Lagos, Ibadan, and Kaduna; the West African Service Brigade; and the 4th Battalion Nigerian Regiment at Ede.[26] The colonial army met the armies of the Egba in a number of battles. By the time everything was over, about 1,000 Egba soldiers had lost their lives, the colonial army had lost about 100 men, and property valued at a staggering 55,638 pounds had been destroyed. The war lasted for over a month, until July 22, 1918, when the colonial government finally declared victory and the Egba armies dispersed to their various homes.[27]

The aftermath was as unsettling as the events that led to the outbreak. Local politics and relations among chiefs were damaged so severely that it took years to repair the damage.[28] The colonial authorities' maximum use of force in response to the uprising upset local Church Missionary Society leaders so much that they protested to headquarters in Britain, while the Nigerian educated elite popularized the idea of the war as carnage.[29] Concerned individuals in Nigeria and Britain called for an inquiry into the

reasons for the rebellion and an examination of how the government officials had handled it.[30] The Colonial Office in London, too, was pressured
(by the media and a number of British politicians) to examine the biggest
rebellion of the period.

The report of the commission the colonial government set up to examine
the causes of the rebellion admitted the obvious causes: the new taxation policy called upon those who worked for free for the colonial government, abandoning their farms and other occupations, to also pay taxes. There was no
doubt that many saw forced labor as an injustice and gross exploitation, and
the rebellions in 1914 and 1918 were partly about an effort to stop it.[31] Those
in rural areas were particularly angry. Not only had they been forced to
"donate" labor and supply cheap food but they were also asked to pay taxes
on electricity without enjoying any electricity. The new taxation policy also
imposed too great a burden: it would require them to pay taxes in their villages and pay another set of taxes should they have anything to do in the city
of Abeokuta, whether it was for social events, employment, or business. The
commission found that the administrative reorganization into districts and
taxation zones was another source of problems. The senior chiefs had been
made heads of districts and had been asked to relocate to their districts, a
move that was unprecedented and in no way rooted in local traditions; this
turned the people against the chiefs. The people saw the chiefs as no more
than tax collectors who relied for their own survival and sustenance on the
monies they collected from poor farmers. Some chiefs had announced that
they would use force to collect taxes and even kill defaulters if necessary.

The commission identified other reasons for the rebellion. One was the
complaint that the government did not have a large enough staff to supervise various agencies and that some staff members had behaved in an irre-
sponsible manner.[32] Many Nigerians blamed Governor-General Lugard for
his inability to prevent the crisis. He was accused of running an "autocratic
government" as a ruler with his hands on "all the machinery of government."[33] Many colonial officers, both in Nigeria and in London, regarded
his haste in introducing taxation in a time of war, economic decline, and
staff shortage as a major blunder. It took many years to restore confidence
in the government and its taxation policy.

Riots in the Owerri Province

Another well-documented case of early resistance to taxation in the south
was that of Warri Province in the Niger Delta in 1928, the first year of direct
taxation.[34] Warri Province was in economic decline as the price of palm
produce, the main revenue earner, dropped. At the same time, the prices of

imported items were high.[35] Some officers warned that it was a bad idea to introduce taxation at a time of economic depression. This economic background was part of the reason for the vigorous anti-tax riots. The trouble began earlier, when the colonial government sought data on the number of taxable adults. The news of the impending tax collection led to anti-tax movements in various locations. Very quickly, these also became movements against the warrant chiefs. The Young Jakri Party was one of the earliest movements, led by Eda Otuedon, a letter writer, a member of one of the new professional occupations that arose with literacy. A letter writer was a sort of public figure who operated in the business district of a town writing letters on behalf of customers who were not literate. He might also be conversant with political events. Eda was a political activist, and he successfully mobilized a group of Itsekiri (the "Jakri" of the colonial reports) to fight the impending imposition of taxation.[36]

Two other issues provoked and complicated the movement Eda led. One was the alleged involvement of the Nigerian National Democratic Party (NNDP), the country's first political party, in Eda's group. The Lagos-based party was led by Herbert Macaulay, who exerted a strong impact on elite politics in Lagos, had put African members in the Lagos Legislative Council. In earlier years, Macaulay, now regarded as "the father of Nigerian nationalism," had fought the British over the alienation of land in Lagos. In the view of the colonial officers, Macaulay was preaching an anticolonial message by lending his support to Eda in 1928. He was even accused of instructing Eda to begin an insurgency, an accusation that cannot be confirmed.[37]

The other issue was the opposition of many people to Chief Dogho, the powerful warrant chief in the area. Dogho, a mighty figure by 1927, started as a warrant chief appointed by the British and later assumed the unofficial title of the head of the Itsekiri people. Dogho was a mediator between the British and the people, but he saw himself more as a king. Obaro Ikime describes him as a powerful politician and a "super warrant chief" with a great deal of power. Dogho's power was not conferred by law; he had acquired it through his ability to arrogate it to himself. The portrait Ikime painted is dramatic—a small man becoming a larger-than-life figure.[38] Like the emirs and the Yoruba kings, Dogho supported the idea of imposing taxation. For Eda and the Young Itsekiri Party (YIP), the name of the anti-tax and anti-Dogho movement, attacking taxation was the same thing as attacking the British and Chief Dogho at the same time.

Eda's first political move was a campaign to prevent the Itsekiri from compiling a list of taxable adults; he reckoned that without a tax roll, the taxes could not be imposed. Eda's anti-tax movement grew bigger when a leader emerged among the neighboring Urhobo people, a man named Oshue, who began a campaign similar to that of Eda. In the words of Ikime, Oshue was "fiery, eloquent and truculent . . . [having] all the qualities of a mob leader."[39] While there are no detailed biographies of either Eda or Oshue, colonial sources, albeit in rather hostile language, describe them as efficient rabble-rousers. While Oshue shared all the concerns of Eda, another issue provoked his anti-tax protest: rumors that the British would change many aspects of the Urhobo economy, especially those dealing with palm oil production, on which the Urhobo relied. Ikime notes that according to one rumor, the British were planning to introduce a plantation system into the oil palm industry and that this prospect "filled the Urhobo with great apprehension and determined them to oppose the new measure, since it looked as if they would be displaced from an industry which was the main source of their economic well-being, at one and the same time as they were being asked to pay tax."[40] To further complicate the matter, another rumor was circulating that the Urhobo would have to apply for a license before they could trade in gin. They believed that such a change would be devastating to their livelihoods.

While the official records do not adequately cover the spread of the anti-tax riots into other parts of Warri Province, it is clear that other groups in the region, such as the Isoko, joined in. Various local leaders emerged who called for opposition to taxation, the warrant chiefs, and a variety of colonial policies. Some of the leaders joined forces, as in the case of Eda and Oshue, who brought the Urhobo and Itsekiri together in July 1927. As various clans sent delegates to Igbudu, a village close to the city of Warri, it became clear that the anti-tax protest could create a political platform. Adopting the methodology of the village assembly of the pre-British era, the delegates at Igbudu reached a consensus. First, they would resist arrest and prevent the police, court messengers, and any officer of the colonial state from arresting anyone; second, the Itsekiri and Urhobo would cease all trade with Europeans and stop the production of palm oil; and third, they would shut down all the native courts.[41] These three items indicate the nature of the people's anger and their resistance methods: closing down the courts was a rejection of the colonial administration; resisting arrest questioned the legitimacy of the government itself (and was not a tactic to promote anarchy, as the government later argued); and stopping trade (an old tactic dating back to the nineteenth century) hurt the government where it was most painful. The agreement was sealed with an oath by all in attendance, and the participating clans were told to punish those who violated the three agreements in whatever way they chose.

The colonial annual report for 1927 indicated that the people began to adhere to the resolutions almost immediately. Even hardened officials had to admit that compiling the rolls of adult taxpayers was difficult in many places and almost impossible in others. Among the Isoko, the Itsekiri, and the Urhobo, the efforts of many people to adhere to the Igbudu resolutions were firm and determined. To start with, they boycotted trade with the Europeans, keeping palm produce at home in the hope that the government would be forced to change its policies.

Second, they shut down the native courts, thereby paralyzing the government in matters of routine administration and the administration of justice. Since the warrant chiefs, court messengers, and scribes needed the courts in order to exercise their power, this was an attack on both the agents and the courts. Young men prevented the messengers, police, clerks, and warrant chiefs from gaining access to the courts, serving summonses, or initiating any new trials. In bitter words, the agents and staff of the government detailed their experiences: some were manhandled by angry mobs; a court clerk was attacked in his home and narrowly escaped being killed; a warrant chief was beaten; the ten warrant chiefs for the Enwe clan were forced to pay a huge ransom, 30 pounds per person; and many other clans imposed levies on their warrant chiefs in exchange for preventing mob attacks on them.

Third, the protesters released prisoners being held in the native court prisons and by the police and court messengers. In addition, they ensured that none of them would be arrested by the police or other agent of the government. For example, while a government official was explaining the need to collect taxes to a crowd that gathered at Sapele on September 30, 1927, a British official accused a man of showing disrespect to the British officer. The police arrested him on a charge of causing a "disturbance in public."[42] The crowd became energized and agitated, urging the police to release the man. The police opened fire on the crowd, wounding many and killing one person. The angry mob, which the police described as very dangerous, ensured that no one would be arrested. The strategy of liberating prisoners was an attack on the power of the government. It also sent a message to members of the anti-tax movement that others would fight for them should the police arrest them. Prisoners were released in various towns, notably Owe, Oleh, Ughienwe, Agbarho, and Aboh.

As the riots spread to other parts of Warri Province, other clans and groups acted in ways that they believed would affect the foundation of the colonial government. At Ode Itsekiri, a town that became the major center of hostility to Chief Dogho, the son of Nana of Ebrohimi, Dogho's former rival and enemy, used the anti-tax protest to revive old family animosity.

The Ijo in the Niger Delta chose to attack centers of trade. A mob of Ijo, estimated at about 800 strong, attacked and closed down the Forcados market, which was located at a major port where palm produce was traded. They stopped all trade and prevented trading boats from using the River Forcados or any of its creeks.

On July 28, 1927, a mob attacked the assistant district officer at Isoko. His counterpart at Warri was attacked on the same day. The district officer at Kwale lost his car to the riots.[43] The people, who were clear about who their enemies were, did not touch public buildings, even those where the native courts met. It was clear that the most hated people were the warrant chiefs. Many residents and district officers later admitted that many of the complaints against the warrant chiefs were justified and that some of these chiefs were corrupt. In 1928, when some clans were forced by the threat of coercion to agree to the tax, they were so hostile to the warrant chiefs that they made the removal of the bad warrant chiefs a nonnegotiable condition of agreement. As many Urhobo clans told the government, they were not necessarily opposed to the institution of indirect rule and the chiefs, but they were opposed to the individuals who acted as chiefs. Some clans simply called for the appointment of new warrant chiefs to replace the unacceptable ones. Where power was taken away from the warrant chiefs as a result of this resistance, traditional mechanisms of government were revived. The elders took over the administration of villages and clans, con-vening meetings and discussing how they would respond to the colonial government and police. As elders and young men held meetings, tradi-tional councils of the pre-British era began working again. The young men took over security and patrol duties, acting as vigilante groups to protect mar-kets, village sites, and shrines. Although the colonial government regarded these young men as misfits who were causing disturbances, their clans and villages regarded them as champions of the right causes.

As with the previous cases of anticolonial violence, the government had to use considerable force and the threat of severe punishment to end the riots. Various police patrols were sent to the hot spots. From August 1927 to early February 1928, Owerri Province was the site of intense security measures as police were drafted from other parts of the country into the area. The police work was long and tough in some areas, as in the creek areas where the Itsekiri stood their ground for over two months. Where possible, police warned people not to join insurgencies. They warned pris-oners who had been released by force to turn themselves in and hunted for "agitators." They threatened local chiefs with punishment, including the removal of their titles.

As in similar cases, the goal was to go after the leaders in the hope that the movement would crumble. They captured Oshue and sentenced him to a two-year prison term. They arrested over 100 others and sent them to jail for terms ranging from under a year to three years. They applied the Collective Punishment Ordinance to many clans and villages, and the punishments meted out included the imposition of small levies. The warrant chiefs who had been forced by anti-tax protestors to pay ransom fees used the police and the threat of force to get their money back again. Some semblance of peace began to return in February 1928, and the government began collecting taxes in the same year.

The violence and massive protests did have an effect on the way taxes were collected. Rather than policing individuals and monitoring thousands of people who were opposed to taxation, the government decided to impose lump-sum taxes on clans and villages, allowing each to work out the best way to collect the amount from its citizens. The clan leaders became tax collectors, a practice colonial authorities justified on the ground that it would allow them to use local "customs" to deal with adult male clan members in ways that would bring peace. The government agreed with the protesters that the warrant chiefs could not be trusted. Senior government officers had been told how a number of warrant chiefs "stole" money meant to build roads, rest houses, and court houses. The British reviewed and abandoned their original idea of asking the warrant chiefs to collect taxes and retain 10 percent of the proceeds in 1928 in favor of using village elders in the same way. The prediction by some warrant chiefs that the elders were too numerous and too illiterate to handle taxes proved to be grossly incorrect: the elders were able to revive traditional institutions in many areas, using them to collect taxes on a household basis in a manner that brought peace.

POST-COLLECTION CRISES

In the east, the lack of an indigenous direct tax system or even regular levies made direct taxation so new as to confuse various people for quite a long time. In the interzone between the north and south, those on the fringes of the north (such as the Akoko) wondered why they had to pay while their neighbors to the south were still exempt (notably between 1906 and 1919). A "feeling of unrest" was reported in the official records for 1914 among the Akoko whose territories adjoined the south. In that year, taxes had to be collected by force. The resident justified the use of force by saying that it was "the only way to show the people that they had to carry out their obligations."[44]

The case of Akoko shows yet another method of anti-tax resistance: migration to other areas in order to escape payment. Migration had a connection with violence: where riots failed or the forces of the colonial power were hard to defeat, one way out was to relocate and some people sought jobs as tenant farmers in other parts of the country. However, relocation sometimes had advantages that ultimately boosted economic production. For example, many people from Akoko and other areas without the export crops needed to generate the cash to pay tax relocated to areas where they could grow cocoa, kola, and cotton.

When the system of taxation was established, sporadic violence broke out in various areas for a variety of reasons. A typical example was the Isin tax riots among the Igbomina in 1933. When the emir of Ilorin visited Oro in 1933, he was confronted by an angry mob who demanded to know why they should pay tax. They chanted slogans, and many followed the emir to the next town, Ajasse, to continue the protest. This is only one example of many small protests and violent outbursts, many unanticipated by the government and chiefs. Individuals and small communities, too, rebelled. One source of anger was the tax rate and the changing principles used to determine it over time. An area that started with a payment of two shillings per adult male might find that the tax was increased in a later year, and in some years people could be asked to pay more than seven shillings. Comprehensive tax assessments were made in different places at different times; the goal was to raise revenue, not to address the concerns of angry taxpayers. The governor in Lagos could adjust the rate, as happened in 1922 when Governor Hugh Clifford increased the rate in some areas from two to six shillings.[45] The people must "realize that there is wealth in the soil,"[46] was a typical colonial response to anti-tax anger, a way of linking payment to increased production of crops to be sold for cash.

The remuneration of the officials who collected taxes produced additional problems. In various local government councils, members of the clan councils and courts believed they were entitled to share in the tax that was collected. Some councils fixed rates for themselves. In some other areas, such as parts of Benin Province, adult males believed that they were entitled to small shares, about sixpence per adult male. In 1940, the district officer in Agbor[47] and the Owa area, both in the Benin Province, decided to introduce the payment of fixed salaries for council workers, to be paid quarterly, primarily to show that the salary payment was a reward "for other duties besides tax collection."[48] The DO decided that a maximum of 10 percent of the total tax collection should be allocated to the payment of salaries to council workers.

In these areas, it was not the procedure of collecting taxes that led to problems but the question of how to share the 10 percent among the chiefs who were the members of the clan council in some villages around Agbor. The first sign of disgruntlement came from some elders in the village of Ogbe Idumu-Ileje, who alleged that the percentage allocated to them was very small because, they believed, some chiefs had stolen money. In the town of Umunede, near Agbor a group of elders complained that the *obi* (head chief) and some of the titleholders had stolen the sixpence meant for each of them. The elders threatened not to attend council meetings again, and their supporters went round the town singing abusive songs directed at the *obi* and some of the chiefs.[49] The DO called for calm and promised to visit the town.

Before the DO could intervene, those who felt left out of the sharing took to rioting on April 27, 1940, first at Umunede, where many people were injured and five houses were destroyed. The Agbor police detachment quickly arrested the eight ringleaders. The DO's investigation revealed that the *obi* had taken the lion's share, followed by the *abani* and *olotu* title-holders (ward chiefs). A category of chiefs known as the *isiulu* were excluded, and it was they who organized the riots. The fact that the taxpaying adults had also been excluded from receiving any money made it easier for the angry *isiulu* to mobilize opposition against the government. When the DO visited the town on May 1, the crisis was still lingering. A reconstituted clan council excluded the *isiulu,* leading to more protests. The DO removed many of the *obi's* relatives from the council and summoned the *isiulu* and other elders to attend. At the meeting, the DO unsuccessfully tried to persuade the angry people that the 10 percent of tax revenues meant for them were "not a reward for the collection of tax but salary for work done throughout the year and that no one is entitled to a reward of 6d merely for performing the duty of paying tax."[50] In the view of the *isiulu* chiefs and other elders in attendance, the council members should not receive any salary, since they were already collecting sitting fees (payment for attending meetings), and they threatened to rally the people to refuse to pay any tax for the year.

Seeing no peace in sight, the government decided to charge the eight people accused of instigating the April riots with "riot, assault and malicious injury to property."[51] Although they were released on bail on May 4, 1940, they were asked to appear before the magistrate. In addition, the DO instructed that none of the town's chiefs should receive any income from the tax revenues until the matter of sharing was resolved, and he reached a depressing conclusion on the town's state of affairs: the Native Authority of

Umunede, as then constituted, was incapable of carrying out the duties imposed by the law and could not exact the obedience of the people. According to the DO, the *obi* was weak, "managed by unscrupulous members of his family"; the titleholders were unpopular; and the *isiulu*, "while able to rouse their people to commit unlawful acts, seem[ed] to have no control over them whatsoever."[52]

By May, the town was in a state of "complete deadlock."[53] The *isiulu* insisted that no other matter would be resolved until the issue of revenue sharing was settled. The court could not sit, and the *obi* was forbidden by many in the town to hold court. Some people made new allegations that the *obi* and some titleholders had stolen the money allocated to the Church Missionary Society school in the town. The DO accepted the criticism that the *obi* was under the manipulative power of members of his family, and he doubted whether the people of Umunede were ready to accept the authority of a hereditary titleholder, a position created only in 1919.

Unable to resolve the issue, the government decided to set up an enquiry in order to formulate new proposals on titles and tax. In this instance, the violence had an unintended consequence: the Native Authority of Umunede had to be reorganized. The *obi* retained his job as the head of a reorganized council, and the eight men who had initiated the violence received only a slap on the wrist.

The Igala Example

The Igala of the Middle Belt present a typical example of the second phase of resistance and violence to taxation. Their protest had a strong link to the first phase of resistance. Contrary to many official reports of the time, anti-tax protests were not limited to the southeast or necessarily instigated by the Lagos elite. As with the Egba, Itsekiri, and Urhobo, the Igala reacted to various colonial policies and to the political and economic transformations of the era. Among the people on whom Nigerians from other ethnic groups were imposed as their local leaders, such as the people in the districts of Bassa Nge, Bassa Komo, and Dekina, all of which are in the northwest of Igalaland, anti-tax violence was compounded by attacks directed against these leaders, who were also regarded as callous tax collectors. When taxation was introduced among the Igala, it came with the appointment of a category of chiefs known as the *onu*, who were authorized to collect tax, administer justice, and ensure peace after 1901. The *onus* were not Igala; many of them were Hausa, Fulani, or Yoruba, former soldiers the British had used in the wars of conquest. Some *onus* were relatives of powerful emirs or local men of wealth residing among the Igala. As the *onus* established a grip on power, they alienated many people. Like the warrant chiefs, the *onus* were unpopular, criticized for exercising power that was not rooted in local traditions. As tax collectors, the people saw them as nothing but rogues who engaged in extortion, imposed arbitrary rates of taxation, and used extreme methods to ensure collection. Even Lugard, who insisted on payment, believed that the *onus* and some other categories of tax collectors were "generally hated" and "became a veritable curse to the country and were the most hated feature of the system."[54]

The Bassa Komo were among the first to revolt, in 1911. The Bassa Komo had grudgingly paid their taxes in previous years. But in 1910–1911, there was a decline in agricultural productivity due to a drought. Because of the crop failures, many were unable to meet their regular expenses, and they failed to pay their taxes. Ignoring the widespread hardship of the time, the *onu*, acting under instructions from the government, used extraordinary measures to collect the taxes. With troops following them, the *onus* set fire to many villages to warn others that a similar fate would befall them if they refused to pay.

Widespread anger mounted, and mobs attacked the Hausa "foreigners" who were living among them, killing about nine in the Bassa Komo area.[55] In another incident, anti-tax insurgents killed six Hausa soldiers who had accompanied the *onus* to collect taxes. Political officers were spared, but not the Hausa, who the people were regarded as the local agents who were exploiting them. Even an administrative officer was sympathetic in his overall assessment:

> The rising of Bassa Komo appears to have been almost justified. They evidently have got provocation and we can only deplore the fact that, in addition to extortion that was practised upon them by tax gatherers, they should have had to suffer considerably at the hands of the troops burning their villages.[56]

Lawlessness spread, and by November, the government had to call a contingent of the West African Frontier Force based at Lokoja to suppress the rebellion. Hundreds fled northwestern Igalaland, and a few people lost their lives.[57] A temporary calm was restored that brought limited success in collecting taxes.

The Bassa Nge in Takete (in Dekina Division) rose in protest in January 1914. As with many groups in the country who seized on the crises that faced the government before and during First World War, they thought that the staff reductions made by the colonial government and the relocation of military personnel away from Nigeria meant that British rule was about to end. The Bassa Nge seized the opportunity to refuse to pay their taxes. When the assistant district officer (ADO) went to them in January to plead for taxes, he met a large crowd of angry people carrying bows and arrows and vowing to kill him. Entering a secure room, he shot at the crowd, who in turn set his house on fire. The ADO had to flee for his life. He was pursued and was injured, but he survived. The government sent troops to Takete and they ruthlessly crushed the rebellion, burning all the villages except those that hoisted white flags to indicate submission and readiness to pay tax. To further punish the people, Takete was downgraded from a district headquarters to a place of no consequence, and Gboloko became the new capital.

The Bassa Nge rose again in violent protest in December 1914. Taru Saidu, the head chief of the Bassa Nge, one of the indigenous chiefs who had been sidelined by the colonial administration, initiated this uprising against taxation. "Why do you pay taxes to the English?" said the agent of a German firm in support of Saidu. "We set up stores and give you goods in exchange for your produce, but the English government officials take money from you and give you nothing. When the Germans arrive, you will be given things you want; don't pay taxes."[58] A rumor had spread that the British had lost to the Germans and that it was time to strike hard at the colonial officers.

In the official version of what happened, Taru mobilized all the males in his town in the first week of December. They chased away the agents of the colonial administration, attacked people who were loyal to the government, and threatened to kill the police. In mid-December, as the town became ungovernable, the government had to send a contingent of police and soldiers to arrest some of the protest leaders.[59] Taru was deposed, and the anti-tax protest was compounded when the people rejected a new chief who was supported by the government.

No sooner did the riots among the Bassa Nge end than their neighbors, the Dekina, began their own riots. The crisis here started with the appointment in 1916 of Ahmadu, a Yoruba, as the onu. The people rejected him and interpreted many of his moves to mean that he wanted to behave like the attah (king) of the Igala people. When rumors circulated that taxes would be raised from 3 pence to 10 pence, the people rose against him, killing some of his supporters and wounding others in various clashes. Ahmadu, too, was wounded, but he escaped to Lokoja, where he found no sympathizers for his side of the story. Indeed, even the administrative officers lost confidence in him, accusing him of extortion that "caused real havoc and civil disorder." He was removed as an onu and put in jail for four years.[60] The situation at Dekina grew worse, turning into what became known as the Mahionu War, which lasted till the last months of 1917. The Dekina attacked anyone associated with Ahmadu, injuring many, burning down many of their houses, and driving them away. The appointment of a Dekina citizen as the *onu* in 1918 put a temporary end to the crisis.

The Dekina riots reveal some other problems associated with taxation. First, the people had to pay with the new British coins, which they complained were scarce and which they had to work harder to obtain. The old currencies of cowries and metals were no longer legal tender. To the people who had subsisted on farming, consuming most of their products, the adjustment required by the need to work for the new colonial currency, in part to be able to pay tax, was a great burden. They had to sell what they felt was too much of their farm produce to obtain money. Second, where the head of a household had to pay for his sons, dependents, and others, he (or she) needed to expand the land used for crops or livestock and find more labor to raise cash resources. Many families experienced tensions arising from the need to pay taxes.

All of this is background for the second phase of tax protests in the region in the mid-1920s. The Dekina took up arms again in 1924. As before, the appointment of a new *onu* (Ocheja) became a source of trouble. In an effort to justify his appointment to colonial officials, Ocheja maintained strict rules in the collection of taxes. And in an effort to maintain a prestigious lifestyle, he collected gifts and levies, a practice that led to violent protests. To solve the problem, authorities removed Ocheja and banished him from Dekina. His successor also failed, again as the result of trying to enforce the payment of taxes in ways that the people found too extreme.[61] The British, who appointed the *onus*, wanted them to perform tasks that automatically alienated them from the people.

Among the Paluwa of the Bassa Komo, the increase in tax from 4 shillings to 5 was the source of violence in 1926. Mamman, the *onu*, was blamed for the increase, although he was simply carrying out the instructions of the colonial political officers. The story had become common: the people would rise, the *onu* would flee, the government would dismiss him and appoint a new one, and the cycle of violence would be repeated. The Paluwa repeated an old demand: the government should either forgo or reduce the taxes whenever there was crop failure due to drought, locust attacks, or other reasons. In later years in other Igala towns and villages (for example, in the Arasamashe rebellion of 1931 and the Bassa Komo uprising of 1932–1933) it was always the same story: when the people complained of serious hardships, the *onus* refused to forgive taxes. Hundreds of Igala migrated in order to escape taxation. Indeed, whenever beetles attacked their yams, thereby reducing productivity, hundreds would realize that they lacked the means to pay tax for that year and begin a strategy of protest or avoidance.

Tax rates were not necessarily based on "income." To the Igala, it was misleading to call the payment "income tax"; it was a head tax that was designed more to punish them than to raise revenue. In poor economies, where the people depended largely on their farms for survival, it was hard to determine the appropriate amount to collect. Rates were based on assessments of farm incomes that the people never agreed with. In determining the "taxable capacity" of an individual, the assessor compiled a crude estimate of what a village could generate, including yields from livestock and trees. In the view of the farmers, nature, the gods, and God were the only ones who could estimate yields. Officials assumed that the farmers were always fully productive and that their trees, goats, and farmlands would always yield the maximum. The *onus* and other tax collectors did not "forgive" the taxpayers when yields were poor, when the rains failed, and when the locusts came. Many Igala complained that they had to sell the labor of their children to others in order to pay their tax. After 1934, based on the history of annual revolts, the government decided to reduce the tax rates, agreeing with the farmers that they lacked the capacity to pay more than a certain amount (4 shillings on average). Violence recorded a success!

CONCLUDING REMARKS

Taxation was highly unpopular during most of the colonial period. The government was asking the people to part with money that they believed would not be spent in ways that benefited them. Where the people believed that the chiefs and kings would be given a portion of the collections, as in the case of the warrant chiefs in the east, they reacted angrily: people argued that they were being forced to "pay" their enemies. The Yoruba and many other groups equated taxation with *owo ori* (payment per head); they interpreted taxation not as a way to make local governments function well but as a way to punish individuals with some kind of mandatory redemption fee. Redemption fees were associated with slaves, who had to pay their masters to buy their freedom; avoiding taxation was a way to avoid being punished by an oppressive government.

Despite the unpopularity of taxation, the government had the force and the machinery to collect taxes, and the people used protests and violence to express their opposition. When the tyranny of colonial agents was combined with their power to collect taxes, many people began to regard the colonial government with hostility, and thus taxation also provoked anticolonial feelings and opposition to chiefs and kings, notably the warrant chiefs. To obtain compliance with taxation rules and regulations, the colonial officers and their Nigerian agents traveled to various parts of the country on propaganda missions, explaining that direct taxation was for the people's good. They made a connection between taxes and public projects as part of the propaganda, creating a lasting impression among a segment of the population, notably those with Western education, that taxation should always be linked to their own interests. Slow progress in development (e.g., road construction or building new schools) became a reason to attack the government and chiefs for "stealing money" meant to benefit the people.

The propaganda had a frightening side to it. It was a carrot-and-stick strategy. Government officials delivered the soft words designed to make people pay the taxes—the carrot. But the real business was the stick, the compilation of names of adults, villages, village elders, the number of farms and their sizes, volume of crops and their prices, and the number of markets and their importance, all in order to determine the tax rate. The sight of an officer collecting this information generated fear among the people, creating the foundation for a lasting fear and mistrust of censuses and inaccurate data. Afraid of paying tax or paying more than necessary, people sometimes gave false information about the number of adults in their households and villages, the sizes of their farms, and their crop yields. Officers made estimates that were not necessarily correct, since their motive was to raise revenue.

Anti-tax violence could be spontaneous or coordinated. It might be well organized. Some episodes had leaders, such as Eda and Oshue. These leaders, who were usually self-appointed, used opposition to taxation as an opportunity to consolidate a variety of grievances into anti-tax riots. The Urhobo combined their opposition to new economic policies that they believed would ruin their key industry with protests against taxation. The idea of opposition spread from one area to another, as we have seen in Warri Province. Support could come from other places (as in the case of the people from non-Egba Nigerian groups who voluntarily joined the Egba armies).

In the southeast, many were angry with warrant chiefs due to their abuse of power. The fact that the people did not destroy public buildings or attack many white officers shows who their real targets were. Opposition to tax was framed as opposition to power—to the local agents of power and to those who used their power from the new colonial system to lord it over the people. In the view of the majority of the people, the British had given excessive power to native court clerks and messengers. They had created "illegitimate chiefs," such as the warrant chiefs in the east and the *onus* among the Igala, and where the British had inherited the kings and chiefs (as in Abeokuta) they had given them "illegitimate power." The official analysis of violent outbreaks after they had occurred, as in the case of Abeokuta in 1918 or Warri Province after 1928, pinned the problem not on the colonial system itself but on the Nigerian agents who were needed to operate it. There was "accumulating discontent,"[62] noted Margery Perham, which officers usually did not pay attention to until it was too late. The British blamed the Egba rebellion on the maladministration of the *alake* (the king) and Edun (the government secretary and "prime minister"). They described the *alake* and his chiefs as corrupt, constituting a council "whose only nature was to acquire personal gain by extortion from the peasantry."[63] The Edun-*alake* administration "combined all the worst forms of injustice and misrule covered by a veneer of apparently advanced methods at the capital of Abeokuta."[64] The colonial government was compelled to dismiss some Igala *onus* and jail the worst of them. The collection of taxes and the administration of justice by the local agents, as in the case of the *onus,* constituted serious threats to peace. Once local agents or chiefs were regarded as corrupt or extortionist, taxation became intolerable, irrespective of the amount required.

The people interpreted taxation as part of an attempt to create progress in ways that undermined or threatened established institutions of society. In other words, many regarded the policy on taxation as part of a package of rapid restructuring of society. In the first two decades of the twentieth century, the colonial government was trying to restructure indigenous politics, impose new ideas on native administration, introduce native courts with judges whose power was new and authoritarian, and implement a policy of taxation. The power of the chiefs was changing, some gaining while some were losing. The power of the Ogboni society (a secret fraternity) to collect its traditional fees was curtailed, while the Parakoyi (a guild of traders) also lost its power to collect market dues and fees. In addition, the British compelled people to work for free to build roads that would enhance the colonial government's ability to move exports to centers of transportation. It "recruited" young Nigerian men into the army during the world war. As the colonial government interfered with various economic and political aspects of life, it alienated many people.

Violent anti-tax reactions produced one substantial result: they forced the government to pay attention to what the people were saying. Indeed, the government became interested in understanding the location and sources of traditional power. After the Egba crisis, Sir Hugh Clifford, who succeeded

Lugard, considered tinkering with the Lugardian administration to deal with the aspects of it that the people found offensive. Between 1928 and 1932, the government undertook various investigations to increase its understanding of indigenous social and political institutions with the aim of reorganizing local governments. The initial process of investigation began in 1928. A large-scale crisis in the following year ensured that more investigations would be carried out and that the findings of such investigations could not be dismissed.

5

GENDERED VIOLENCE

If most of the leading officers of the government and their local agents thought the anti-tax riots were over by 1928, they were about to be disappointed, even shocked. A year later, the biggest of the riots occurred in the Bende District of southern Nigeria, known in some records as the Aba Riots of 1929.[1] It should properly be labeled the Aba Women's War, the name the rebellious actors coined for their actions; it was the first gendered violence of note since the beginning of British rule. Three issues that precipitated the 1929 Women's War had also triggered protests against taxation in 1928. First, the government announced through a network of local officials and by word of mouth that taxation would be imposed on the people. These announcements were not always direct; sometimes the act of counting people and resources in an attempt to determine the appropriate tax rates was the mode of announcement. Second, the announcement was preceded by rumors that the palm produce trade and industry would be reorganized in ways that would injure the economic interests and livelihood of the people. Third, the tax collectors were to be the much-despised warrant chiefs, whom many had already accused of corruption, arbitrary arrests, and illegal trials of innocent people. Like the Urhobo and Itsekiri, the Igbo received the news of taxation, which came at a time of economic decline, with outrage.

However, there was a major difference between the war of 1929 and all the previous outbreaks: women were central in the anti-tax resistance of 1929. In that year, a widespread rumor passed through eastern Nigeria that the government would soon require women as well as men to pay taxes. Although the Women's War emerged as a broad-based social movement without a particular female leader at the helm, the gender lines were very clear; not many men were drawn into the Women's War as fighters. There was yet another important departure: although the previous cases were confined to one ethnic group, the 1929 war was multiethnic, involving Igbo, Opobo, and Ibibio women, all in the eastern part of Nigeria. In addition, the impact was also more widespread, precipitating a series of government measures to reform the colonial administration in southern Nigeria.

Colonialism undermined and subverted the position and status of women in many African societies. The Women's War of 1929 represents an early response of African women to their disempowerment and the subservience colonialism perpetrated and legitimized. The 1929 riots also reveal traditions of women's activism among the peoples and groups of eastern Nigeria. While there were other examples of protests by women in other parts of Nigeria, the 1929 example offers rich data with which to understand the role of women in the colonial setting.

BACKGROUND TO THE VIOLENCE

The Igbo were constituted, along with the Ijo, Ogoja, and Efik-Ibibio, as part of the Eastern Provinces. The districts of these provinces were administered by colonial officers and hundreds of local agents, chiefs, and kings. Although the British claimed to have imposed colonial rule by June 5, 1885, it took them thirty years to fully establish control in the east.[2] As chapters 3 and 4 have shown, anticonquest resistance was strong among the Igbo, who had never before been conquered or dominated. The Igbo found their experience of the British conquest new and humiliating. Without powerful kings for the British to negotiate with, diplomacy in many villages and towns was long and drawn out, and they eventually concluded that it was quicker to fight wars than to negotiate treaties. Before 1914, it was difficult for the British to know when an Igbo village had been totally subdued. Many villages used the trick of offering peace but later reverting to aggression, refusing to surrender to the new authorities. In 1915 alone, the British mounted a dozen expeditions against resistant Igbo villages and towns. Tired of the trickery of resistance, the colonial forces burned down villages and houses and maltreated the elders who represented the people. In the 1920s and beyond, the Igbo sought reconciliation with the British, but only after they had lost many wars, many men, and a great deal of property.

It is clear that the administrative system that evolved to govern the Igbo was a result of their resilience and their propensity for aggression. The initial phase of the administration began in 1891 with the appointment of Sir Claude Macdonald as the consul general.[3] Macdonald created divisions headed by vice-consuls, who supervised large areas. These areas were policed by local agents in hundreds of small villages. The Igbo paid a price for losing the wars against the British: in the new political order that emerged after 1914, power went to "new men" who were not lineage heads or titled elders. The "new men" became collaborators; the British expected them to supply men to work for free, arrest offenders, and carry out many instructions that annoyed the people.

With the 1914 amalgamation of the southern and northern provinces, changes were made to the structure of the administration of Nigeria. The three large provinces in the south were broken into nine. Four—Ogoja, Onitsha, Calabar, and Owerri—were in the east. These four provinces were in turn broken into divisions and districts. The amalgamation preserved the hierarchical nature of the colonial government. The central government in Lagos, headed by a governor, coordinated all the work of the subordinate white officers heading the provinces, divisions, and districts. Residents (who were called commissioners before 1914) headed the divisions and supervised the district officers, who headed the districts. The residents and district officers performed both political and administrative duties as the heads of the departments of agriculture, education, and prisons.

Local governments were created, to be administered by Nigerian agents of the government. Local rulers were used in large part to save money, since not many white officers could be used. The policy of using local Igbo rulers as part of the larger system of indirect rule caused trouble for the colonial government. The major problem (and this affected the nature of anti-tax violence) was the assumption that chiefs were necessary to govern the Igbo, as they were for the Yoruba, the Edo, and the Hausa-Fulani. The British ignored the Igbo village assemblies of the past and the role of elders in running "representative assemblies." Instead, they appointed the more powerful chiefs. The new chiefs and the new policies, the British hoped, would begin the process of moving the Igbo to a stage of "civilization." The assumption, sometimes stated very clearly, was that the Igbo were primitive, far behind the Edo, Hausa, and Yoruba in their political development. This primitivity thesis stated that African groups like the Igbo who had failed to develop strong monarchies lacked the capacity to do so. Rather than try to understand the age-old political institutions of the Igbo, the government created a new institution for them to manage law and order.

After 1912, Lugard began instituting reforms that constituted the preface to the taxation crises of the 1920s. Lugard believed the system the British had used was too lax and too slow to raise up the Igbo politically and economically. A. E. Afigbo provides a catalogue of Lugard's criticisms of the way the Igbo were being managed:

> He inveighed against the arrangement by which [British] political officers sat as presidents of Native Courts, the fact that appeals lay from Native Courts to the British Courts thus creating a loophole for legal practitioners to intervene at some stage in the settlement of native disputes, the fact that there was no system of direct taxation which could form the basis of Native Treasuries, the fact that there were no paramount chiefs and so on.[4]

Lugard was unrelenting in extending the system of indirect rule, as practiced in the north, to all the southern provinces, including the native revenue system, native authorities, and native courts. Afigbo notes the changes Lugard introduced in the Eastern Provinces:

> He insulated the Native Courts from the British Courts, interposing between the two the Provincial Courts manned entirely by political officers and from which legal practitioners were excluded; abolished the rudimentary system of native treasuries attached to the pre-1914 courts; abolished the practice of political officers presiding over Native Courts; curtailed the number of court messengers attached to each Court, and introduced the idea of sole Native Authorities through the creation of paramount chiefs and permanent presidents.[5]

Lugard was not completely successful in his reform efforts in southern Nigeria. He could not reduce the number of village councils to create bigger areas managed by more powerful chiefs. More important, he could not implement a policy of taxation. A large number of British officers in the south objected to the Lugardian changes and implemented them only with reluctance. The reduction in both British and Nigerian staff during the First World War and Nigerians' objections to many of the changes also affected Lugard's ability to implement his reforms. The warrant chiefs, clerks, and messengers grew more powerful and corrupt. By 1919, complaints that the reforms were a failure had become more frequent and more vociferous.

By the 1920s, Lugard's regime had ended and colonial officers were debating how to govern the Igbo. Two themes dominated discussions in official circles: first, the Igbo needed chiefs, and second, their native authorities needed money. Taxation was introduced in the 1920s in order to solve the problem of the lack of money. As in the north, collection was preceded by attempts to determine the incomes of individuals and villages, a move that aroused great suspicion. The taxation policy and the fear that warrant chiefs would acquire more power became the preface to the series of protests in the 1920s and the Women's War of 1929.

Anti-tax protests took various forms. Very early on, the people protested against being counted and having their incomes determined for what they believed were illegitimate reasons. The relationship between taxation and the counting of yam mounds, palm trees, and livestock was very unclear to many people, who had not previously paid levies determined by such types of income. Also, the measurement of farmlands created panic among those who believed that the government would seize the land. The very idea of collecting money on a regular basis in form of taxes was resented. Rather than seeing the funds as meant for their own upliftment, they regarded taxation as a form of punishment.

As with the Yoruba, Itsekiri, and Urhobo, taxation became one of the reasons for the Igbo to fight the British. They were feeling the impact of economic depression by the late 1920s. Prices of a number of essential commodities and luxuries such as calico and tobacco had increased because of the government's decision to raise import duties to collect more revenue. Income had decreased, due largely to the decrease in the prices of palm oil and palm kernels, the main cash crops in the area. In the view of the Igbo, taxation would compound their economic woes.

THE WAR OF 1929–1930: CIRCUMSTANCES AND CONTEXT

In 1928, taxes were collected in many Igbo towns and villages for the first time. The collection generated bitterness. Some of the warrant chiefs were not happy with their role as tax collectors because of the insults such activities generated. Many who paid their taxes did so reluctantly, mostly to avoid punishment. Many people refused to pay; they would not yield to official pressure and threats of severe sanctions. By 1929, anti-tax complaints and protests had increased everywhere. To start with, those who had paid in 1928 began to protest more than they had before, saying that taxation was nothing but a policy of forcing them to lose money. Anti-tax activism was aided by an increasingly depressed economy. As the prices of palm products continued to fall, diminishing earning power, the people became more angry about taxation. When people compared their tax rates, they began to realize that their warrant chiefs had exaggerated the incomes and population of their areas, in part to boost their own power.

Then came the rumor in 1929 that women, too, would begin to pay tax. The circumstances surrounding the rumor were connected with the assessment to determine the rate of taxation to be imposed on each person.[6] The British had made assessments before but had explained them as collecting information for the census rather than as collecting information for taxation. The warrant chiefs agreed to the 1929 assessment, and their job was to announce it to their people. The methods varied; some used the language of force and alienated the people. The chiefs asked heads of household to provide data about how much livestock they owned and how many adults their households sheltered. To add to the tension, chiefs could also ask everybody to gather at the village square or market so they could be counted and the numbers of goats and sheep they owned could be estimated. This assessment, regardless of the methods used to do it, was the basis for the total tax that was imposed on a village; warrant chiefs left it up to the villagers to divide the burden. The tax burden affected women indirectly, since the entire village was being taxed.

In Oloko in 1929, the power of the colonial officer and the warrant chief combined to make taxation a source of conflict. To confirm the accuracy of the population counts for some areas and the amount that was expected of these areas, a junior colonial officer decided in November to check the numbers reported for the village of Oloko in Bende Division. As usual, he directed a warrant chief to do the job of counting the men, women, livestock, and farm yields. The warrant chief delegated the job to a schoolteacher named Emeruwa. The trouble began when the schoolteacher reached the home of a woman named Nwanyeruwa. The questions about the number of crops, men, women, children, and other items in the household angered Nwanyeruwa, who had recently lost her son's wife and was in mourning. Demanding to know the number of a person's children was also considered "evil" in many Igbo households due to a belief that the knowledge would be used supernaturally to kill the children. Many people did not understand the need to count women, who compared themselves to the fruit-bearing trees (which, incidentally, were also taxed) needed for the survival of society.

A scuffle ensued between the schoolteacher and Nwanyeruwa. Refusing to supply data, she angrily asked the schoolteacher "Was your mother counted?"[7] Smarting at the insult, the teacher threatened to report her to the powerful warrant chief. She hurried to mobilize other women, holding a meeting to discuss a variety of issues that included taxation. More angry words followed, and the belief gained ground that the census was a prelude to announcing the imposition of taxation on women. To calm down the women, the colonial officer who had started it all conducted a summary trial, arrested the schoolteacher and the warrant chief, and gave the women the cap of the warrant chief as a sign of peace. This effort was a little too late. The women had sent the symbolic palm leaves—a signal of trouble and a summons to a crucial meeting—to various villages, inviting them to Oloko. A huge gathering of women had assembled by November 24. On that night of November 24, the Women's War began, with merriment and resolution to resist: "They danced and sang outside the Mission compound all night, eating, and drinking palm wine, and singing. . . . They became hysterical as their number increased."[8]

The changing conditions of women in the colonial situation made the rumor that they would be taxed believable. In more ways than one, women had fared poorly in the colonial era. Men had been appointed as warrant chiefs and gained in power. The young men who went to school and adopted Christianity were also benefiting; they were able to obtain new jobs with wages that enabled them to live comfortably. Other young men began to profit from the trade in palm produce. Men with bicycles dominated the middleman trade between the farms and the markets, selling products in ways that hurt the women's chances in the marketplace. Many women feared they would lose their children to growing cities and to new occupations located far away from the villages (for example, on the railroad or in coal mining at Enugu). Women located in the big towns saw "foreigners" from other parts of Nigeria coming to work among them, young people who (from the women's perspective) tended to behave rather strangely. Either because they were unable to fully grasp the nature of the changes or because of the strong psychological impact of the changes, it was common for many women (and men, too) to blame the colonial government for many of their woes. Thus they blamed the British for the devastating influenza epidemic of 1918 and inflation and decreasing prices for palm oil and palm kernels in the 1920s.

Many women were also persuaded by the revivalist movements of 1926–1927, which featured religious leaders who predicted the end of British rule and preached about the positive changes that would ensue. Rumors that the Germans would come to rescue them from British rule circulated. There was certainly evidence of restlessness among many women in the 1920s.[9] While it is clear that many cases were not recorded in the official records, the events of 1925 were major enough to be noticed. In that year, hundreds of women organized dancing groups to complain about colonial rule. Talking and singing, they marched to the homes of warrant chiefs in various parts of southeastern Nigeria to present far-reaching verbal demands. They demanded that men be less involved with local trade;

that men work more on the farms; and that the native courts be abolished if possible because they were too powerful. They also said that rich men were exercising too much power over the poor. It was also clear that the women were disturbed by the changes of the era, and they demanded a reduction in bride-price, attention to sanitation and compound cleaning, and the restoration of many of the older values that were being eroded.[10]

Perhaps the rumor that women would have to pay a tax was the straw that broke the camel's back. The rumor led to a major protest and a series of riots among Igbo, Ibibio, and Opobo women in various communities in the city of Aba and in many villages and towns within a 20-mile radius of the city. The women at Oloko gave the rumor the wings to fly as they sent word to many villages and towns that women were about to be counted and taxed. There was no need to convince most women to rise in rebellion; they had been waiting for the day to arrive. "Our grievances are that the land is changed," declared a woman in an oral interview:

> We are all dying. It is a long time since the Chiefs and the people who know book . . . have been oppressing us. We are telling you that we have been oppressed. The new Chiefs are also receiving bribes. Since the white men came, our oil does not fetch money. Our kernels do not fetch money. If we take goats or yams to market to sell, court messengers who wear a uniform take all these things from us.[11]

These powerful reasons fueled the women's anger and resistance. Some even believed that their activities would bring down the government. A mass movement emerged, not with Nwanyeruwa as the sole leader—there was no single leader—but with various groups and leaders acting in various places.

The Women's War came as a shock to the government. A small incident quickly spread beyond the government officials' control. Before local colonial authorities could deny the rumor or people could change their minds, the protest had become violent. Thousands of women were spontaneously radicalized against the government. As had happened in the previous years among the Itsekiri and Urhobo, the casualties were the warrant chiefs and native courts, who were attacked with the maximum force available to the women involved. They also destroyed official buildings and the houses of those who symbolized the new power elite. The women called for an end to the authority of the warrant chiefs and demanded that no more cases to be heard at the native courts, whose judges they associated with the abuse of power and corruption. When the riots reached Aba, the women added European trading firms to the list of objects of attack.[12]

While many grievances against the colonial government provoked the violence, certain preexisting social arrangements enabled it to spread. Many aspects of the precolonial structure and institutions were still in place, providing ideas and networks that the women could tap into to energize themselves and generate protest actions that were not led by any particular person. The women had experience in wielding political authority in their villages. While they could not be heads of households or lineage leaders, they were not excluded from decision making. Women connected one village to another through a system of "village exogamy," in which a woman married a man from another village while maintaining her connections with her place of birth. Women had limited rights in the village into which they married; their power and rights were in the village where they were born, where they were entitled to land. The war of 1929 enabled the women to work through a complex network of villages and social relations.

Various organizations were also in place that the women were able to mobilize. The wives in each village belonged to a social club in which membership was mandatory. These clubs regulated conduct and imposed sanctions on wrongdoers. Each club had a recognized spokesperson who had been chosen for her leadership qualities. Clubs were forums for discussion of many issues: agricultural and trade matters, assistance to the needy, the role of government, the impact of new policies, and so forth. In 1929, taxation became a subject that united the women against the government.

Their declining incomes from palm produce also occupied women's attention, adding to their anticolonial sentiments. The economic downturn hurt women who had made their livelihood as "middlemen" selling exports of palm oil and palm kernels and imports of cigarettes, spirits, tobacco, and cloth. The prices of key products fell within a short time: the price for 50 pounds of palm kernels fell by over 1 shilling between November 1928 and December 1929; that of four gallons of edible oil fell by 2 shillings. Complaints were widespread, and some women sent delegations to the European trading firms to complain. According to the angry women, it would take hard work by various members of a household to make 4 shillings a month from their trading activities.[13] The women also complained that they were paying more for imported items. This was true; in 1928, the government had increased the duty on a number of products in an attempt to raise additional revenue. The increases in the duty on items imported from Europe such as gray baft and tobacco, both of which were widely used, added to women's hostility to the government.[14]

Furthermore, the administration system did not favor women. Most women were poor and unable to obtain a Western education. They were thus not qualified for administrative positions because of lack of education and because of their gender. Some of their traditional power was being eroded as well, especially in the area of judicial control over members of women's associations who had violated sanctions.

Women's grievances against the colonial government were comprehensive and complex, and taxation became the one policy that united all the other grievances. Although the taxes of 1927 and 1928 were levied on men, men and women were joint producers, which meant that the burden affected women as well. Many women had to help their husbands and other male relations earn the money to pay the tax. A tax on a goat was a tax on the women who reared it. A tax on farm products was a tax on women who worked as farmers. When the "news" (or the rumor) came that they, too, would pay, it meant double taxation, not to mention the cultural objection to asking women to pay. When an entire community was assessed, the community shared the burden. When individuals were assessed, gender roles in households were displayed in ways that displeased many people. The government was apparently perceiving women as independent money earners and apparently had an expectation that they would pay taxes as well as male heads of households. Some women wondered, in oral testimonies, whether the taxation policy was assuming that they were heads of households, to be treated the same as men.[15]

As the official records tend to suggest, the most important source of anger that defined the women's movement was the political structure under which they were governed and the habits of those who exercised power. The women wanted an end to the power exercised by the warrant chiefs. In this desire, they were no different from most men. Attacking the warrant chiefs was the same as questioning the right of the British to create such a new political class, demanding the restoration of the traditional elite, and saying that the new basis of power was corrupt. The women wondered why warrant chiefs could not be appointed on a short-term basis after serving a probation period that would allow the unacceptable ones to be removed. The women also insisted that all the warrant chiefs they had attacked be permanently removed from power.

Process, State Reaction, and Outcome

The first battle occurred at Oloko itself. As would be expected, the focus of the grievances was the local warrant chief. The women besieged the house of the warrant chief, Okugo, for many days. They asked him to leave his house to explain why women, who were "dependent on the men for subsistence,"[16] should be taxed. They attacked his compound and looted his property, and an open fight broke out. S. N. Nwabara, who collected oral information on Okugo, described him as rich and powerful. He was carried in a hammock like a colonial officer when he traveled. He lived in a large palace with his many wives, and his wealth in livestock attracted the respect of some and the resentment of others.[17] While there were other chiefs in the area, the women attacked Okugo because he had subordinated other lesser chiefs and was openly identified with the colonial government.

Next, the women contacted Captain J. Cook, the acting district officer, asking him to issue a written statement that there would be no taxation of women. After reading a police report on the violent activities, Cook sent a sergeant to Oloko to assure the women that they would not pay taxes. He followed this with a visit in late November to repeat his promise. He also agreed to arrest Chief Okugo and to initiate a formal trial in Bende. On the day of the trial, December 4, the doubting women were present in the courthouse in full force. Captain Hill, the district officer, now back from leave, was stunned by what he saw:

> The women numbering over 10,000 were shouting and yelling round the office in a frenzy. They demanded his [Okugo's] cap of office, which I threw to them and it met the same fate as a fox's carcass thrown to a pack of hounds. The station between the office and the prison and just round the office resembled Epsom Downs on Derby day. The crowd extended right away through Bende Village and the pandemonium was beyond all belief. It took me two hours to get an opportunity of sending the wire asking for more police.[18]

Although he called for police reinforcements, Captain Hill had essentially capitulated by giving the women the cap of office of the warrant chief. He did more. On the same day, Chief Okugo was convicted of "spreading news likely to create alarm and of assault."[19] This was a decisive attempt by the government to blame its action on a local chief, saving its own officer, who had authorized the warrant chief to conduct a census. It was a victory for the women; their action had led to the fall of a powerful warrant chief. Okugo went to jail for nine months.[20]

But the problem of anti-tax sentiment could no longer be solved by punishing just one chief. The victory emboldened the women to ask for more changes, including the removal of many warrant chiefs. The women immediately held mass meetings and demonstrations; thus began the Ogu Umunwanye (Women's War) that consumed the month of December. The movement spread like wildfire, touching many parts of Owerri and Calabar provinces. Many of the women still believed that taxation was about to be imposed on them, and their action received support from men who were not happy about paying taxes. Following the court hearing in Bende where Okugo was convicted, hundreds of women took to the streets, moving from one village to another, chanting antiauthority and war songs. "If it were not for the white man," their favorite song declared, "we should have killed chief Okugo and eaten him up. If it were not for the white man we should have killed all the chiefs and eaten them up." The colonial officers were shocked by the rebellion. In a telegram to Lagos, the district officer attributed the war to taxation, low prices, and preaching by the church that weakened parental control over children.

Songs gave way to battles. The women destroyed court buildings and records at Nguru, Okpuala, Ngor, Isu, Uratta, and Aguata. The intensity of the attacks was such that by December 13 the government needed military operations to stop them. The government's strategy was to use excessive force to disperse the women and break the mob into smaller units that could be dealt with. Both sides were making plans; the women were spreading the battles to other locations and the government was mobilizing troops to destroy them. As the war spread, the government mobilized troops in places such as Aba and Port Harcourt, although this did not stop the women from continuing a looting rampage in some areas. Over the course of the war, the army confronted more than 15,000 women in a number of locations over an area of 6,000 square miles.[21] In Aba and Owerri, they repeatedly dispersed the women with force, but the women regrouped each time. In smaller villages and towns, the women had the upper hand.

In mid-December, fearing more trouble, the colonial officers requested Lagos to send more troops. Lagos ordered caution and suggested a political solution, working through the chiefs to redress the grievances. But Lagos authorities felt that villages needed to be reminded of the Collective Punishment Ordinance. They told officers to threaten participants with a fine of 500 pounds and a two-year prison term.[22] The chiefs of Azumuri were the first victims of the Women's War policy of harassing villages; they were forced to pay a heavy fine of 2,000 pounds. As more cases of violence erupted, local officers began to use force. The most excessive use of force occurred in Calabar Province at Abak and Utu Etim Ekpo, where many were injured and twenty-one women were killed.[23] The killing did not particularly disturb the officers. Indeed, they discussed their need to improve on the methods of killing. The governor in Lagos told district officers to first order mobs to disperse with a strong warning that demonstrators would be shot if they failed to do so. With the threat or use of force, order was gradually restored in the period from the last days of December 1929 to January 10, 1930.

Some broad features of the movement emerged after the December 4 conflicts. As Nwanyeruwa retreated into the background, more activist women took over, described in the report of the commission that investigated the Women's War as "the intelligent trio of Oloko women: Ikonnia, Nwannedie and Nwugo." The "intelligent trio" that were the initial spokeswomen energized others to become a powerful militia. The participants were not confined to any age or generation; the women's unity was fostered by a common objective. Even the daughters and wives of chiefs participated, and some relations of the much-hated warrant chiefs and court clerks were active in the riots. This was a well-ordered movement even though it grew rapidly. The orders the women leaders issued were obeyed. In addition, the movement was well supported by local people. The fighters received support from various villages in the form of food and weapons. Colonial officers did not anticipate such a massive uprising and did not believe that thousands of women could act in a well-organized and coordinated fashion.

Women took on some elements of male identity in this war. Many women described themselves as having the energies of men. In becoming ready for battle, many protected themselves with charms and amulets and performed war rituals as male soldiers would do. Medicine men assured the women warriors that no bullets could kill them, but on December 16, 1929, many were shocked at Opobo to see twenty women shot and killed and their corpses scattered.

Although women adopted some aspects of male identity, their rhetoric contained a strong critique of male behavior. They criticized the warrant chiefs as "useless men," characters who would do anything for money and were not needed as husbands or as members of society. The women constructed their solidarity along gender lines that featured the women's associations and women leaders, and they excluded men from participating in the war. Interests were also defined along gender lines: women should not pay taxes that could undermine their economic and political power. In defending their interests, women saw the enemy as men who imposed taxes on them. Some even spoke of men's oppression of women that needed to end, citing the corrupt activities of male court clerks as an example. For those who saw the movement's goal as an end to male oppression, taxation was not the beginning of the crisis or its sole cause but the result of a series of objectionable actions and behaviors by men.

The government was interested in knowing the religion of the initial instigators of the war in order to find out whether an ideology had provoked the rebellion. The Oloko trio claimed to be Christians, but it is difficult to link their actions to Christianity. They were not literate in the Western sense and were unable to read the Bible. As farmers and petty traders, they probably suffered along with others from the economic decline. However, aside from the initial mobilization, the trio did not have much power beyond their own village. When the rebellion became heated, the trio could not stop other women from looting and burning down courthouses. No central leadership structure emerged, as women in each village decided what to do, where to attack, and whom to insult. At the village level, the women appointed their own leaders, usually people in their late twenties or early thirties and others who were unencumbered by childbearing responsibilities. In some areas, leadership simply fell on the existing "head women," who moved seamlessly from their traditional power to a radical form of power. The government reports described Nwanyeruwa as a personality that could move people; the three leaders of Oloko as intelligent; and the two "prominent leaders" of Nguru, Mary Onumaere and Chinna, as leaders who were widely accepted by other women, trusted for their judgment, and strong enough to lead over 3,000 protesters. Nnete Nma, the woman who led the others in the village of Obohia, was reported to be so quick in decision making and so angry that she took no time in ordering that the Obohia courthouse should be burned down. Nma was perhaps the only leader to be sentenced to a two-year jail term for her activities, which the government described as excessive.

The objects of attack were similar to those in previous outbreaks of violence. The warrant chiefs were the primary targets but not the only ones. The women destroyed ten native courthouses and damaged many others. They also destroyed houses of court clerks and other personnel and looted trading factories in Anaba, Aba, Imo River, and Mbawsi. The objects of attack provide some evidence about the objectives of the riots and protests. Although some officers of the government portrayed the women as irrational, it was perfectly clear that the women knew what they were fighting for, knew the endgame they desired, and were aware that they could not get everything they wanted. It was abundantly clear that the warrant chiefs were a major source of their anger. It was widely believed that the warrant chiefs were the ones who had advised the colonial government to impose taxation on women. Many of the women believed that the *ezeala* (traditional chiefs) would not have treated them as the warrant chiefs had done. Indeed, a large number of the women separated the activities of the warrant chiefs from the colonial government itself. In the eyes of the women, the warrant chiefs had misled the government into calling for taxes. In various testimonies before the commission of inquiry held on the matter, the women made a distinction between the warrant chiefs and the government: they were fighting the warrant chiefs, not the government. "We did not come to fight," declared a woman protester from the village of Ahiara, "but simply to tell government that the chiefs have been oppressing us." The government did not agree with the women that it was different from the warrant chiefs. In other words, for government officials, an assault on the warrant chiefs was an assault on the government itself; the government, not the warrant chiefs, had put the taxation policy in place.

When the colonial government reacted with the use of force, the human casualties were high. Colonial forces killed thirty-two women and injured thirty-one at Opobo. In the town of Utu Etim Ekpo, the police killed eighteen and injured nineteen. The number of deaths recorded in official records was about fifty; oral testimonies give a higher figure. We can never know how many were injured. The government believed that it could easily intimidate the women, but this was not the case. Guns and threats did not frighten them. Indeed, after the most serious outbreaks were put down, many continued with their protests in various places until July 1930. The women were motivated by their objectives: their men should stop paying taxes; women should never be taxed; market prices for their products should rise; and native courts should be reorganized to make them less corrupt.

To assuage the protesters, the government decided to review the performance of a number of warrant chiefs. Some chiefs were disgraced and some were fined, an admission by the government that some of its agents had been behaving unacceptably. This met one of the most important conditions the women had demanded. But the government's most far-reaching response was its decision to establish official inquiries to examine the causes of the riots and suggest ways to prevent further outbreaks.[24] It was only after the publication of the reports and indications that changes would come that the riots ended in the mid-1930. By this time, it was clear what the women's victories were: they would not pay taxes; the government would reorganize the native courts as they had suggested; and many warrant chiefs would be prosecuted and punished.

While the violence by the women was eventually ended with the use of force by the government, the women were certainly not completely defeated. First, women were not made to pay tax and the issue of taxation for women was not raised again until the 1950s. The government did not change its mind about collecting taxes from men, but its assurances that women would be exempted were clear enough. The government emphasized that it had not even set out to tax women and that an overzealous officer was responsible for initiating a census that counted animals, children, and wives.[25] However, the government's enumeration procedure and the visitations to villages and towns by its agents had made it appear to the women that they would be asked to pay tax.

The women were not opposed to development, and they did not equate antigovernment behavior with opposition to modernity. A few of them wanted women to become involved in the administration. Although they attacked courthouses, their complaint was that court clerks and judges were corrupt. They were not opposed to the judiciary as a concept; some of them were happy that the courts could grant them divorces from bad husbands. Although some in the government wanted to associate the violence with an approach that was hostile to Christianity, the women provided no evidence of this. They did not attack churches or mission houses and they spared the lives of white men even when they had the opportunity to attack and kill them. The only white person who was assaulted was a certain Dr. Hunter, but this was in revenge for the fact that he had knocked down and killed two women with his car and then fled the scene. There was a radical tone in some of the women's testimonies to the commission of inquiry that suggested a desire to transcend both the traditional and colonial societies: they wanted equality with men, the ability to dictate what they wanted, and changes in law to benefit them.

In the aftermath of the war, many continued to draw inspiration from it. A number of women kept an eye on colonial agents and used the legal system to challenge some warrant chiefs. The women took an interest in and complained about various issues: prices, their increasing economic and political marginalization, the abuse of power by colonial agents, and even the impact of the taxation of men on women.

The government responded to the women's criticism: in London, the Colonial Office was critical of the taxation policy of its Nigerian administration. After the commission of inquiry submitted its report, steps were taken to abandon the system of warrant chiefs, bring back to power the traditional officeholders (*ezeala*), and reorganize the native court system to include women as members. The administrative reorganization that followed was such a permanent legacy of the Women's War of 1929 that it merits a brief discussion below, following a discussion of the punishment that was meted out to villages involved.

POST-VIOLENCE CHANGES: PUNISHMENT AND ADMINISTRATIVE REORGANIZATION

The government blew hot and cold at the same time. It used force to achieve its initial goal of suppressing the rebellion, but it used the law to achieve the goal of preventing future wars by women. For many weeks, colonial officers went around to remind the chiefs and elders of the Collective Punishment Ordinance, which had been revised in 1926. The relevant chapter gave the government the power to punish a town or village for a crime committed by any of its members. As chapter 80 of the 1926 ordinance stated:

> The Governor may impose fines on all or any inhabitants of any village or district of members of any tribe or community if, after inquiry, he finds:
>
> That they have willfully disobeyed, or neglected or refused to carry out, any lawful order given to them by an administrative officer or by a native authority.
>
> That their conduct has been such as to require the bringing of soldiers or police to the village or district or the employment of soldiers or police against them for the purposes of preventing or suppressing disturbances, or enforcing lawful orders or the payment of taxes leviable under any law of the Protectorate.[26]

During the Women's War, the colonial officers immediately began using the ordinance by asking various villages to pay an advance deposit for good behavior with the assumption that refunds would be offered if there was no more trouble. The idea of a deposit was to force village elders and chiefs to call the women to order. Colonial officers asked twenty-nine villages and towns to pay deposits, some of which were punished with very heavy amounts. The ordinance required that a crisis should be over and the community tried and found guilty before a fine could be imposed. After the violence ended, colonial officers traveled throughout the region in the initial months of 1930 to document villages' roles in the Women's War. They forced many chiefs to document the role of their villages. A few letters by the chiefs written in the Igbo language surfaced that highlighted the role of certain women and places that were touched or damaged. Colonial authorities used these letters to extract more information. In one of these documents, the women of Oloko were said to have contacted others, inciting them to rebel, to demand the removal of many warrant chiefs, to demand that the courts be abolished, and to demand several other changes. Almost thirty communities were punished for listening to the Oloko women, for sending delegates to Oloko to host an anti-tax rally on December 17, for refusing to disperse when they were ordered to do so by a government agent, and for looting.[27] They were accused of disobeying laws and behaving in such a way as to invite the police and army to their communities. All adult members of communities were asked to contribute to a combination of taxes and fines, as listed in Table 5.1.

TABLE 5.I. Fines Imposed on Villages That Participated in the Women's War of 1919

Town	No. of adults	Tax	Fine
Abuwa	166	£41.10s	£10.0s
Ahaba	184	£46.0s	£11.10s
Amaba	407	£101.14s	£25.0s
Amizi	189	£47.5s	£12.0s
Awomuku	282	£70.10s	£17.10s
Azuiyi	92	£23.0s	£5.10s
Ekeberi	81	£20.5s	£5.0s
Ekpiri Ala	101	£25.5s	£6.0s
Ekpiri Elu	64	£16.0s	£4.0s
Eriam Ala	316	£79.0s	£19.10s
Eriam Elu	150	£37.10s	£9.10s
Nbiopong	64	£16.0s	£4.0s
Nchara	382	£95.10s	£24.0s
Ndeoro	91	£22.15s	£5.10s
Ndi Oriwea	69	£17.5s	£4.27s
Nnang	288	£72.0s	£18.0s
Ntalakwu	75	£18.15s	£4.10s
Obohia	374	£93.10s	£23.0s
Obuebile	161	£40.5s	£10.0s
Ohuhu	186	£46.10s	£11.10s
Okwe	189	£47.5s	£12.0s
Oloko	223	£55.15s	£28.0s
Umugo	139	£34.15s	£8.10s
Umuigwu	191	£47.15s	£12.0s
Usaka Elogu	55	£13.15s	£3.10s
Usaka Ibionu	140	£35.0s	£8.10s
Usaka Ndieke	50	£12.10s	£3.0s
Usaka Obogu	113	£28.5s	£7.0s
Usaka Obon	86	£21.10s	£5.10s
Usaka Okoro	36	£9.0s	£2.0s
Usaka Uku	192	£48.0s	£12.0s
Usaka Ukwobon	52	£13.0s	£3.0s
Usaka Upa	72	£18.0s	£4.10s

Sources: "Inquiry under the Collective Punishment Ordinance," NAE, CSE 1/85/3624, EP 6784; S. N. Nwabara, *Iboland: A Century of Contact with Britain, 1860–1960* (London: Hodder and Stoughton, 1977), 195–196. Calculations per head are not included in the archival sources.

The table provides more evidence on the nature of the violence. It confirms the widespread nature of the Women's War, which affected the nearly thirty towns that were punished for their participation and the other towns that were compelled to pay advance money. The amount might appear small if calculated per person, but in an agrarian economy, it would have taken several months to generate enough money to pay it. The difficulty would have been compounded by the economic depression and the withdrawal of women activists from their regular economic activities. The fines and taxes demonstrate the excesses of the legal system: whether a town participated in the Women's War or not did not count. All towns were taxed where mobs had gathered. Although some officials regarded the application of the ordinance as a violation of human rights, the commission of enquiry supported the action, if only to punish a so-called "recalcitrant primitive community."[28] A few officers were not too happy with the idea of collective punishment and said so once in a while, as E. Falk, the senior resident of Calabar Province, did in January 1930:

> In assessing these fines it should be taken into consideration that all damage to buildings was repaired by the people, who turned out in hundreds to perform the necessary labour; further that where villages refused to come in to sue for terms huts were burnt as a warning example. It is my considered opinion that heavy fines should not be levied, since the main objective after restoring law and order with a firm hand should be to avoid any impression that Government desires to punish vindictively those who were stirred up by false rumours spread by unscrupulous agitators.[29]

The commission of inquiry that the governor of Nigeria set up in February 1930 included two famous Nigerians, Sir Kitoyi Ajasi, a barrister-at-law, and Eric Olawolu Moore, also a barrister-at-law; a representative of the European firms (Valentine Ronald Osborne, the agent-general of John Holt); an advocate of law (George Graham Paul); and a colonial political officer (William Edgar Hunt). The commission was headed by Donald Kingdom, the chief justice of Nigeria's Supreme Court. The commission was set up with the following goals:

> To inquire into the origin and causes of and responsibility for the recent disturbances in the Calabar and Owerri Provinces and the measures taken to restore order and to make such recommendations as may seem fit.
>
> To inquire into the responsibility (if any) of any person or persons for failing to take in anticipation of such disturbances adequate measures to safeguard life and property.[30]

Various interest groups and villages were represented, some of which came with counsel. The work of the commission lasted from March 10 to May 26, 1930, during which time it interviewed 485 witnesses and submitted many reports and memoranda. The comprehensive report blamed the Women's War on "the widespread belief throughout the affected areas that government was about to impose a direct tax upon women."[31] The commission denied that government wanted to impose taxation on women, but it concluded that the women "had good grounds for supposing that such a measure was afoot."[32]

The recommendations of the commission laid the basis for the administrative reorganization of the Eastern Provinces. Arguably the most important outcome of the Women's War was the government's recognition of the need to understand indigenous political institutions and create changes that people could tolerate and live with. Fresh studies were commissioned to understand Igbo cultures. Noted colonial anthropologists were drafted to work on the Igbo, led by C. K. Meek, who was assisted by Margaret Green and Sylvia Leith-Ross. Ida Ward, a linguist, began a separate project on languages. Although the books emanating from their research began to appear from the mid-1930s onward, some of their initial findings were reported earlier to colonial officers.[33] In addition, almost 200 fact-finding reports, known as intelligence reports, appeared, all of which discussed aspects of the people's way of life. The Women's War and the knowledge generated after it led to both judicial and administrative reforms.

In the pre-1929 era, the membership and practices of native courts and native authorities were inconsistent and were set up in ways that many people disliked. In some places, a warrant chief constituted the native court. Many villages and clans could be grouped together into one native authority and native court even when they were located far from the court. Citizens who needed services had to travel long distances, and many courts were slow and inefficient. In 1930, the government empowered the resident of each province to establish more native courts and native authorities, using his discretion to locate them in appropriate places.[34] After 1930, many native courts were established to serve smaller population units.

Another important change was the differentiation between the native court and the native authority. After 1930, native authorities were no longer required to perform judicial functions and were limited to other administrative tasks to manage towns and villages. Section 2 of the 1930 ordinance defined a native authority as "any chief or other native of Nigeria or other person or any native council or group of such natives or other persons appointed to be a native authority under the Ordinance for the area concerned."[35] Native courts were to be constituted by the government with clear instructions about their judicial functions. In addition, the native courts were reformed to allow appeals and their powers were reduced. They were also prevented from exercising jurisdiction over many offenses.[36]

Finally, the native courts were divided into four grades, each with defined jurisdictional powers:

> Grade A Full judicial powers in all civil actions and criminal causes, but no sentence of death to be carried out until it has been confirmed by the Governor.
> Grade B Civil actions in which the debt, demand or damages do not exceed one hundred pounds. Criminal cases which can be adequately punished by imprisonment for one year, twelve strokes, or a fine of fifty pounds, or the equivalent by native law or custom.
> Grade C Civil actions in which the debt, demand or damages do not exceed fifty pounds. Criminal causes which can be adequately punished by imprisonment for six months, or in the case of theft of farm produce or livestock by imprisonment for twelve months, twelve strokes, or a fine of ten pounds, or the equivalent by native law or custom.
> Grade D Civil actions in which the debt, demand or damages do not exceed twenty-five pounds. Criminal causes which can be adequately punished by imprisonment for three months, or in the case of theft of farm produce or livestock by imprisonment for six months, twelve strokes, or a fine of five pounds, or the equivalent by native law or custom.[37]

The resident had the power to designate the grade of a court, appoint the members, decide on the judicial fees to be paid by winners and losers in cases, and encourage appeals by dissatisfied people in order to minimize charges of unfairness and corruption. When the courts went into operation after 1930, residents chose the members of the courts, and residents retained the power of the veto over judicial decisions.

Similarly, the administration was reorganized to make use of traditional institutions. As with the courts, the native administration was divided into first, second, third, and fourth classes.[38] Only the third and fourth classes were relevant to local areas. Called a "tribal council," the third-class native administration consisted of low-ranking chiefs who were appointed as "headmen" to exercise administrative power over their areas. The fourth-class native administration combined the councils of village elders, clans, and subclans. The real challenge was over appointments, as many put forward claims. The limits of power were badly defined, while the colonial officers retained the crucial powers. For example, colonial officers controlled the native treasuries.

The 1930s thus inaugurated important reforms in the administration of the Igbo at the local level, all in an attempt to prevent another uprising. The government's major recognition was that most of the societies in the east had no kings and chiefs with autocratic powers. Its new approach was to make use of more elders and "fragment" the political units. Elders were sought to represent various interests and political units. Lineage heads were drawn into the administration, appointed to serve in hundreds of village and clan assemblies. The idea behind the change was to take power away from one man (the warrant chief) and give it to many men. The clan council became important, and lineage elders decided many issues and ran the administration in a way that was more "gentle" and acceptable to the people. Village assemblies were put under native authorities in which colonial officers were able to issue orders and supervise the management of local governments. The focus on village assemblies and the way they were grouped ensured that each ethnic group (Igbo, Efik, Urhobo, and so on) was separated from the other so that differences in culture and institutions did not stand in the way of administration.

The power of local chiefs was also reduced. The creation of two agencies—the native authority and the native court—split the organs of government into the executive (the native authority) and the judicial (the native court). Before the 1929–1930 war, the warrant chiefs had enjoyed both executive and judicial powers, and, together with the colonial officers, had also had some legislative power. Warrant chiefs, messengers, and clerks had been more interested in the judicial aspect, since they were able to make money from people in trouble. After 1930, the clerks and messengers of the previous years were removed and replaced by local youth. The belief was that the local youth would respect their people and would be less tempted to collect bribes or show disrespect, unlike the strangers who had previously been recruited as clerks and messengers.

The 1930s was a decade of calm, thanks in part to the Women's War, which created the conditions for reform. There was jubilation across the land that the warrant chiefs had been removed. It was as if taxation was the poisoned arrow that many had been waiting to throw at the hearts of the much-hated chiefs. Power was also redistributed to local communities in ways that favored the traditional elite. (Indeed, some elders misunderstood the arrangement to mean the restoration of traditional power, while the greedy ones among them wanted to imitate the warrant chiefs.) Although taxation was not abolished, the government asked the elders involved in administration as council members to explain the need to pay to their people. Also, council members were responsible for ensuring that assessment was fair and collection was peaceful and noncoercive. More important, the council members would know how the revenues were spent, as they were also expected to discuss projects and estimates and fund disbursement.

The colonial officers, too, were happy; they regarded the changes as an opportunity to fully implement the Lugardian principles of indirect rule and expected rapid progress. The colonial officers expected cooperation in various ways: the elders and co-opted youth would collect tax and assist in the propaganda that encouraged people to produce more cash crops. Also, they expected peace: they hoped that the elders and youth, now part of local administration, would no longer create problems.[39] As it turned out, however, although the changes of the 1930s produced calm for a while, they created the foundation for the anticolonial resentments of the 1940s. The native courts were not "native," in that much power was still exercised by the colonial officers, and they became very unpopular among the people. The basis of the legal system was changing as local laws were replaced by new ones. Respect for elders was weakening and elders' decisions were not always binding, especially on those with the resources and knowledge to use other courts. No one could foretell the impact of the changes in the early 1930s. What most were talking about at that time was the reward the Women's War had brought to many.

6

VERBAL VIOLENCE AND
RADICAL NATIONALISM

We the enslaved peoples, know certainly well that imperialism
and African irredentism are two irreconcilables. We know also that
the redemption of Africa lies in the hands of Africans themselves
and must be achieved by either violent revolution or by non-violent
revolution.

—OSITA AGWUNA, MEMBER, ZIKIST MOVEMENT,
KANO BRANCH, 1946

Nigeria entered an era of militant nationalism in the 1940s. The anti-imperialist mood was fed by the desire for the rapid disengagement of the British from power and the belief that previous leaders and parties had been too gentlemanly. The rise of activist leaders, notably political leaders such as Nnamdi Azikiwe and critics such as Nduka Eze, instigated the rise of a militant movement. Trade unions were similarly radicalized and changed their strategies from oral negotiations with the government to strikes and violence to realize their goals and possibly bring down the colonial government. The literature and media of the 1940s fired the imagination of youth, leading many young men and women to develop a political consciousness that led to political activism and aggressive nationalism. Various young people in their twenties captured the mood of the time when they publicly stated that they saw a revolution in the making and were sure that their combative actions would set Nigeria free.[1] The words they used, the words they read, and the words they heard all became inspirational. It was as if a generation of young men was waiting for such words to empower it. Young people began to feel as if they could challenge whiteness and the colonial order and "deflate the pride, arrogance and perfidy of the colonial rulers and create a new society for Nigeria."[2]

The literature of the 1940s was politically engaged and ideologically focused. Some dwelt on the glories of the African past, pointing out the achievements of the kingdoms of Ethiopia, Ghana, Mali, and Songhai. Some noted the cultural advances of the past to make the point that blackness could not be equated with primitivity. Many writers questioned the colonial ideology of European supremacy and promoted positive ideas of blackness. In this writing, we cannot discount the worth and power of words expressed with violence in mind.[3] Words embody ideas, and even if they do not always translate into concrete actions, as they did in the Women's War, these ideas reflect the mood of the time, the possibility offered to a young generation of expressing itself.

Resistance and nationalism became two sides of the same coin. One side fought to protect the old order of traditions and precolonial nations and the other side fought to create a new order in an emerging nation-state. Anticolonial protests began a few years after resistance to colonial conquest of the period 1885 to 1916 had failed. Demands for reforms, political agitation, and complaints about imperial exploitation were common during the period 1914 to 1939. Elites led agitations for reform that were mainly peaceful; this group used writing to express dissent or seek changes. Elites could be aggressive and radical, but many of its members chose not to use violence. They put their Western educations to good use to articulate nationalism,[4] and their demands for incremental changes to constitutions eventually led to independence.[5]

The Western-educated elite in the 1940s and 1950s knew what they wanted. Some had tasted privilege in the colonial service and enjoyed good incomes in self-employment. Those who had been educated in Europe and the United States were able to compare Nigeria with other countries and develop an idea of progress premised on the idea that they would use their education, knowledge, and skills and imported technology to move the country forward. For this reason, the conduct of elite politics in Nigeria, by and large, was moderate. For example, the Northern Peoples' Congress (NPC), which acquired power in the 1950s, regarded itself as traditional and deliberately promoted an agenda that drew from Islam and supported chieftaincy institutions. In the late 1950s, many political party leaders went so far as to distance themselves from the radical Pan-Africanist activities associated with W. E. B. Dubois and Kwame Nkrumah. The National Council of Nigeria and the Cameroons (NCNC) and the NPC felt that such activities were premature.[6]

The literature on the constitutional steps to Nigeria's independence overlooks two important areas.[7] First, it overlooks the acts of violence in the years of decolonization (as in the case of resistance by unions, for which see chapter 7). Second, it overlooks the expressions of radicalism in words and actions that called for revolution and popular uprisings, the actions that form the core of this chapter. Neither can be ignored as part of the resistance and nationalism that was shaped by the imposition of colonial rule. Osita Agwuna, quoted above, was not a lone voice crying in the wilderness. Rather, he belonged to a generation that wanted to combine fiery words with concrete action to bring about changes.

In this chapter, the violence that we see is a combination of militant criticism of the colonial order that demanded independence and messianic nationalism that asserted that a Nigerian hero and leader was ready to take over. A generation of young men and women arose that claimed that they were not afraid of the government or its army or its police. They criticized a colonial education that had inculcated a mindset of excessive respect for white rulers and fear of the machinery of the colonial government. They regarded the colonial government as illegitimate, refusing to call it "the Nigerian government." They saw British leaders and the Nigerians who supported them as enemies. Militant nationalists expressed frustration with a gradualist approach to reforms and constitution making, saying that "actionism" was better than writing petitions to the Colonial Office. Nduka Eze, one of the young activists of the 1940s, maintained that "in an age with special reference to Nigeria where the governmental structure is not democratized, it becomes obvious that constitutionalism is not an effective weapon to be used by anybody who calls himself a nationalist."[8]

Both the radical and ideological phases in Nigerian politics were marked by revolutionary demands and violent words. Young leaders emerged who made highly combative statements, emphasizing that they were not afraid of being killed or jailed for their views. Nduka Eze was just one of many. Perhaps the most prolific among them was Mokwugo Okoye, who served in the army from 1941 to 1942 and became a political activist thereafter as well as a famous anticolonial critic. His book *Vistas of Life,* which he wrote in prison from 1950 to 1952, is one of the classics of the era.[9] Okoye wanted to restore African communalism, which, he argued, had been destroyed by imperialism. He borrowed a strategy of civil disobedience from Gandhi to call for mass action against the colonial government. He wanted Nigeria to adopt a socialist ideology, arguing that this was the only available option for creating progress. Agwuna focused on racism, asserting that white domination was hurting Africa.[10]

Nationalism built around anti-imperialism became very strong during the 1940s. In addition, as in previous decades, there were many physical attacks on agents of the state, specifically policemen, clerks, and messengers. The most abused and assaulted victims were the court messengers,

Nigerians who served on the lower rungs of the ladder. To beat a court clerk was to defy the government, settle a score, take revenge. While senior officers lived far apart from the people and were protected by the police, court clerks lived among the people and were vulnerable to violent encounters. Court clerks brought home the reality of corruption; they collected bribes and gifts on behalf of chiefs and kings, delivered unpleasant summonses from judges, maintained order inside and outside offices and courts, and watched over the movements of British and Nigerian colonial officers in order to report fellow Nigerians to the police.

As colonial policies and the changes of the era incited nationalism, pioneer leaders emerged to challenge the colonial regime. Although many were famous, such as Herbert Macaulay and Nnamdi Azikiwe, others were not so famous. These lesser-known individuals were active in mobilizing market women for action (as in the case of Alimotu Pelewura of Lagos), organizing labor unions, or carrying politics to the grass roots. Their demands were legion, varying from involving Nigerians in local politics to bringing more amenities to the people. Although the literature on nationalism has focused on the Christianized Western-educated elite, it is clear that a broad spectrum of society was involved, including highly educated people and peasants, men and women, young people and elders, Muslims and Christians, and people in a variety of occupations, both traditional and modern.[11] There were many ways to articulate nationalism, including closing markets, participating in strikes, mobilizing the masses against government policies, and participating in violent protests. In this chapter, I focus on the ideas of a new generation of anticolonial activists, and in chapter 7 I discuss their actions.

THE CONTEXT OF RADICALISM

The radical phase of Nigerian nationalism began in the 1940s. It was a departure from the pre-1939 phase when political parties and their leaders, mainly based in Lagos, pursued reformist goals and were content with gentle criticisms of colonial authorities. The events and changes brought about by the Second World War, including the participation of African soldiers in the war, the increased cost of living, the loss of Europe's prestige and power, and the rise of the United States and the Soviet Union as superpowers, all served to change the course of the nationalist movement in Africa.[12] After the war, colonial authorities initiated political and economic reforms that brought health centers, more roads, and even the first university. Nigerians asked for more.[13] The political atmosphere became far more intense than ever before. Anticipating a transfer of power, aspiring Nigerian politicians began to compete with one another. This competition produced the collapse of two parties, the Nigerian Youth Movement (NYM) and the Nigerian National Democratic Party (NNDP). The NCNC and its leader Azikiwe rose to prominence, but challenges came from other ambitious politicians who began to create political-cum-cultural unions toward the end of the 1950s that became regional political parties.

Radically oriented movements also established their own political space. Radical anticolonial nationalists sought to unite people of different ethnicities and groups to create a Pan-Nigerian platform. They were quick to see the growing rifts among the elite in the 1940s and the danger these would pose to the independence struggles. Thus, the radicals began to refer to one nation, regional and ethnic cooperation, and the unity of the educated elite and the masses. In highly charged words, radical nationalists pointed to the political and economic exploitation involved in colonial domination and began to call for the total rejection of the British.[14] The revolutionaries among the nationalists advocated the use of violence to end the colonial relationship.

The cultural element that we found in the early expression of anticolonial resistance (see chapter 2) was revived as radical nationalism in the 1940s. A number of people began to call for an emphasis on African food, attire, clothing, and other aspects of culture to make a powerful statement that the British were not wanted in Nigeria. Boycotting European objects became a way of expressing radical anticolonialism.

In the interest of fulfilling the dream of a united country, activists searched for a national leader who would replace the British governor-general and represent the vision of a new Nigeria. In the 1940s, many gravitated toward Nnamdi Azikiwe and the NCNC. Azikiwe's arrival on the Nigerian political scene in 1937 sped up the political tempo. In that year, he established a combative newspaper, the *West African Pilot,* that reflected the militant tone of a new generation of politicians and has become one of the most valuable primary sources of the era. His political ambitions were large, and some of his strategies were new.[15] Azikiwe combined ideas from Pan-Africanism, Fabian socialism, and African cultures to advocate a new set of reforms. He also called for the rapid Africanization of the country.[16]

In *Renascent Africa,* a collection of his speeches, Azikiwe formulated ideas about what he called the "New Africa."[17] He projected the members of his generation as the new leaders, saying that the old elite had failed to resist the conquest and challenge colonial domination. Those who have

studied his speeches, most recently Ehiedu E. G. Iweriebor, have divided
them into five themes: spiritual balance, social regeneration, economic determinism, mental emancipation, and national or political "risorgimento."[18]
These five themes include the following concepts: African youth must tolerate other people's ideas and a multiplicity of opinions (what Zik called
spiritual balance); Africans must ignore their differences and regard one
another as brothers (the principle of social regeneration); and the leaders
and the government must create job opportunities for all youth (the principle of economic determinism). In addition, Zik wanted African youth to
become mentally emancipated through an education system that was free
of racism. In terms of political emancipation, he believed that Africans
must control their own countries.[19] These ideas appealed to various groups
of people: Nigerian businessmen eager to make money; youth in search of
education; and politicians who wanted power. While the ideas were not
necessarily coherent or revolutionary, they motivated a number of aspiring
politicians. Azikiwe's ability and persistence in his quest to obtain a higher
education in the United States impressed many young men who wanted to
do the same. His energy and political entrepreneurship also impressed
many people. In the words of Anthony Enahoro, a contemporary observer,
Azikiwe "appealed to the masses. They flocked to his lectures to enjoy his
oratory. They did not, perchance, understand his long words nor many
of his 'scintillating, titillating and vibrating' editorials of the *West African
Pilot* of those days, but they respected this man who had such a copious
vocabulary and loved him because he stood up to the whiteman."[20] M. C. K.
Ajuluchukwu, a Zikist and later a famous party organizer, added, "Little
did Nigeria ever fathom that a messiah was forthcoming who would sound
the death knell of imperial atrocity and preach the gospel of Nigerian rena-
scence, African redemption and international fraternity."[21]

In addition to discovering a messiah, the militants and activists also
discovered that they had access to a body of literature on political radicalism and communism published outside Nigeria. One set of ideas in the
literature dealt with socialism and/or communism, to which many were
attracted. The colonial government believed that exposure to this kind of
literature was subversive and that drawing from it was an offense close to
treason. All works branded as "communist literature" fall into this category, which included many works of the socialist literature from the Soviet
Union. It did not hide its belief that communists were traitors and violent
men. A second set of ideas, which came from India, provided the theories
and methods needed to create distance from the colonial state, delegitimize
an alien government, and replace it with a Nigeria-controlled government

that would be active in promoting economic development.[22] The Indian literature taught that people could be mobilized against the colonial government by political parties and leaders. Some activists were even thinking and talking as if they could govern Nigeria, as if a shadow state was already in the making.

When anticolonial activists chose Azikiwe as a leader and hero, they questioned the legitimacy of the British governor-general and in effect appointed a leader of their shadow state. They considered both violent and nonviolent ways to dislodge the colonial government. Kola Balogun, a notable activist in the 1940s, promoted ideas from India such as the strategy of civil disobedience. In a public lecture entitled "India Is with Us," Balogun noted that the success of India in getting rid of the British was the result of the emergence of good leaders, astute political planning, and the use of civil disobedience.[23] Pointing to many similarities between India and Nigeria, Balogun praised Gandhi and Nehru for their leadership and their ability to interact with rich and poor and applauded the readiness of Indians to suffer and die for the cause. The idea of attacking the British on several fronts began to take deep root.

RADICAL MANNERS, VIOLENT WORDS

The pioneer and arguably the most notable example of a radical organization was the Zikist Movement (ZM), which was established in 1946. The British design for Nigeria was a gradual transfer of power through a series of constitutional reforms. In the Zikist view, the constitutional approach was too slow. Instead, Zikists wanted what they called "positive action," which included three violent steps: armed sabotage, labor activism, and civil disobedience. The agenda of "positive action" changed the language of politics from mere words to political actions, from constitutional reforms to violent national liberation, from conservative steps by "gentlemen" to radical actions by angry youth. The ideas and activities of the ZM show the extent to which Nigerians could go to formulate revolutionary ideas and attempt to use violence to overthrow the colonial order. The ZM operated under the umbrella of the Azikiwe-led NCNC, the major Pan-Nigerian political party of the 1940s.

The original instigators of Zikist ideas, although they were not members of the Zikist Movement, were NYM members Nnamdi Azikiwe and Nwafor Orizu. Azikiwe split from them in 1941, when the NYM divided. The ZM also owed some of its ideas to Nwafor Orizu, an Igbo who, like Azikiwe, attended colleges in the United States. While Azikiwe laid the foundation for Zikism, Orizu was the "codifier of the philosophy of Zikism."[24] In 1944, Orizu, influenced by Azikiwe, published *Without Bitterness*,[25] a book that called for African youth to mobilize for political action. Orizu, like Azikiwe, admonished a new generation of Nigerians to decolonize their minds and to develop a new set of ideas and values (patriotism, hard work, and combativeness) in order to take their country back.

Kolawole Balogun, a young Yoruba based in Lagos, founded the Zikist Movement on February 16, 1946, in collaboration with three other young men: M. C. K. Ajuluchukwu, Nduka Eze, and Abiodun Aloba. All four were journalists with the *Nigerian Advocate,* a newspaper owned by a Lebanese merchant. All four lost their jobs because, they alleged, they supported Azikiwe. Eze became a union leader, while the three others joined the Zik Group of Newspapers. Balogun, who convened the initial meeting of the ZM, wanted to end the divisions among nationalists and create an effective force to combat the colonial powers. As a testimony to his influence, over 200 young men and women attended the meeting on February 16, where they listened to speeches urging them to radicalize themselves; accept Azikiwe as a leader; reject "tribalism, jealousy and Uncle Tomism"; and opt for a radical ideology and progress. Balogun urged young people to "rise up and decide between leaders and misleaders, between philosophies and pseudo-philosophies."[26] A tract was immediately published to publicize the objectives and mission of the ZM. It called for the emergence of a strong nationalist front with an ideological bent that required men and women who would not waste their time talking but would take action.[27] In the view of Ehiedu Iweriebor, the leading scholar on this subject, the Zikist movement "was one of the most self-consciously and explicitly ideological political movements in Nigeria's history."[28]

It was an enthusiastic moment, with many acting as members of a new generation destined to lead and transform their country.[29] The number of members, impressively, reached a total of almost 3,000 and spread across the country; most were political activists ready to fight for the great cause.[30] The Zikists resolved to work to make "a new Nigeria a happy home."[31] The key participants felt that they should accept Azikiwe as their leader. They credited him with transforming anticolonial struggles and speeding up the pace of the movement leading to independence. They were impressed by Azikiwe's ability to invest the black race with pride and to formulate what they regarded as an ideology of rapid development. The challenge was selling Azikiwe's ideas to the masses. As part of this effort, they established Zik Day on Azikiwe's birthday, November 16, to reaffirm their values and their support for their leaders. As they declared in their first publication:

Never more shall we allow the John to cry alone in the wilderness.

Never more shall we allow this evangelist to cry his voice hoarse when millions of youths of Nigeria can take up his whisper and echo it to all world wide.[32]

The ideas of the Zikists received a great deal of publicity in Azikiwe's newspapers, in the *African Echo,* established in 1948, and in their own journal, the *Zimo Newsletter,* established in 1949. In addition, they invented an ideology of militancy that they expressed using radical words and presented to their audience with anger. This ideology was described as a "social faith" and a religion whose practices brought its risks: "In the course of propagation, martyrdom, persecution and oppression might creep in like disease."[33] Zikists described themselves as socialists who believed in God ("the God of Africa") and material and spiritual wealth and were determined to reclaim Africa from the evils of colonial domination.

"Positive Action": Zikism and Political Activism

Who can bell the white cat which is spreading evil in Africa?
Who can cure our mental and physical diseases?[34]

The answer those who framed these questions provided was that only activists and Zikists could do it. Nigeria now had a homegrown ideology of radical nationalism, born, according to a Zikist booklet, by a "revolt of youth against the desecration and vicious influence of imperialism in Africa and against the complacence and reactionary tendencies of Old Africa in a fast changing world."[35] The ZM also identified with the NCNC that Azikiwe had founded. It affiliated with the NCNC in May 1947 and tried to expand it, act as its vanguard, and promote its agenda.

In addition, Zikists tapped into the Ethiopianist ideas of the late nineteenth century to further the thread of cultural nationalism. They equated colonialism with exploitation and advocated that the illegal British rule should be overthrown by any means necessary. To Nduka, the colonialists were "foreigners who have no right to exist in our territories."[36] The activists believed that after the overthrow of colonialism, Nigeria should move forward through a socialist program and a revolution. They put their hope in the working class to lead this revolution, which they expected would follow the model laid down by the Soviet Union.

In the ZM's first year, 1946–1947, under the leadership of Kola Balogun and M. C. K. Ajuluchukwu, the goal established a national political movement, demanded major reforms from the colonial government, and pushed for rapid change through political means. The ZM sought to create a Pan-Nigerian nationalist movement, making use of legitimate means but going beyond the bounds of caution imposed by the colonial authorities. To their credit, they began to talk of a nation as a united territory with a socialist ideology strong enough to withstand ethnic divisions. They also began to think of ideas that could be used to strengthen national consciousness and to believe in the notion of a Nigerian nation-state. If the British had created symbols to promote colonial domination (such as Empire Day, May 24, or the anniversary of His Majesty's coronation), the Zikists sought alternative ideas and symbols to promote the idea of a Nigeria owned by Nigerians. The ZM replaced the colonialists' symbols with Zik Day, All Heroes Day, and Foundation Day, all of which involved public celebrations. Zikists invented a flag, a uniform, a national pledge, and a song, all to create alternative symbols that would generate a new spirit of national consciousness. They chose a flag with white, blue, gold, and red, colors that symbolized "untrammeled freedom and undisturbed peace," "unity," "love," and the "blood of martyrdom and victimization."[37] An anthem reclaimed Nigeria from the British:

Land of Our Birth
We pledge to thee
Our love and toil in years to be
Land of Our Pride
For whose dear sake
Our fathers died
O Nigeria we pledge to thee
Head, Heart and Hand
Through years to be.[38]

This was a definite rejection of the colonial government. Instead of singing in praise of the king or queen of England, Nigerians could now sing in praise of Azikiwe or the Nigeria of their dream. Zikists and other activists of the time believed in the capacity of the black race to manage its own affairs. They extolled the great contributions of the past in order to embolden themselves:

When we realize that it was a black man, Mr. Henry Blair, a full-blooded Negro, who in 1836 invented the corn harvester; when we realize that Tarik Ibn Ziad who led the Moors into Spain and conquered that country in 711 A.D. was a black man; and when we remember that as far back as 760 A.D. the black man was not only fit to rule himself but did govern an empire; you will agree with me that the harder we strive to put this bleeding continent back on her rightful place the better for us and posterity.[39]

Zikists also created a "religion." Azikiwe became a prophet, the head of the National Church of Nigeria and Cameroons, which used Christianity to seek freedom and terminate alien rule. The church preached a theology of political liberation to mobilize people to fight and to promote indigenous religions and indigenous leadership. It had an invocation for a new generation of leaders who would "lead all Africa out of bondage."[40] In addition, it prepared a creed for its members to memorize and recite:

I believe in Herbert Macaulay, the Prophet, the doyen of Nigerian journalists and politicians and in his only political son Nnamdi Azikiwe, who was conceived by mother Nigeria, born of the noble Chinwe Azikiwe, suffered persecution under the regime of the new autocrats; whose life assassination was attempted in Lagos. The third day he escaped assassin's bullet to Onitsha and sitteth at the right hand of Obi Okosi, whither he was consecrated the "Oracle of Onitsha" from thence he shall show the light to the people. I believe in Zik's philosophy of freedom from want and oppression, the communion of the NCNC and the Zikist Movement, repentance of our detractors and redemption of Mother Nigeria from Alien Domination. Liberty Everlasting.[41]

Several incidents in 1947 further radicalized the ZM. The government shot striking workers at Burutu in 1947, the Colonial Office rejected many key demands an NCNC delegation to London made, and tensions between Yoruba and Igbo politicians in Lagos increased. Under new leaders—Habib Raji Abdallah and Osita Agwuna—the ZM chose what it called a revolutionary strategy. It promised that it would not hesitate to use violence. In 1948, the ZM called for a revolution and mass civil disobedience against the colonial government.

In 1947, Mbonu Ojike added another dimension: a boycott movement. The idea was to restore indigenous institutions and customs in food, names, attire, religions, and festivals. To attain this, Ojike appealed to the urban-based elite to do away with imported culture and habits and asked other Nigerians to embark on cultural renewal and assertion. Ojike had been inspired by Azikiwe and had benefited from the opportunity to receive an American education, coming back to Nigeria in 1947 with two degrees. He worked for the *West African Pilot* as its general manager and maintained two successful columns where his ideas received publicity. A believer in the indigenous control of businesses and power, he wrote two books that outlined his ideas about how Nigeria could move forward.[42] Ojike became famous for his campaigns to promote Nigerian names, clothes, music, religions, and literature. He succeeded in persuading Nigerian civil servants to wear African attire to their offices.[43] His boycott movement, launched in 1948, was designed to generate local savings to create businesses, revive pride in African objects and ideas in order "to give us an invisible armour of psychological independence," and "arm our politicians with the dynamites of visible and invisible propaganda."[44] He toured the country to publicize his ideas, wearing a sweater over a loincloth, asking people to call him Mazi (an Igbo form of address commonly given to a senior man who was not a chief) instead of the English "Mister," and pleading with the people to boycott European "food, drink, fashion, marriage system and all imported luxury."[45] The idea was not to stop all imports: "Let us import machines and helpful books, make movies of African life, buy from abroad all those essential commodities that will ultimately raise us to the economic level of Britain, Russia and the United States of America." Ojike became known as the "Boycott King" and the advocate of "Boycott the Boycottable," an idea that had a strong anticolonial thrust. When Ojike also called for Christianity to be boycotted, the churches responded, asking students not to read his columns and describing him as an anti-God communist.[46]

An incident of racial discrimination in February 1947, now known as the Bristol Hotel Incident, provided the ZM with the opportunity to mobilize the youth of Lagos against the government. A black officer in the colonial government was refused accommodation in the hotel, although a reservation had previously been confirmed for him. The Greek manager of the hotel took the confirmation as a mistake. As the incident became public, it created an uproar, leading to accusations of racism.[47] It was an opportunity for the ZM and the labor unions to launch a public attack against the colonial regime and its racist attitude. The ZM organized a mass rally and sent a letter of protest to the governor that asked him to expel the hotel's proprietor from the country. As the event generated more unrest, the manager of the hotel was dismissed, but the ZM and other protesters asked for his expulsion from the country. A planned siege of the hotel was aborted by the police, which also denied the organizers a permit for a three-mile protest march. Nevertheless, a number of angry people moved close to the hotel to throw stones. Michael Imoudu, a militant labor leader, was wounded in the police counterattack and was later charged with participating in a "disorderly assembly."[48] The incident forced the government to declare that racial discrimination would no longer be tolerated in hotels, public places, and hospitals.[49]

The Zikists were emboldened by their relentless attacks on the Richards Constitution, a 1947 revision of the constitution that reserved much power to colonial authorities; by major instances of racism in Lagos and Kano; and by their effective monitoring of new bills that they believed were not in the interest of Nigerians. In 1947, criticism of the Richards Constitution focused the goals of the ZM, and it ultimately decided to embark upon what it called "positive action" to liberate the country. "Positive action" included an element of insurrection. The new attitude began with the annual general conference of the Zikist Movement in August 1947 and the appointment of new officers.

One of the new leaders was Habib Raji Abdallah, a staff member the Post and Telegraph Department who had been posted to Kano in 1940. He and others had joined the Kano branch of the Zikist Movement in 1946. In December 1946, he joined others to establish what the government regarded as a political party, the Northern Elements Progressive Association (NEPA), which he used to spread anticolonial ideas in various parts of the north. The ZM elected Abdallah as president-general at the 1947 general conference. Abdallah was the first northerner to head a Pan-Nigerian political movement. His militant activism and his northern origins were positive assets that enabled the ZM to claim that it was working to unite the country. In his inaugural address, Abdallah made it clear that his ideas of liberation were not compatible with imperialism and that angry and oppressed people like Nigerians could not be expected to cooperate with their conquerors.[50] He affirmed that Nigerians would not allow their spirit to be destroyed and their energies to be consumed by service to the colonial government.

The government saw Abdallah's lecture as subversive and asked him to disclose any plans he had to cause violence. He responded to his boss's recommendation that he be dismissed from the colonial service in the north with an insulting letter to the chief secretary in Lagos, telling him that he would continue to be active in politics, that he believed imperialism was "satanic," and that he would work to liberate his people from "merciless and ungodly exploitation" through any means possible.[51] He said that "a chasm of destruction" awaited British imperialism in Nigeria. He was dismissed from his lucrative senior position in January 1948.

Abdallah's dismissal enabled him to go into politics full time. He gave lectures in various parts of the country and became a paid officer of the NCNC as an under-secretary. Abdallah's deputy in the ZM, Osita Agwuna, was equally rebellious. He openly advocated the use of violence to end British rule. He was also a strong believer in the politics of civil disobedience.[52]

The Abdallah-Agwuna leadership now began to think of how they could put their ideas into practice. Many lectures and newspaper articles had spoken of ideas about ending colonial rule and transforming Nigeria quickly. Abadallah now wanted to add armed sabotage and demonstrations and providing support to trade unions that wanted to organize strikes. The idea of civil disobedience now needed violence to make it work.

The ZM started by organizing demonstrations against the government. On October 4, 1947, it mobilized about 3,000 people to complain that the NCNC had been badly treated and ridiculed for leading a protest to London against the Richards Constitution. Some weeks later, another demonstration mustered about 100,000 people, all shouting "Down with imperialism."[53] In response, the government proscribed the demonstrations the ZM had planned for 1948. In response, the ZM issued a combative document in 1948, "A Call for Revolution," that included a series of insurrectionary statements that attacked the colonial government on all fronts and were designed to mobilize Nigerians for violent civil disobedience. This document marked a turning point in radical politics, generating a chain of reactions that were hard to control. Before issuing the document, the ZM Central Executive Committee decided on two courses of action: first, they would attack the British; and second, they would push their opposition to a level at which Azikiwe would be arrested and imprisoned. It was their hope that imprisoning Azikiwe would anger many Nigerians and rock the foundations of the government, while making Azikiwe the Nehru of Nigeria.[54] The members of the executive also believed that their action would put an end to the interethnic rivalries in Lagos politics, unite Nigerian politicians, and create a clearer focus on the anticolonial struggles.

In an address delivered on October 27, 1948, Agwuna blamed the colonial government for dividing Nigerians and creating rifts among their leaders. He called on Nigerians not to be afraid of the government but to see themselves as slaves who must be liberated. Agwuna told his audience that the country was a police state, and he called on Nigerians to mobilize in order to fight. He wanted young men and women to develop a "fanatical philosophy" that would entail death and suffering for the cause of overthrowing the colonial regime. The leaders must be ready to attain martyrdom as well. All must believe that there was nothing good about British rule and must be prepared for civil disobedience, a boycott of most imported and foreign objects and ideas, and a firm rejection of alien authority and allegiance to any imposed constitution.

Agwuna was not simply speaking in general terms. His lecture included a specific plan that involved the establishment of a Nigerian-led government by the NCNC, lectures around the country by activists on the nature of colonial exploitation, and demands from unions for higher pay and an end to deductions from their wages for taxes. In addition, he wanted workers to engage in strikes to paralyze the country, and he wanted all locally trained doctors who had been discriminated against to withdraw their services. As if the list was not long enough, he asked Nigerians not to participate in Empire Day celebrations and students in schools abroad to take courses on the military so they could acquire the skills needed to fight.

The colonial government regarded the lecture as an act of treason. The police raided the offices of the NCNC, confiscating a copy of the speech as evidence of "a certain seditious publication."[55] Abdallah and another officer of the ZM were arrested on October 28 and released after a lengthy interrogation. The police served Agwuna with a search warrant and confiscated many documents from his house, including his "Call for Revolution" essay. On October 30, Agwuna and other officers of the ZM were arrested and charged with sedition.

The ZM and other political activists eagerly awaited a mass uprising, but in vain. They had calculated that their words and the harassment by the government would provoke the people to protest. However, people did not go to the police stations to be arrested and workers did not go on strike. A civil uprising did not take place. The ZM expected Azikiwe to be arrested too and believed that his arrest would generate national protest. But Azikiwe was not arrested. He had not attended the lecture, although he had been expected to attend as the chair. After this incident, Azikiwe began to put some distance between himself and the ZM. Azikiwe's position on radical, violence-oriented politics was ambivalent: he needed the support of the young men but did not need their violent ideas. Azikiwe's *West African Pilot* did not carry Agwuna's revolutionary speech. The media outlets that had always been critical of Azikiwe, the NCNC, and the ZM, notably the *Daily Service,* took the opportunity to denounce Agwuna and his ideas.

The ZM had exaggerated the support of the masses. Its campaign to incite "hate and disaffection" against the colonial government was yet to take root. Many of its ideas were known only to certain segments of the population in a few urban centers, and there was no indication that a radical, revolutionary, and pro-violence political culture had gained widespread support among the populace.

The public inaction and the arrest of ZM members did not dampen the enthusiasm of the Zikists and their leadership. Indeed, they reaffirmed the call for a revolution on November 2 and registered new members. On November 6, the *African Echo* made a call to the nation:

Citizens of Nigeria, elect of God, what are you waiting for? Why do you wallow in quagmire of lethargy? Although we had thought that Nigeria is ripe for freedom, but she lacks one thing—an army of liberation. Dare you talk of non-violence when the world is built on violence?[56]

This statement created a problem for the newspaper, as it was regarded as a seditious attempt to incite the public to violence. The editor and one of his journalists were arrested and charged on November 15. The core Zikists were angered and continued to call for action to overthrow the government. Abdallah publicly declared that he no longer owed allegiance to any colonial government. He asked all Nigerians to declare themselves free of the British and face the consequences. To Abdallah, violence was the only language the colonial government would understand. The Zikists planned a series of youth demonstrations, but the police refused to grant them permits. When a crowd of about 2,000 gathered for one of the rallies on November 12, the police dispersed them. The next day Abdallah was arrested; he spent three days in jail.

Prominent members of the ZM were again arrested on November 20 for sedition. The preliminary depositions against the main leaders began six days later. Agwuna and three others were prosecuted for uttering seditious words and circulating seditious publications. Agwuna and the others used their trial as an occasion to demonstrate their anticolonial position by wearing African clothes, answering questions in a stubborn manner, and lending support to the large crowd that attended the trials. Agwuna did not hesitate to insult the judge, saying that he did not consider the court properly constituted to try him: "I do not expect any justice from a court which is serving the very government towards which I am preaching disaffection."[57] Agwuna refused to defend himself and was found guilty and sentenced to a one-year term in prison. Unrepentant, he wrote a letter to Nigerians, presenting himself as oppressed like others and calling for unity among all youth and greater dedication to the anticolonial struggles.[58] Other trials proceeded, and the publishers of *African Echo* were also sent to jail on charges of sedition. In yet another case, Agwuna, Abdallah, and two others were charged with various seditious activities. The charge reveals how the colonial government interpreted the activities of the ZM and the revolutionary-minded activists:

They called for the forcible removal of the governor from office.
They asked His Majesty's subjects, or the inhabitants of Nigeria to procure the alteration by force of the Government of Nigeria, as by law established.

They urged that the laws of Nigeria should not be observed.

They described the governments of the United Kingdom and Nigeria as the common enemy of Nigerian people.

They asked people to give their allegiance exclusively to the NCNC.

They stated that "The revolution against the Government of Nigeria has commenced: the people of Nigeria must continue the common struggle by violence."[59]

Agwuna and Abdallah used the trials as an opportunity to strengthen their revolutionary credentials by abusing the government and the judicial process. When the judge found them guilty and imposed jail terms, they even thanked him.

The trials and sentences did not destroy the movement. The ZM continued to make its call for concerted action against the government. It asked all its branches to mobilize all unions, schoolteachers, and family associations to engage in struggles against the government, saying that should the leaders of the ZM be sent to prison, all workers must go on strike and market women should refuse to buy and sell and that by December 24, 1948, acts of sabotage should have destroyed many mercantile houses, police stations, and post offices. Some branches of the ZM, such as those at Enugu and Onitsha, responded to the call. On November 20, markets at Onitsha were closed and many businesses did not operate. Mass demonstrations were held that directed verbal abuse at the government.[60] In December, the Central Executive Committee of the ZM decided to continue its revolutionary action by setting up various secret organizations to challenge the government and finding ways to steal rifles and ammunition from police and military barracks. The executive committee resolved to begin armed sabotage and to seek ways to create an armory, train people to fight, and pressure trade unions to organize damaging strikes.[61]

In 1949, two self-avowed socialists, Nduka Eze and Mokwugo Okoye, took over the leadership of the ZM. They not only advocated a socialist path for Nigeria but announced the adoption of a policy of armed sabotage. By this time, many in the Zikist movement no longer regarded Azikiwe as a hero and were willing to chart a totally different course. The revolutionary elements in the ZM maintained their commitment to "positive action" and criticized others, including Azikiwe, as mere reformers. The new leaders believed that they could popularize their ideology of socialism and armed sabotage among the working class. They began to think about how the country could embark on a general insurrection and worked through labor unions to radicalize some of the unions' activities.

Nduka Eze became the president of the ZM on April 3, 1949. He promised to bring freedom to the country—the freedom for people to choose their own government and constitution, determine their politics and economy, and shape their foreign policy.[62] Freedom, Eze warned, would come only after a war against imperialism. Eze's crucial connections with labor unions (he was the secretary-general of the Nigerian National Federation of Labour) gave him a dual platform from which to sell his revolutionary ideas. Okoye, the new secretary-general of the ZM, was an equally fearless socialist-leaning leader. That year, he began publishing the monthly journal, *Zimo Newsletter*, which popularized the movement's activities. After the NCNC distanced itself from the ZM, the ZM sought other alliances, notably with progressive and radical movements in Britain (the British Communist Party), India, the Gold Coast (the Convention People's Party), the United States (the Universal Negro Improvement Association), and the Soviet Union.

The ZM was associated with the 1949 protests following the Iva Valley massacre in November (see chapter 7). In 1950, it formulated a plan of violence at a conference held in Kaduna from December 26 to 28. At the conference, the ZM passed a vote of no confidence in the government because it was "destructive." It demanded a "people's government" that would take effect in April 1951, the release of all political prisoners, the creation of more jobs, and the implementation of socialist planning policies. Recognizing that the British would not negotiate with the movement, the ZM called on its members to refuse to cooperate with the government and begin civil disobedience. Its goal was to "destroy all storage centres, Government Houses, Government Department[s] and so on."[63] In addition, the ZK declared it legitimate to assassinate British officers, from senior officers to junior officers such as district officers. A majority vote approved a plan for an insurrectionary public lecture to start a coordinated program of civil disobedience all over the country. The ZK argued that schoolteachers should preach hatred for the British, no one should pay taxes, the police and army should disobey orders, and young men should be militarily prepared to fight and die if necessary for the success of the revolution.[64]

As the government, which had earlier planted agents within the ZM, learned of the plan, it took preemptive action that prevented the organization from embarking on its violent cause and ultimately led to the end of the ZM itself. In February 1951 (and again in May), police and security agents descended on the offices and homes of key members of the ZM in Lagos, Kaduna, Kano, Aba, Gusau, Enugu, Zaria, Sokoto, Ibadan, Jos, Ilorin, and Jebba, looking for seditious documents and weapons. The raid yielded many documents that the government considered incriminating. These were found especially in the ZM's secretariat in Lagos and the home of Okoye, who was later prosecuted and sentenced to nine months in prison. Many other members of the ZM were arrested, tried, and incarcerated.

One person kept his commitment to the use of violence: Heelas Ugokwe, a postal clerk and war veteran who tried to assassinate Hugh Foot, the chief secretary to the Nigerian government. In the premises of the Nigerian Secretariat, Ugokwe used a jackknife to stab the secretary in the back.[65] Another Nigerian quickly wrestled him down. Foot sustained a minor wound, and Ugokwe, who initially fled the scene, was later arrested. Ugokwe was charged with murder and brought before a Nigerian judge and an all-Nigerian jury, which gave him a life sentence. The West African Court of Appeal later reduced the sentence to twelve years. Throughout his trial, Ugokwe was unrepentant. Rather than defend himself, he gave lectures on the brutality of British rule and expressed his regret that he was unsuccessful in killing Foot.

The colonial government formally suppressed the ZM in April 1950. In an official gazette detailing the proscription, the government gave three reasons for its action:

> Conclusive evidence has been obtained from many parts of the country that the Zikist Movement is an organization which aims to stir up hatred and malice and pursue seditious aims by lawlessness and violence.

> The movement has a membership of only a few hundreds and its teachings and methods are condemned by the overwhelming majority of the people of Nigeria who wish to maintain law and order and pursue economic and political progress without resort to violence.

> Although the movement is small and unrepresentative its purposes and methods are dangerous to the good government of Nigeria and it is essential to make it quite clear that such purposes and methods will not be tolerated. The Governor in the Executive Council has therefore declared the movement an unlawful society under section 62 of the Criminal Code.[66]

As if to spite the colonial government, on August 8, 1950, a group of radicals issued the Sawaba Declaration, which led to the formation of the longest-lived and most well-supported radical party in northern Nigeria, the Northern Elements Progressive Union (NEPU), whose mission was to rid Nigeria of all "oppressors" irrespective of their color. Other leftist-leaning associations also emerged, even though their overall influence was marginal.

Radical groups continued their message in a variety of ways, but in 1950, it was reform-minded Nigerian politicians who obtained power.

CONCLUDING REMARKS

As the colonial regime firmly established itself in the 1920s and 1930s, nationalist expressions intensified. The Western-educated elite of Nigeria became more assertive; many believed that the country belonged to them and that they had legitimate rights to a number of privileges. The Nigerian-controlled media was not shy in criticizing colonial officers and giving space to activists to express their sentiments. A solid foundation was being laid for Nigerians to eventually attain power. The literature on Nigeria's decolonization slights the roles of women, youth, labor, and radical political elements in order to privilege the mainstream political parties; some of this literature maligns the most radical among these groups. Regional or "tribalist"-oriented political parties have claimed the credit for ending colonial rule. In the view of the radicals, the British encouraged these "tribal" parties because they essentially served the interests of the colonial government.

The radicals and the marginal parties believed that their violent words and actions were necessary to obtain "complete independence" for Nigeria, end dependence on the West, and liberate Nigerians from all forms of external domination. Zikists believed that nationalism and patriotism needed to be anticolonial and that socialist-oriented leaders had to mobilize the masses to build a new economy and society. Many of the expressions of socialism and Pan-Africanism during the 1940s were not new, but their impact in creating a generation of anticolonial activists and putting the word "violence" into the vocabulary of nationalist agitation was significant.

The chapter has examined the case study of the Zikists to explore the radical orientation in Nigeria and the trend toward the adoption of a violent revolutionary strategy that began in the 1940s. For five years during that decade, from 1946 to 1950, Zikists changed the tone of politics from one of dialogue and negotiation to one of violence and civil disobedience. Zikists promoted the idea of cultural nationalism, asking people to change their names and clothes and use politics not only to seek independence but also to attain cultural liberation. A new generation of political activists emerged that promoted socialism, labor radicalism, social welfarism, and revolution.

Not all who fought against the colonial state subscribed to the use of violence. Two strategies for obtaining Nigeria's independence predominated in the 1940s and 1950s. Those who resorted to violence and those who promoted elitist methods of forming political associations likely had the same ends in mind. Whether violent or otherwise, those who took part in nationalist struggles chose strategies that they believed would be successful. However, the strategies of the educated elite began to take precedence by the 1950s, and the wars of resistance and rebellions began to give way to peaceful negotiations conducted by the educated elite and the implementation of various constitutions.

Radicalism and a belief in revolution, with or without violence, was one way to express black consciousness. Those who resorted to violence and spoke of revolution used racial terms, rejecting the superiority of the white/colonial order. They believed that a notion of racial inferiority would incapacitate activists who were attacking colonial officers and their tools of domination. The racialized vocabulary of the radicals was designed to argue that blacks had the resources and talents to manage themselves. This rejection of an inferior status on the basis of color attained the status of a religious faith.

The colonial administration responded to violent and radical expressions with vigorous attacks. Repressive laws enabled the police and the army to focus their attacks on radical leaders and their followers. In northern Nigeria, the colonial government, which was in a panic about the establishment of branches of the Zikist Movement, tried to root the radicals out of the region. The case of Habib Raji Abdallah provides an example of how the government responded to radicals; it regarded him as a dangerous person who could destroy the peace of the north. In the eyes of the government, he was paving the way for the penetration of southern political influence into the north, thereby importing subversive, antigovernment people and ideas.[67] He and his associates were trailed, and when possible, prevented from speaking in public, in order to prevent the corruption of the values of the north.[68] When Abdallah was dismissed from his job, he had to move NEPA to Lagos. Even though the government tried to suppress radicals like Abdallah, his brand of violent nationalism was crucially significant in the history of Nigeria. The struggle itself—that is, the ability to mobilize the people to fight—was an achievement that introduced a new discourse and a new strategy. The question of whether or not violence was necessary for revolution generated its own dialogue, one that continues to this day.

7

Labor, Wages, and Riots

Nigerians in the service of colonial authorities described themselves as "workers." Even though they might work for the colonial government or foreign-owned companies, they distanced themselves from the idea that they were stakeholders in the colonial regime. Rather, the word "workers" had begun to suggest to many Nigerians a spirit of nationalism and the opportunity to convert labor power into political power. By the 1930s, many workers were beginning to be drawn into political parties; and by the 1940s, many more had become part of the critical mass on which the nationalists relied to overthrow the colonial government. The colonial state could no longer count on the loyalty of many of those who worked for it. One can be paid by the government and at the same time be critical of one's position, one's bosses, and the existing political institutions.

The major employers between 1900 and 1945 were the colonial administration, about thirteen Levantine firms, and European mining and trading firms, notably the UAC, John Holt, G. B. Ollivant, Paterson Zochonis, the Compagnie Française de l'Afrique Occidentale, the Société de l'Ouest Africain, the Union Trading Company (UTC), and Thomopoulus. After 1940, other companies joined these ranks, including European commercial banks, insurance companies, oil-prospecting companies, and a host of manufacturers. As radicalism developed among Nigerian workers and their unions, political rhetoric promoted the idea of violence. Angered by the fact that the government and the companies that employed them were foreign, workers believed that the government was an exploiter interested only in using Nigeria's resources to develop Britain and that all foreign companies were profit seekers that were bleeding labor and the country for their own narrow goals.

Workers' paramount concern was wages, as indeed it should have been, given the nature of the Nigerian economy. From their point of view, the failure of the government to provide for them was a form of violence. The politicization and radicalization that precipitated the violence of the 1940s reveal not just the development of the unions but the development of a politics of decolonization that made a new generation of Nigerians more assertive and aggressive than their predecessors.

The role of workers and labor unions became important in the 1940s, which were characterized by three major labor crises: the General Strike of 1945, the Burutu Workers Strike of 1947, and the Enugu Colliery Strike of 1949. These three strikes reveal the face of postwar radicalism in Nigeria. The purpose of this chapter is not to discuss the broad canvas of unionism and politics, but to isolate the communication of anger, riots, and aggressive responses to the colonial state. Workers' use of violent language and union leaders' ability to mobilize their members for strikes show the important role of labor in political activism and the movement toward independence. A number of labor leaders were unafraid of the colonial state, the colonial army, and the colonial police. In 1945, labor leaders ignored messages of intimidation from the governor. As the General Strike succeeded, it revealed that militancy could pay off in the long run if the people could be organized. Indeed, a small number of people were even talking about violence and strikes designed to end the colonial regime. Thus, we see a merger between the interests of politicians and those of organized labor. The former group was demanding constitutional changes, and the latter demanding improved wages and conditions of service, but both sets of demands led in one direction: nationalist expression. The merger created its own problems, between so-called moderates and so-called radicals in the various trade union organizations. The moderates tended to be suspicious of politicians, and they argued that the workers should fight for their own cause rather than for the concerns of politicians. In the eyes of the radicals, the future of the workers and the future of Nigeria were intertwined, and they should, therefore, merge workers' concerns with those of the nationalist politicians.

The circumstances behind most labor-related aggression and violence were no different from those that shaped the events and the radicalism discussed in chapter 6. The recession, uncontrolled inflation, scarcity of essential imported items, and high rate of unemployment of veterans after the Second World War all triggered a response by labor. Unsatisfactory constitutional changes that were slow in transferring power to Nigerians angered both politicians and union leaders aspiring for power. In addition to all these circumstances, some members of a new generation of workers emerged were eager for change, ready to fight, and not afraid to adopt the strategy of violence. By the 1940s, the belief had become widespread that Nigerian workers were being cheated by the government and foreign companies, that wages and working conditions were poor, and that those who had worked for many years had little to show for it. To change what many Nigerians regarded as their "deplorable situation," they began to organize in unions and make their demands aggressively. The activities of workers cannot be understood without an understanding of the rise of the labor movement and its increasing radicalization.

THE LABOR MOVEMENT

The emergence of unionism in Nigeria illustrates how strikes can be interpreted as economic violence to combat the structured violence of the colonial economy. Wage labor in what became Nigeria began during the nineteenth century with a small number of people employed by the church, European firms, and (later) the colonial government. As the colonial government established itself, it needed paid workers in several departments. It established schools to produce literate individuals who could meet the new and increasing demand for an educated workforce. The construction of the railroad after 1898 intensified the demand for labor. The urban setting for many of the new jobs encouraged interactions at work and in social spaces. Indeed, as early as 1897, the concentration of workers in Lagos generated a labor strike.[1] Although Nigeria's first union, the Nigerian Civil Service Union, was formed in 1912, it was created mainly to enable a few senior members to socialize, and its members declared that they would not support strikes or any form of disruption to services.[2] Seven years later, the clerks and mechanics working for the railroad established the Railway Native Staff Union to promote the welfare of members and encourage devotion to duty. A few other unions also emerged with similar aims. The inflation caused by the First World War pressured wage earners to complain and unions to demand salary increases. A 10 percent increase failed to satisfy some unions. In 1920, the Nigerian Mechanic Union, which was comprised of both skilled and unskilled laborers employed by the Nigerian Railway, decided to go on strike in Lagos to demand a pay raise and a war bonus. A number of branches in other parts of the country joined in. The railway management declared the strike unconstitutional since no formal grievances had been presented. The king of Lagos called the union leaders to his palace on January 16, 1920, and advised them to call off the strike.

The striking workers not only agreed to resume work but apologized for their action. Reflecting the mood of the time, the *Lagos Weekly Record* wrote about the strike and its harsh editorial criticized the workers: "We say strikes are altogether undesirable here, not only that, but extremely dangerous; they are just like sharp-edged tools in the hands of children."[3]

Various reports in the 1920s described labor unions as either dormant or calm, but some unions used strikes as a weapon to press their demands. For example, laborers in coal mines embarked on small-scale strikes in 1920.[4] However, the mood of workers changed in the 1930s as the depression created economic crises and panic. As a result of cost-cutting, many workers lost their jobs, salaries were cut by 10 percent, and the work week was cut to four days. Many unions became moribund and new ones were formed, notably the Nigerian Union of Teachers, established in 1931, and the Nigerian Railway Workers Union, established in 1932. Young people were beginning to take over the leadership, but the government used its power to transfer those who were considered rebellious to different parts of the country or deny them promotion.

The circumstances that radicalized labor began to develop during the 1930s. To start with, the retrenchment that came with the economic depression created an atmosphere of job insecurity. Those in the civil service could no longer take their jobs for granted. Even among those who were lucky enough to have jobs, the worsening conditions of living led to alienation. As the decade closed with the beginning of the Second World War, conditions became even worse. Joining trade unions and being active within them became one strategy for survival. Many "house unions" emerged in government departments, and by 1937 many people were beginning to use strikes as a weapon. For example, in 1937, the Motor Transport Union organized strikes to protest the increase in the cost of truck licenses and coal hewers struck at the Iva Coal Mines in the east for better conditions of service.

By the 1940s, the era on which this chapter focuses, a number of Nigerians had acquired experience in managing unions. They had learned the value of strikes, especially how to make them effective in attaining their goals. By that decade, it was clear to many that they had to either merge their unions or create umbrella organizations that would lead to better organization and unification. Several unions representing employees of the Nigerian Railway took the initiative in beginning consolidation, and by late 1939, they had created the Nigerian Union of Railwaymen (Federated). A set of young leaders emerged in the 1940s who chose radicalism and began to see workers as possible political managers. Indeed, they began to think of creating a labor party that could take over power and began to identify possible sources of external support.[5] Labor leaders chose to create alliances with political associations in order to create stronger anticolonial platforms. A noted figure in the 1940s was Michael Imoudu, who radicalized the railroad unions and took part in some of the events analyzed below.

Imoudu and the railway unions started off the decade with a major demand early in 1940. The Railway Workers Union called on the government to raise wages and abolish hourly rates of pay. The negotiations between railroad management and the union were protracted and led to no major concessions. By mid-July 1941, tension between the union and railway management had increased. On September 27, 1941, Imoudu organized a demonstration and protest march. The alarmed government was forced to improve the conditions of service, make small changes in wages, abolish hourly rates of pay, and remove a senior officer about whom the union had complained.

In July 1941, the Railway Workers Union persuaded nine trade unions representing technical employees to merge into an umbrella organization, the African Civil Service Technical Workers Union (ACSTWU). Now empowered, the various unions began to pressure the government to pay a cost of living allowance (COLA) to all workers who had been suffering from the high cost of living. The government responded quickly by setting up a committee on November 14, 1941, to review the COLA. Meanwhile, on December 5, the government awarded a bonus of 3 pence per day to all employees whose annual income was less than 36 pounds. It also increased the wages of temporary and daily laborers.

The COLA committee had to balance the political and economic circumstances of the war years with the general dissatisfaction among the workers. When the committee submitted its report on June 22, 1942, it recommended a minimum wage of 2 shillings per day and 2 pounds 12 shillings per month for laborers employed by the government in Lagos. This was an increase of almost 1 shilling a day. The salaries of government workers who earned between 48 and 220 pounds per year were also increased by 2.7 percent to 40 percent. The committee responded to workers' complaints about rising food costs by asking the government to control prices, provide subsidized food for workers, and give free meals to laborers.

The Nigerian Railway, the employer of members of the increasingly powerful Nigerian Railway Workers Union, responded by applying the wage increase, moving about 5,000 staff members from day wages to permanent pay, and moving another 6,000 from daily rates to monthly rates. Many were promoted. This initial success increased the reputation of trade unions and their leaders among Nigerian workers.

The 1940s were years ripe for labor-government confrontations. The unions wanted economic progress and political power, while the government sought ways to send profits to Britain and close control of its colonial subjects. The government could no longer use repressive measures against the rising number of union leaders. To be sure, it could victimize a few and dismiss them from service, as it had with Abdallah (see chapter 6) and Imoudu, but this would not stem the rising tide of labor radicalism. As unions increased their demands to include even better pay, price controls on housing, subsidized food, and price controls on key food items, a frustrated government turned to reform in the hope that political and economic changes would placate the majority of the population. Thus, in the 1940s and 1950s, the government introduced new constitutions that gradually transferred power to Nigerians and began economic plans, notably the Ten Year Development Plan, which outlined a series of concrete measures for transforming society.[6]

However, the government also resorted to control and regulation. The first regulatory move was made in November 1938 when a bill was introduced to the Legislative Council that required all unions to register with the government and allow the government to audit their funds each year. In addition, the bill specified that the Inspectorate of Labour would supervise unions and see that they were managed effectively. The announcement of the law generated panic and fear among unionists, who regarded it as an effort to cripple them. In some cases, registering a union was a long process during which the government was able to exercise some control over the union. The need to complete the paperwork needed to register unions and to run them as stipulated by government created a new set of Nigerian professional experts on labor law. In the 1940s, the first generation of "labor experts" began teaching would-be unionists how to register, negotiate with the government, and pursue legitimate means of embarking on strikes.

A successful strike by the Nigerian Railway Workers Union in 1941 pushed the government to think of other forms of regulation to deal with labor disputes and the resolution of demands. The Trade Disputes and Arbitration Ordinance and Workmen's Compensation Ordinance of 1941, which attempted to resolve conflicts by dialogue, was an attempt to minimize the use of strikes. Under the new ordinance, the government could choose to mediate between unions and employers; it mandated the Department of Labour to establish a conciliation unit to arbitrate in disputes. The Nigerian General Defence Regulations of 1941, enacted under the Emergency Powers/Defence Acts of 1939 and 1940, set limits to the use of labor power: "An employer shall not declare or take part in a lock-out and a work-man shall not take part in a strike in connection with any trade disputes unless the dispute has been formally reported to the Governor."[7]

New unions known as COLA trade unions emerged that were driven by demands for cost-of-living adjustments to wages. Between 1941 and 1942, seventy such unions were formally registered. The government responded by preaching a system of mutual conciliation and peaceful arbitration. However, the COLA trade unions used the demand for better wages as a justification for resorting to violence to make their case for better living standards. Many unions objected to a 1941 regulation that made strikes illegal; the working assumption was that the government would respect them if they engaged in violent protest.

In the 1940s, unions forged alliances with political associations such as the Nigerian Youth Movement, the NCNC, the Zikist Movement, and other radical groups. Union leaders also encouraged house unions to federate so they could gain a stronger voice. In November 1942, the Nigerian Youth Movement and the ACSTWU called a meeting of twenty-three unions to establish the Federated Trades Union of Nigeria (FTUN), which immediately called on the government to involve it in the formulation of labor regulations. The context of the crises of the Second World War strengthened workers' demands for improvements, and in March 1943, the FTUN offered a list of demands:

> Full citizenship, free collective bargaining, free articulation subject only to ordinary rules of courtesy, timely consultation on labour and kindred matters, logical wage schemes, equality or opportunities and privileges, protection against ignorance, want, disease and exploitation.
>
> Continuity of employment as a counterpart of compulsory service.
>
> Protection against victimization.
>
> Guarantee against intrusion by unauthorized persons or agents into the privacy of trade unions.
>
> Reasonable respite in form of leave and adequate leisure and recreation.
>
> Guarantee against labour laws being unilateral in nature.
>
> Guarantee of substantial gratuity on retiring through certified physical incapacity as a result of occupational accidents.
>
> Pension as a result of old age or incapacity after 10 years of employment.
>
> Unemployment benefits.[8]

Three months later, the FTUN convened a meeting with delegates representing fifty-six trade unions. A new name emerged: the Trades Union Congress

(TUC). The federated union officers sought links with other unions in Europe. Trade unions were not only becoming better organized but they were also turning into a political machine. The most critical demonstration of their power came in 1945 with the first major national strike.

THE GENERAL STRIKE OF 1945

Although signs of labor unrest had been appearing before 1945, the 1945 general strike brought home to the government and even to the unions that their power was stronger than previously realized. The economic problems of the war years were already leading to mild militancy among workers in Lagos. Then came the complaints by those discharged from military service about resettlement and compensation policies. In 1944, an ex-servicemen's division was established in the Department of Labour to register veterans and servicemen. The division registered 3,000 veterans, but the government could find jobs only for 150.[9] The government was not unmindful of the problems of creating jobs for the veterans. In March 1945, the Legislative Council passed the Employment of Ex-Servicemen's Ordinance, which authorized the government to restore veterans to "civil life."[10] This ordinance led to the establishment of the Nigerian Ex-Servicemen's Welfare Association, which took over the assets of the various pro-war funds and organizations established during the Second World War. Within months, veterans realized that the funds committed to their rehabilitation were inadequate and that joblessness awaited many of them. Distrust of the government led to agitation as veterans demanded jobs, an increase in their gratuities, and assistance in adjusting to civilian life.[11] To pursue their agenda, they established the Nigerian Union of Demobilised Soldiers, some of whose members made strong anticolonial statements. Veterans use the training they had received in military organization to their advantage as they pressured the government.

A group of labor leaders who organized their protest around the issue of increases in wages and the cost of living allowance (which included, notably, Michael Imoudu) was far more assertive and militant than veterans' groups, however. The government awarded a cost of living allowance of between 10 and 40 percent in 1942 in response to this pressure. Organized workers did not feel this was enough and continued to complain, pointing out that the cost of living had increased by 200 percent between 1942 and 1945. While the government did not dispute that there had been inflation, it put the increase at only 176 percent.[12] These disputes over how much inflation there was did nothing to reduce the growing tension.[13]

In March 1945, the ACSTWU, by that point an umbrella organization of twenty-two unions that included about 90,000 workers, made a formal demand for a 50 percent increase in the COLA allowance for all junior workers and a minimum daily wage of two shillings and sixpence. The government delayed its reply to this demand. It finally replied on May 2, 1945, that a salary increase would not help workers unless the supply of goods and foods increased and said that inflation was a temporary problem created by the failure of members of the public to ensure that price control measures succeeded, by an increase in the prices of imports, and by the overall staff shortage in the administration.

Workers did not see these as cogent arguments and began to make plans for direct action. They organized a mass rally on May 19 that demonstrated the growing power of trade unionism in Nigeria. Combative speeches at the rally repeated workers' demands. The leaders threatened that if their demands were not met by June 21, 1945, they would mobilize the "workers of Nigeria . . . to seek their own remedy with due regard to Law and Order on the one hand and starvation on the other." The government immediately announced that the planned strike was illegal. While some labor leaders called for a postponement in order to negotiate with the government, a radical faction led by Michael Imoudu insisted on a massive strike and a further radicalization of the trade unions.

The rise of Michael Imoudu marked a turning point in labor-government relations. Imoudu took over the leadership of the strike committee and persuaded the other members of the committee to attack the government and embark on a strike. He became the hero of Nigerian trade unionism, a status he maintained until his death in 2005. He began as an apprentice with the Nigerian Railway, but his interest in labor unions led to his appointment in 1940 as the president of the Railway Workers Union. For two years he was tireless in fighting for the cause of railroad workers. His style was regarded as extremist by the government, and he was not shy about using nondiplomatic means to call for better conditions of living. For example, in 1943 he led a protest march to the house of Bourdillon, the governor himself. The march was a threat to colonial and racial power. This militant action cost Imoudu his job; he was also detained and later banished from Lagos.[14] When he returned two and a half years later, he received a hero's welcome as Nigeria's "Labour Leader No. 1," as the Lagos media styled him.

Imoudu lived up to this name in 1945. He energized the radicals in the union, winning them over with the argument that labor should play an active political role and should assert itself more aggressively, using violent tactics as far as was possible.

The country's first general strike began on June 21, 1945. Various trade groups, notably railroad workers, were involved, and a large number of people embarked upon a strike for between thirty-seven and forty-four days; estimates of the number of strikers vary between 32,000 and 100,000.[15] Deeply angered by the general strike, the government tried to minimize its impact and punish the main organizers. Prisoners and about 900 "scabs" were drafted to work to make the point that the striking workers were replaceable. Ten union leaders were arrested, and the air was filled with the government's threats that the labor leaders would be jailed and threats from angry workers about using force to release them if that happened. The government formally charged the leaders with organizing an illegal strike.[16]

The government accused the *West African Pilot* and the *Daily Comet*, the newspapers that Azikiwe had founded and used effectively to further his political career, of contributing to the crisis. Indeed, the government was right: the *West African Pilot* and the *Daily Comet* strongly supported the strike. It offered encouragement to strike leaders and headlined the event. Azikiwe astutely used the strike to position himself as a nationalist and a humane leader who was far better prepared than the foreign governor to help workers.[17] The government decided to punish the *West African Pilot* and *Daily Comet* by banning them on July 8, using as an excuse the reports the two papers had carried two days earlier on their interview with the country's public relations officer. In the view of the government, the newspapers had presented the interview in such a way as to ridicule the public relations officers and moderate trade union leaders who called for caution.

A week after the ban, Azikiwe publicly alleged that the government had a plan to kill him. To popularize the alleged plot, he contacted the colonial secretary, Oliver Stanley, and liberal media in the United Kingdom. These actions strengthened Azikiwe's nationalist credentials. Using the banning of his papers and the alleged plot to kill him, he turned himself into a crusader and a victim of colonial power.[18] Not only did he devote his newspapers and writings to the cause, he was also able to turn radical members of trade unions into NCNC party men. A number of union leaders became members of the Zikist Movement. In an adroit move that aligned his interests with those of youth activists, Azikiwe called for help to recover income lost due to the banning of his papers, a loss that he put at close to 5,000 pounds. The Zikist Movement established Zik's Press Defence Fund, raising money through boxing events, public speeches, soccer tournaments, and dancing.[19]

Once the strike began, the stakes became very high. Workers needed to come away with something so they would not become demoralized and their leaders would not be humiliated. The government, also, did not want to appear too weak or too reckless. In their negotiations with the government, the workers won a concession that a 20 percent increase in the COLA would be paid immediately. Now emboldened, the ACSTWU workers rejected the increase as too small. It called on the government to institute a commission of enquiry to look into the merits of all its grievances. In addition, the ACSTWU set conditions before it would call off the strike: none of the leaders could be sued; the order banning the two newspapers had to be lifted; and no worker could be victimized for taking part in the strike. The Colonial Office in London, acting on a recommendation from the governor in Lagos, set up the Tudor Davies Commission to investigate the workers' claims; it began its work in November 1945. For three months, the Davies Commission traveled around parts of the country to take written and oral evidence; it completed its work in January 1946. The commission's report was published in October of that year. Its conclusion supported the main demands of the workers and it recommended a 50 percent increase in the COLA with arrears backdated to 1945.[20] The pay of low-paid government workers was increased and measures were put in place to control food prices.[21]

The strike brought significant changes. The power of labor was enhanced, and many workers were able to see that gains could be made by supporting strikes and political radicalism. Indeed, after 1945, the labor union was the strongest method of putting pressure on the government. This led to increased union membership, competition for leadership positions, and the creation of new unions. Many unions threatened to strike during this period.

The 1947 strike at Burutu (Warri Province) was the next major strike. Increases in the salaries and benefits of government workers encouraged those in commercial firms to seek similar privileges, and the African Clerical Workers Union, the African Mercantile Workers Union, the African General Workers Union pressured their employers for salary increases. (The three unions had all formed in 1942 and affiliated with the TUC.) The London office of the United Africa Company (UAC) had approved a new salary structure for its Nigerian office, but it was not enough for the workers, and on June 14, 1947, the unions called a strike to demand better pay for all workers in private industry. Riots erupted, first between strikers and nonstrikers. Mediation by the Department of Labour was unsuccessful and the UAC management decided to dismiss all the striking workers. More violence followed and the police had to intervene, using excessive force that sent thirty-five people to the hospital. When the situation calmed down, 535 of the 1,384 workers that had previously been dismissed were rehired and 462 workers and their dependents were sent away from Burutu to different locations in order to prevent them from uniting to foment more trouble. A sole commissioner was appointed by the government to examine the causes of the disturbances. As with other commissions, blame was spread around.[22]

Labor radicalism intensified after 1945. Two ideologically divided factions began to emerge among the unions and their leaders. Both felt they were pursuing the correct strategy in fighting for the interests of workers. On the one hand were those who argued that the unions should limit themselves to the issues of wages, pensions, and better conditions of service. On the other hand were those who wanted the unions to play the same role as nationalist political parties and help capture power from the British. The division ultimately became bitter and led to a major split in the labor union movement. Creating an umbrella labor organization, the TUC, had been a major achievement. The debate after the 1945 General Strike was whether the TUC should become affiliated with a political party. The party of choice was the NCNC, with an understanding reached in 1947 that an affiliation would be temporary until the time when the TUC could create its own labor party. A year later, when some TUC members argued that the links with the NCNC should be retained, others objected, saying that the TUC should not be affiliated with any party and that trade unionism should be separate from politics. Although the Sixth Annual Delegates Conference of the TUC opted not to affiliate with a political party, the faction that believed in being part of the NCNC—notably the Railway Workers Union, the Domestic Workers Union, and the Public Utility Technical and General Workers Union—decided to withdraw and form a new organization, the Nigerian National Federation of Labour (NNFL). The new organization described leadership of the TUC as weak and accused it of collaborating with the government.

The NNFL and its associates believed that unions and their leaders needed to be active in politics. They chose to participate in the NCNC, create a working-class consciousness, and seek the establishment of a socialist government. By 1949, the leading members of the Zikist Movement had created a trade union platform. Nduka Eze and Imoudu were two of the best-known figures in this movement, but there were numerous others. By 1948–1949, this cast of radical labor-cum-political leaders had decided to use a working-class movement to promote armed struggles and the spread of socialism in the country. These leaders argued that the aims of political parties and labor unions should be the same. They criticized unions that worked exclusively for better living conditions for pursuing limited goals instead of focusing on the larger goal of overthrowing the colonial regime. The radicals recruited new members to unions and to their movement with the idea that they would become militant revolutionaries who would be ready to fight. In 1949, Zikists recruited high school dropouts into unions and gave them small stipends with the hope that they would become militants who could use both words and arms to fight the colonial government.

The NNFL decided to test its strength as soon as it was born in March 1949. True to its goals of creating a socialist country, it sought full employment for all. It regarded the Labour Department as useless because it had not met the needs of workers, and it argued that the work of the Labour Department should be transferred to labor unions, which were better placed to work in the interests of workers. It demanded additional training (both locally and abroad) for various categories of workers so they could earn promotions. It wanted fewer privileges given to foreign workers so that they would have the same status as their Nigerian counterparts. The NNFL's most popular demand was more money for all: generous leave and transport allowances for all workers, increases in wages, and an assured annual increment. Even the person without a job must be paid: 5 pounds a year with an annual increase of 5 shillings.[23] The government, alarmed by this demand, regarded the leaders of the NNFL as dangerous.[24] As the NNFL threatened to initiate strikes, the government began to think of ways to curb its excesses.

Another labor-government confrontation was on the horizon. The government believed it was doing more than enough to respond to the high cost of living and to control soaring rents in urban areas. What the government saw was a politicized set of union leaders who had ulterior motives in mind.[25] All unions wanted more money and complained about low wages, high rents, and high prices of goods. However, the NNFL was using an approach that the government considered very uncivil. For example, when the NNFL called a mass meeting on September 3, 1949, in Lagos, it sent an invitation to the governor. In a politically charged letter, to which it demanded an immediate reply from the governor, the NNFL painted the colonial government as constructed on the basis of racial discrimination.[26] The government banned the meeting and warned that it could not respond to an invitation written in such a tone. To the NNFL, however, all approaches were legitimate, including the resort to violence.

The NNFL convened the rally at another location where its leaders, especially Imoudu, poured venomous words on the government. It also embarked on a five-week tour of the country to build workers' consciousness and organize a national strike.

THE 1949 IVA VALLEY VIOLENCE AND PROTESTS

The Coal Miners' Strike of 1949 in the Iva Valley in the Eastern Provinces of Nigeria ended the decade on a militant note. The Enugu area was the center of production of coal, a natural resource needed to fuel the country's railroad system.[27] Coal miners and management began their disagreement in 1944 over issues that were well known all over the country: inflation, demands for better wages, the payment of arrears, and the recognition of their union (the Colliery Workers Union; CWU).[28] None of the issues were resolved to the worker's satisfaction, and tension mounted. On November 7, 1949, the miners embarked on a "go-slow" action, a policy of working only minimally, to press home their demand for a minimum wage of 5 shillings 10 pence per day and the payment of arrears for 1946 and 1947. Two attempts by the government to mediate between the workers and the Colliery Board were unsuccessful.[29] To punish the workers, the mine authorities decided to dismiss over 200 hewers between November 10 and 12. Tensions increased, and the dismissed miners decided to stay at the mines so they would not be replaced by new recruits. The wives of the striking workers demonstrated at the colliery offices on November 14 and 15, shouting, destroying equipment, and smashing windows. When the coal company asked police to disperse the women, some of them were injured.[30]

Positions hardened: the striking workers needed to fight to get their jobs back and management wanted to assert its power. Colonial authorities interpreted the actions of the workers not just as a strike but as an attempt to use armed resistance to undermine the government, believing that the strike was a "terrorist plan" to create havoc. The government dispatched about 900 soldiers and policemen from the Northern Provinces, almost 150 of them armed with rifles. When the soldiers and policemen arrived on November 17, their major goal was not just to disperse the striking workers but also to remove explosives from the mines. The government believed that some of the miners were working with "communists" and radicals, such as members of the Zikist Movement, to create widespread acts of violence all over the country and claimed that it had knowledge of the plans of certain organizations to steal rifles and explosives in order to fight for independence by blowing up government buildings and key installations.

Armed policemen moved to the mines at Obwetti and Iva Valley to remove the explosives. At Obwetti they were successful. At Iva Valley, the miners' resistance made things difficult for the police. First the miners and police engaged in a war of words, but then one of the officers, F. S. Philip, fired a shot, and his colleagues began firing on the miners. Within a short period of time, twenty-one miners were killed and fifty-one were injured.[31]

The tragedy energized the nationalist movement.[32] As the news spread, the event came to be seen as a deliberate massacre. Speculation spread that the government might kill more Nigerians. In Lagos, the media revealed the angry mood of its readership. In the east, protests against the government occurred at Enugu, Owerri, Aba, Onitsha, Port Harcourt, Umuahia, Awka, Calabar, and elsewhere. The government put the police and army on alert. At Enugu, where anger was manifested immediately, European men were drafted into the police, supplied with arms, and put on twelve-hour shifts. In Lagos, the killings united many labor unions and political associations. The representatives of the NCNC, the NYM, and various labor unions decided on November 17 to establish the National Emergency Committee (NEC) to defend the rights of workers, to publicly denounce the government, and to investigate the shootings.[33]

Enugu became a center of anticolonial protest. A mass meeting was held on the day of the killings at which many angry people spoke. A memorial service was also held for the dead. The government, which was afraid of what the crowd at Enugu might do, used the police to disperse it with tear gas. As people fled in different directions, they became more and more embittered. The police, now strengthened with the armed Europeans, were ready to fight back. All European women and children were sent to military barracks for protection.

Enugu was just the beginning of what became a widespread protest.[34] By November 22, various leaders of political parties and ethnic organizations had met at Aba to plan their own protest, and branches of the Zikist Movement, the NCNC, and the Ibo State Union were able to unite in a common anticolonial cause. By November 23, the economic life of Aba was paralyzed. Stores and government offices were attacked and looted. Many people came out to demonstrate. The police responded with violence, beating many people in the crowd and using teargas to disperse it. Many were wounded and one person was killed. Many were arrested, later to be tried and jailed. The leaders, notably Margaret Ekpo, S. O. Masi, and Jaja Wachuku, all prominent political activists, were arrested and put under police surveillance after they were released.[35]

Riots and demonstrations started in Port Harcourt on November 24 that lasted for three days. The police reacted with brutality, killing two people, shooting thirteen, and injuring many more. The demonstrators moved about the city chanting anticolonial slogans and looting European stores.[36] When the Zikists called a meeting to plan their own action in Onitsha on

November 26, the police dispersed about 200 of them. Nevertheless, the Zikists declared November 26 a day of mourning, demonstrated around the city, and forced European stores to close. As elsewhere, the police used maximum force to disperse the crowd, wounding about three people.[37]

By November 26, the colonial government was worried that if the demonstrations spread to other cities, curtailing them could be very difficult. It proclaimed a state of emergency all over the country. In Lagos, where many activists were concentrated, the government proscribed any form of demonstration and assemblies of a political nature. It imposed a curfew on the eastern part of Nigeria. All news about the Iva Valley massacre and violent reactions to it were censored.[38] The government decided to work through the NEC to bring an end to the crisis. (While there were radicals in the NEC, it was dominated by reformers and conservative politicians. Indeed, the report of its fact-finding mission after the demonstrations was mild, although it disagreed with the government's claim that the miners had been armed and had aimed at killing the police.) The NEC called on the miners to resume work.

The demonstrations and pressure from various quarters forced the government to set up a four-man commission of enquiry to examine the labor disputes at the Enugu mines. The commission began its work on December 12, 1949, and ended its work on January 5, 1950, but its report was not published until June, after things had cooled off.[39] The report tried to spread the blame among the leaders of the miners; the chief commissioner of the Eastern Provinces, whom it accused of treating a labor dispute as political agitation; the Zikists and other politicians, whom it accused of heightening the tension; and the media, who spread the news. The NEC and the labor unions chose to turn July 4 into an annual National Day of Mourning, and the first such day was marked with memorial services and processions in Lagos and other parts of the country.[40]

CONCLUDING REMARKS

A clear shift emerged in colonial policy toward granting concessions and transferring power to Nigerians, a strategy that ultimately minimized the use of violence. The chapter records two clear cases of the use of violence by the government: one at Burutu and the other at Enugu. The overwhelming tone of these events is the surprising and uncharacteristic reticence and reluctance on the part of the colonial authority to use violence. Imoudu's 1941 demonstration and protest march to the governor forced the government to meet the protestors' demands. What made this march to be so effective? Why did the government make important concessions to the workers, including raising wages and sacking a senior official as the protesters demanded? How and why did the colonial government suddenly become responsive to workers' demands when in the past the protests would have been dismissed off hand and the agitators jailed or even shot? What happened to the government's usual posturing and high-handedness in dealing with protests and agitations? The answers are all connected to the reforms that began during the Second World War and the need for decolonization after 1945.

The government chose a new approach to crisis management after the war. While workers became more emboldened and more confrontational with every concession they were able to wring from the authorities, the government became less willing to use force. Instead of answering protests, venomous speeches, and even violent demonstrations with intimidation and maximum fire power, it negotiated with workers, controlled unions with cumbersome regulations, and used intermediaries, appeals, compromises, and concessions. This was a major turnaround in colonial policy.

The involvement of labor in protest broadened the range of possibilities for expressing nationalism. Sometimes nationalism was expressed through angry words and political rhetoric. We see the use of strikes as a weapon, as in the case of the 1945 General Strike. Imoudu gained in stature, drawing labor to the center of anticolonial struggles.[41] Astute politicians such as Azikiwe profited immensely from labor radicalism. Azikiwe was able to connect his aspirations with those of the labor movement. As elsewhere, labor unions were able to connect the larger interests of workers with politics and policies.[42]

The activities of the Zikists and unionists discussed here reveal a dimension to violence and radicalism that cannot be established in previous cases: this new dimension is the domination and leadership of young men in their twenties. The political activists were mainly urban-based educated young men.[43] They included clerks, teachers, union leaders, students, exservicemen, traders, and members of the working class.[44] Many had secondary education, and the professionals among them used their influence to publicize their activities in the media and mobilize the workers to rise against the government. Unlike their predecessors in the 1930s, they were able to produce pamphlets to advertise their cause. They had a clear vision of what they wanted, even if their philosophy was full of inconsistencies.[45] They were vigorous in attacking the colonial government and clear about their goal to get the British out of Nigeria.[46] They had a hero in Azikiwe.[47] They regarded themselves as courageous; they were not afraid to go to jail, lose their jobs, or be killed by the colonial government.[48] Their political activities were not totally devoid of personal interests. They were educated men whose ideas privileged the rise of the educated elite to power. They sought professional and career mobility, regarding the transfer of power to Nigerians as an opportunity to advance themselves. The leaders were able to mobilize the workers only on issues around wages, and once salaries and conditions were improved, workers' interest tended to wane. Cities played a central role, as many who participated in unions and strikes were residents of urban centers, a pattern that became a permanent feature of trade unionism in the country.[49] In turn, the high cost of living in urban areas contributed to the widespread discontent among workers.[50]

In the present chapter and chapter 6, we see the radicalization of nationalism. When the activities of the Zikist Movement are combined with those of labor unions, we begin to see the attempts to create a national platform to express nationalist consciousness. Previous organizations and political movements had not been national. In the language and actions of the unions and the Zikists, violence was one legitimate weapon to use against the colonial authorities. A clear vision of political action emerged: it was opposed to colonialism, opposed to the British, and opposed to capitalist exploitation. In the articulation of political action, the leaders did not espouse ethnic nationalism, and they tried to focus on the issues rather than the ethnic origins of those who espoused them. It was a great moment in the articulation of nationalist consciousness: radicalism infused with ideas that accepted the use of violence for anticolonial struggles.

The political process was not necessarily dominated by radicals or by combative trade union leaders. The 1940s produced the men who would become prominent in the country's politics for the next four decades. However, the visions of these men were divergent, from the radicals to the conservatives, from the nationalists to the tribalists. At the same time that radicalism was on the rise, the forces of ethnicity and regionalism were beginning to grow stronger, eventually leading to the adoption of federalism in the 1950s. The Nigerian Youth Movement (NYM) had become weakened and factionalized by the early 1940s. While Azikiwe was using the *West African Pilot* and the *Daily Comet* for his political ends, others were acting similarly. The *Daily Service,* a rival newspaper owned by the NYM, saw Azikiwe as a propagandist and claimed that the story of the plot to kill him was a hoax.[51] A bitter fight among the members of the political elite who were competing for power had begun by 1941. As with many major political struggles, this had its beginning in a small issue. Kofo Abayomi, a member of the Legislative Council on the ticket of the NYM, resigned in order to travel abroad for higher education. Two candidates for council membership emerged, Ernest Ikoli and Samuel Akinsanya, both backed by powerful factions. Azikiwe supported Akinsanya, who lost, and both of them decided to leave the NYM. This schism destroyed what was developing as a pan-Nigerian political party and inaugurated the trend toward the politics of ethnicity. In 1945, when the radical labor movement was claiming victory, the power of ethnicity was rapidly growing. In that year, the NCNC won the municipal elections in Lagos, defeating the NYM candidate. Interparty rivalry began to take the form of ethnic competition between the Yoruba and the Igbo. Each formed ethnic-based unions that became the major arenas of constituency politics. Divisive battles were launched by two antagonistic media outlets: the *West African Pilot* and the *Daily Service*. As labor leaders were drawn into the war, they began to lose the power to build a coherent anticolonial labor movement. The radicals of the Zikist Movement grasped the dangers posed by ethnicity but they failed to understand that choosing Azikiwe as their leader added to the ethnic tension. They regarded Azikiwe as a radical ideologist rather than a politician competing for others with power. It was one thing to rouse the spirit of national consciousness, as Azikiwe did, but it was another to create a platform from which to acquire power. The radicals promised to fight not only the British but also their Nigerian collaborators and all those opposed to the liberation of the country from imperialism.[52] When the TUC met in 1948, the controversy over whether or not to be part of the NCNC led to a split, which gave birth to the more radical NNFL. The Iva Valley crisis reunited the unionists, leading to the formation of the Nigerian Labour Congress in 1950. Their fight was sabotaged not by the British but by Nigerians who opted to conduct politics not in class but in ethnic terms. The unity that followed the Iva Valley violence was short lived. When Nigeria entered the 1950s, the strikes by unions and the voices of the socialist-oriented leaders became only background sound, as political leaders organized themselves on the basis of ethnic and regional political parties. The moment for building a new nation constructed out of anticolonial anger was lost. As an eyewitness observer who later became a prominent politician put it, a great opportunity had been lost for a truly national and nationalist movement to take hold of and give leadership to Nigeria.[53]

CONCLUSION

VIOLENCE AND
POLITICAL CULTURE

If politics is about the ability to define the middle ground and make compromises, violence may be about the ability to avoid the middle ground in order to establish one's power and make one's opinions the new hegemony. Violence has become an integral part of Nigerian political culture, where it is often used to resolve major arguments and conflicts between the state and its citizens, between the state and its component units (as in the case of the civil war of 1967–1970), and between civil society and the state. Intracommunity disagreements in Nigeria are also often resolved through recourse to violence rather than through a slow deliberative process of dialogue and persuasion. The coercive mobilization of people in Nigeria for or against policies has strengthened the power of ethnicity, which is often used there in combination with acts of violence to produce political outcomes.

Violence is not an irrational behavior. The British used violence to unsettle and conquer the precolonial states and their leaders. This book has provided key examples: the large Sokoto Caliphate crumbled, the powerful Empire of Benin destroyed, and the arrogant Ijebu humiliated. This violence had a clearly defined political agenda: to attain political domination. The British justified the atrocities that accompanied violence by pointing to the supposed barbarity of their would-be colonial subjects, who were preventing the march of progress. They presented the Aro as brutal slave traders, the Ekumeku as murderous insurgents, and the Muslims as bloodthirsty crusaders. These were no more than labels used to justify the use of violence against precolonial states and many of their innocent citizens. Yet the colonial power that unleashed various acts of violence pursued its mission with a sense of moral justification for all its actions, acquiring territory as if it had some kind of divine right to it. The British believed that they could seize land by peaceful means where possible and by violence when necessary. Although they criticized Nigerian groups that fought back as "barbarians," they had no moral qualms about their own motives and the instruments they used to attain them. They regarded their own acts of treachery, duplicity, and fraud as normal, and they treated those who implemented them as justified.

On the Nigerian side, the women fighting against the policy of taxation in 1929 were neither irrational nor careless. They mobilized themselves for violent resistance in order to communicate a clear political message: women must not be asked to pay taxes. The women had the support of the male population, they defined the targets to be attacked, and they knew their enemies. They were intelligent enough to realize that their actions would not bring about the end of the colonial regime, but they knew that they could challenge the power of the colonial officers over them. They understood the symbolic meaning of attacking warrant chiefs and courthouses. Their methods varied, from the strategy of those who used control of the Lagos markets as leverage for negotiations, to that of those who fought against both the colonial government and against the kingship at Abeokuta.[1] Their politics were very active at the grass roots, where people discussed issues of common interest, political leaders, and their overall future aspirations for themselves and their children. Similarly, union leaders who used angry words knew that they needed to mobilize thousands of people to instigate mass rebellion. They did not always make public their goal of using violence in part because they realized that if they did so, the authorities would use the power of the police and army against them.

Today, Nigerian citizens realize that they have yet to translate their numbers into the power to exert pressure on the state to make it deliver positive goods and services. Those in power have achieved that power through violence and have used violence to maintain their control of state power. The police and the army are not agencies of development or progress but instruments of state terrorism. Members of the political class have effectively co-opted the police and the army to actualize state terrorism. The successful men in power have converted themselves into mini local governments that include security apparatuses to protect themselves against both armed bandits and poor people who seek change. The competition for power is always intense, and it involves thuggery, ritual murder, and the assassination of opponents. Members of civil society who seek change and opposition political parties also believe in the power of violence and armed protests.

So prevalent is the culture of violence in relation to political leadership in Nigeria and other parts of Africa that Ali Mazrui, writing many years ago, pointed to a pattern that he labeled a warrior tradition: "As a reaction and rebellion against dependency, this wears the face of proud promise. But as an initiation into the culture of violent valour, the resurrection of the warrior tradition in African political culture also carries its own special hazards."[2] Another scholar is of the view that the cult of violence has become so firmly established that it now constitutes a danger:

> Throughout their history, with the possible exception of the armies of Shaka Zulu, Africans had observed limits to the use of violence, sometimes even substituting ritual and symbol for physical force. It is not clear that Africans understand those limits any more. If they do not, this may be the saddest of all the unhappy legacies of the wars of imperial conquest.[3]

Yet in Nigeria, the violence Nigerians employed during the colonial period was not intense and its casualties were not staggering. And although radical labor unions spread propaganda about the utility of violence, they did not necessarily embark upon many acts of violence. However, the belief is widespread that violence is a useful political tool. The message would appear to be that it is necessary to destroy before it is possible to build. Even today, angry university students destroy campus property in order to argue that they need more hostels. Radical nationalists have accepted the idea that to defeat those in power, one has to attack them—the idea that violence can precede orderliness.

But order has not followed chaos; no revolution accompanied the end of the civil war in 1970. Even the minimum political requirement after a major crisis, that of political compromise, has yet to occur. Political leaders who complained in the 1940s and 1950s that colonial officers were tormenting them oppressed their own people after 1960. Ideas about democracy, development, and social justice have met with violence and brutal repression from political leaders—both military and civilian—who have no respect for their people. In turn, civil society has become radicalized, taking to violence to fight the state. The Maitatsine rebellion in the 1980s is a case in point. Drawing on the power of Islam, the Maitatsine took to violence to protest against the decadence of society as well as the widening gap between rich and poor.[4] In the 1990s, antimilitary protests took a violent turn as people demanded an end to military regimes.[5]

The history of how Nigeria reached this depressing political culture has been told in part in the preceding chapters. Violence is an integral aspect of the imposition of colonial rule, the maintenance of the colonial order, and the Nigerian struggles to end colonialism. The Nigerian political system was marked by violence when it obtained its independence in 1960, and a civil war occurred within the first decade. The scale of communal, ethnic, and religious violence has been intense and unabating. In what follows, the essential features of violence in relation to politics are identified for discussion.

To start with, the Nigerian state was created largely by colonial conquest and violence. The motives were clear: the British sought to acquire territory for purposes of economic exploitation and political domination. The imperialist motives, by their very nature, created violent encounters. The method was also clear: small wars (now known as "low-intensity conflicts") were directed at various groups. The British justified this violence in ethical ways: it was the responsibility of the "civilized nations" to uplift Africa. As "barbarians" and "primitives," those who opposed the advance of civilization deserved to be killed. There was no need to mourn those who stood in the way of a righteous cause, a mission divinely given to the "superior" West to carry out on "barbarous subjects." The colonizers justified their violence, as they had justified slavery, by racism—Africa was a "burden" to the white man.

Even though the British pursued "small wars," the devastation could be similar to that of "big wars." Colonial forces often pursued a strategy of attrition, destroying everything of value in order to weaken their Nigerian enemies. Many attacks on the Igbo destroyed farms and crops, livestock, and villages. For example, the village of Satiru was set on fire in 1903, with a curse placed on it against rebuilding. The caliph of Sokoto, who took to flight, had to become a war commander at Burmi, eventually losing his life together with others as the town suffered an attack.[6]

Colonial officials made calculations about which strategy to use in response to protests. In the case of the Women's War of 1929, for instance, the British did not immediately resort to violence, a decision that allowed the riot to gain momentum and spread widely. Confronted with a revolt and a protest rally by thousands of women, the British chose consultation and compromise, agreeing for the most part to one of the women's demands by publicly removing, disgracing, and jailing the most notorious of the warrant chiefs, Okugo. In the end, even though the British did use violence, there were very minimal casualties among the rioting women. Instead of gunning the women down indiscriminately, as they had done in response to protests in Ijemo and Abeokuta, British officials chose to impose heavy collective monetary fines on the thirty or so towns involved in the uprisings.

However, the specter of resentment and rebellion lurked behind the semblance of peace. The British strategy of pacification through brutal demonstration of power failed to win the people to full acceptance of colonial rule, and this fact instigated anticolonial nationalism.

Resistance to the conquest involved the use of violence, but Nigerian groups lost more lives than the imperialists did. Some resistance wars were carried out on a relatively large scale, as in the case of the Benin Expedition of 1897 or the wars directed against the Aro in eastern Nigeria from 1901 to 1902. The decision to fight the invading forces was based on the need to preserve sovereignty, defend power, or even protect established religion, as in the case of the emirates of Kano and Sokoto, which fought to preserve kingship and Islam. A dangerous pattern emerged, as we saw in the case of the Ekumeku guerrilla wars, where the British justified brutality with their need to destroy the Ekumeku or so-called cultist groups (such as those of Awka). In the pursuit of what was called a civilizing mission, the colonial authorities found nothing wrong with the use of violence.

When Africans found it difficult or impossible to reach white officers and others in positions of power, they focused their energy on their Nigerian agents and collaborators. Nigerians killed other Nigerians in the process of fighting the British or in conflicts over power, and black-on-black violence became common. Violence was directed at agents of the state even if they were Nigerians. Property associated with the state or its agents who Africans perceived as exploitative constituted another set of targets. Thus, we saw that the Ekumeku insurgents attacked the trade headquarters of the Royal Niger Company and that Africans destroyed many courthouses in the 1920s. Attacks on government buildings and vehicles were designed to devastate the enemy and undermine the prestige of the government and its officers.

Local chiefs—for example, warrant chiefs among the Igbo—suffered as well. As the British reordered precolonial institutions to meet the needs of the colonial era, they imbued them with authoritarianism and violence. Local chiefs who arbitrarily exercised power in an authoritarian manner generated widespread hatred, and deep cynicism with regard to government began to take root. In the past, as a reaction to the changing status of chiefs, cults and secret societies were formed to create networks that would make it possible to negotiate and manage relations with colonial authorities. Some cults operated in ways that met with drastic retaliation and punishment from the government, as in the cases of the Ekpe Ikpa Ukot (Man-Leopard Society), the Idiong (Society of Diviners), and the Atinga ("witch hunters").[7] Many reworked themselves to meet the demands of the new era, as in the case of the Reformed Ogboni Fraternity, which combined elements of an indigenous cult with Christianity in order to appeal to a new set of Western-educated people.

Violence and coercion inevitably generated anticolonial feelings. Resentment followed conquest, and colonial policies about issues such as taxation generated hostility that further stoked the fires of anticolonialism. Whether they were successful or not, cases of resistance constitute powerful elements of historical memory. The oral traditions in some parts of the country's Middle Belt are replete with cases of bold actions. Leaders that the British conquered became heroes to their own people, as in the case of Jaja of Opobo. They were resisting the penetration of European power, and they also understood some of the consequences of the penetration of Western capitalism. European influence, as they realized, could undermine or destroy them.

It was possible for the British to attain their colonial objectives in part because they used coercion. People had to be put to work, even against their wishes, if the British were to make a profit. When uprisings occurred, they had to be crushed. Those who refused to obey laws and regulations had to be incarcerated in the prisons built to hold resisters. The British invested in security and defense so that efficient police and military forces could intimidate, scare, or kill local people. They co-opted local chiefs and kings into the administration as collaborators. In a strategy of "diplomacy" after the conquest, they allowed indigenous rulers to benefit from the exercise of colonial power by way of steady incomes, collection of taxes, and administration of justice, which enhanced their power over their people.

The time of decolonization, when anticolonial sentiments ran deep, was the period when the academic writing of Nigerian history (indeed, African history as a whole) was born. The courage of Jaja of Opobo and his contemporaries who resisted colonial conquest has enhanced their status in Nigerian historiography, which interprets them as "proto-nationalists." Nigerian historians argue that the consciousness of the nations created by people like Jaja of Opobo was turned into a source from which to create a consciousness for modern Nigeria. Anticolonial fighters in the 1940s also eulogized the resisters as they sought the origins of anticolonial nationalism. Historians regarded colonialism as an embarrassing phase and those who resisted it as heroes, a position that characterized many others as "collaborators."[8]

While the distinction between collaboration and resistance is sometimes overdrawn and the connection between resistance to colonial conquest and later anticolonial struggles is sometimes exaggerated, it is hard to deny that the heroism attributed to Jaja of Opobo and his contemporaries has influenced the thinking of their people up till today. For instance, the Igbo linked their ability to declare their secession in the 1960s to their long struggles against the British. Many modern-day Igbo nationalists link the history of the resistance to the civil war to make a case for political assertiveness and radical political projects. Thus, the Igbo continue to draw inspiration from previous revolts and violence, even if these were unsuccessful. In addition, although it might be far-fetched and in some cases misleading to postulate a grand (single) nationalist narrative of Nigeria that links Jaja of Opobo with Azikiwe, it is also erroneous to argue that Jaja of Opobo had no notions of resistance or of nationalism. Certainly, Jaja of Opobo did not have the idea of defending Nigeria, since the modern country of Nigeria had not yet been created, but he had the idea of protecting the sovereignty of his own people and preventing them from losing their independence. Jaja of Opobo wanted to retain his independence; Azikiwe wanted to gain independence.

Colonial rule restructured the economy and politics in a way that made competition inevitable. Power struggles and contests over land and boundaries added to the incidence of violence. The politics of managing local areas created tensions among chiefs and between communities. Rivalries for power intensified during colonial rule at two levels: within a city, a king could clash with other chiefs, notably powerful lineage chiefs, over power and prestige; and between cities, kings could fight with one another for superiority. Conflicts among chiefs and kings could become communal conflicts, leading to riots and physical attacks on key individual actors. The key to understanding many of these conflicts is the introduction of indirect rule. Conquered chiefs that the British put in positions of power began to look for fresh opportunities offered by British rule. They were active in collecting taxes and they took control of communal land in order to benefit from rents and royalties. As chiefs and kings looked for more power and opportunities, they stepped on the toes of the Western-educated elite, who regarded education as the major criterion for participation in modern politics and argued that power should be transferred to them.

The extension of indirect rule to the south laid the conditions for antagonisms and protests. Before 1914, there was no single power in the south. Subordinate officers who did not want to antagonize Lugard told him that the policy used in the north would work among the Yoruba. Among the Yoruba, the Egba State was under the Egba United Government, a kind of anomaly, with power given to the local elite and the king (the *alake*). Other groups were constituted into provinces independent of one another. In 1914, Lugard decided to break the Yoruba into smaller provinces, each to be controlled by a powerful resident accountable to the governor in Lagos. The policy of indirect rule assumed that Yoruba kings had autocratic power over their people, fellow chiefs, and land. The new powers granted by the British made the kings less constitutionally accountable to their people and their chiefs than had been the case in precolonial times. There were many challenges to kings from their chiefs. The particular configuration of local governments the British put in place and the chiefs they assigned to govern generated many protests and conflicts. One chief could be denied the opportunity to chair an area court because of the way the boundaries were defined, as was seen in the protest of the Isin, who fought for the right of their king (the *olusin*) to chair the Oke-Onigbin court instead of a rival chief, the *ajia*.[9] In the east, the policy of indirect rule was a failure, but the colonial government did not initiate changes not until after various conflicts and riots had defeated the idea. Lugard called for a greater understanding of the Igbo and their institutions, but his subordinates interpreted this instruction as a mandate to look for chiefs even where none had existed. The Women's War of 1929 helped bring this configuration of indirect rule to an end; to restore peace, the colonial government made structural changes to its administration that led to the establishment of village councils in over a hundred places.

Nothing represents the permanence of violence in Nigerian political culture better than the police and the army. The main purpose of both was to maintain domestic order and security. During the two world wars, the size of the army expanded as thousands were recruited to serve as soldiers and carriers outside the country. Involvement in colonial wars turned soldiers against their own people. The goal of maintaining an army was not to defend the interest of Nigerians but to defend the colonial state. British authorities took steps to ensure that the police and the army gave their full loyalty to the colonial state. For one thing, they owed their wages and promotions to the government, and the promise of long service ensured good incomes and pensions. British officials also promoted a spirit of obedience to government officers and policies. Unlike indigenous practices, in which armies lived among the people, the British separated both the army and the police from society. The barracks were located far away from the people, constituting small villages on their own. The idea was that keeping them away from others would mean they would have no sympathy for the people whenever they had to use force to maintain order. As a result, the people regarded them as nothing but servants of the alien rulers.

The British recruited men to their military forces in the early years of colonization in a way that exploited ethnic differences. Soldiers from one group were made to work among other groups, a strategy based on a belief that ethnic animosities would make them efficient and, perhaps, ruthless. Officers and rank-and-file members could be separated by ethnicity to promote divisions within the army and limited loyalty to the country.[10] By the 1950s, many senior officers were from the south, fueling the regional competition for power that was one of the reasons for the coups of 1966. During the 1950s, violence directed at the state was not necessarily violence against the colonial government. As Nigerians formed political parties and acquired power, they began to direct violence at one another.

Nigeria did not experience the equivalent of the violent struggles for liberation in Algeria, Kenya, or South Africa. Nor was there any revolution directed at cleansing the system. Instead, the pioneer political elite, motivated by self-interest and the defense of ethnicity, competed in dangerous ways. This is not to suggest that independence was not fought for; labor movement radicalism and the combative activities of nationalists and the media illustrate that the notion of freedom was accompanied by a realization that violence could become a legitimate means to attain it.

CHARACTERISTICS AND PATTERNS

The prevalence of violence has led to attempts to find "universal" explanations for it. Studies of African military systems have seen violence as inevitable, since officers shoot their way to power. Some see violence as one of the traumas of the colonial era. Frantz Fanon even argues that Africans need violence to "cleanse" themselves. Drawing from the Algerian war of independence and related experiences, Fanon argues in *The Wretched of the Earth* that meaningful decolonization involves using violence against the colonizers. His thesis has been read to mean that liberation without a violent fight for it is inadequate, given the overwhelming force used to conquer Africans and to force them to live under colonial rule. To use violence against Europeans, Fanon believes, is to turn it into a regenerative instrument, one that allows Africans to torment and humiliate their oppressors.

Ali Mazrui has accepted and extended Fanon's argument, regarding violence as a cure for the psychological wound inflicted by colonialism. To Mazrui, although the precolonial society linked virility and martial valor, the colonial society became disconnected from both: the warrior of old became a dependent new man. With the spread of Christianity, the "new" African who did not serve in the army became "demilitarised and emasculated."[11] In Mazrui's view, African dictators who take to violence simply want to restore a warrior tradition and others who take to violence are seeking to recover a lost manhood. All of these are controversial arguments, but they point to a strong interest in explaining the persistence of violence in African politics.

In colonial Nigeria and elsewhere, violence and racism were combined to ensure that the system worked. Prejudice and brutality were clear to see. White officers beat Africans not because they were sadists, argued some contemporary observers such as Charles Elliot, but because their remote location and solitary existence were not conducive to their well-being.[12] The limitation of this argument is that violent officers were not necessarily based in remote locations or isolated from other Europeans. Some officers, such as Sir Walter Egerton, the governor of Southern Nigeria from 1903 to 1912, said that many officers were probably mentally ill and that this was the probable explanation for their violent practices. No evidence exists that can be used to ascertain the mental status of many officers, although we cannot dismiss the connection between mental illness and violent behavior.

What is clear is the pervasive belief among officers, even those who were sane and rational, that Africans were uncivilized children and that violence was needed to tame the majority of them. Such negative ideas were pervasive and prevalent for the whole period of European rule in Africa.[13] There was a connection between the stereotypes and violence: primitive Africans were conquered by guns and were expected to become economically productive by means of flogging, while those who were unredeemable were put in prison. For many officers, violence became the quickest way to prove that they had the right to rule.[14]

No consistent organized resistance movement existed that was committed to the use of violence during the colonial era. Rather, cases of violence occurred in various locations, and attacks on individual agents could be spontaneous. In some cases, leaders emerged, including those who organized pitched battles. The opinions of the educated elite in the media fueled some communal rivalries. Violence was not always directed at the colonial state or system; it was sometimes directed at specific policies (as in the case of taxation) or personnel (such as warrant chiefs, court messengers, and court clerks).

LEGACIES: POSTCOLONIAL DISORDER

It is striking that Nigeria is torn from within rather than from any external conflict or threat from its neighbors. There have been skirmishes over the Bakassi Peninsula with Cameroon and over small islands in the Lake

Chad region, but by and large, no one has threatened the territorial integrity of Nigeria. Violence has revolved around the inability to stabilize internal politics and use national revenues wisely to ameliorate poverty. Although Nigeria was a pioneer in the new wave of wars that followed the end of Africa's independence, anticolonial nationalism failed to produce any lasting foundation for the creation of Nigerian patriotism. The fragmentation of Nigeria's nationalism into ethnic and religious nationalisms has ensured the continuity of violence. Far more Nigerians have killed one another than were killed by the British.

The causes of the violence in post-independence Nigeria have nothing to do with a so-called renaissance of "primitive barbarism," as some are inclined to characterize African wars,[15] but are found in factors that connect with the nation's past and the way that violence has become "legitimate" as a strategy of politics. The colonial government did not resolve the issues of how to reduce tensions in society, how to limit state power, how to placate a radicalized civil society, how to deal with a variety of complex social struggles, and how to resolve conflicts between rich and poor, between one ethnic group and another, and between minorities and majorities. The colonial system thrived on the use of violence; the postcolonial era sees the monopoly of violence as a tool for creating a stable nation-state. Unresolved issues of the past, including the conflicts they generated, have a bearing on contemporary problems and their attendant revolts and other violence.

Party politics and violence inaugurated Nigeria's independence in 1960. Violence was triggered by elections, ethnic conflict, and power struggles. The political system lost legitimacy, eventually leading to a civil war in 1967. The linkage between parties and violence began early. The post-1940 political parties were formed in an atmosphere of distrust and ethnic competition. Each major political party represented a region: the Nigerian People's Congress in the North, the National Council of Nigeria and the Cameroons in the East, and the Action Group in the West. Each successfully kept control of its region and all struggled bitterly to control the center. The task of national integration was complicated.

All the troubles of the 1950s were continued after independence. The federal system was still a basis of contention, as the three big regions struggled to retain their autonomy while at the same time their key political leaders wanted to control federal power. The Northern Region, the most privileged of the regions, was able to do both, as its leading politicians took control of their region as well as the seat of the federal government in the southern city of Lagos. The competition among the big regions was aggressive and manifested violence, real and threatened. Angry parties warned of secession. The minority ethnic groups in each of the big regions experienced nothing but domination and marginalization.

By 1962, just two years after independence, there was a feeling that Nigeria might not survive as a geographical entity. The country survived, but at the high cost of the collapse of the First Republic and a civil war, both within the first decade of independence. Even the lessons of the civil war were quickly lost or ignored, and the politicians of the post-1980 era reimposed "tribalist" politics that created the conditions for instability and violence. New recruits to politics accepted the rules and limitations of "tribalist politics" and sought followers to help them defend their corrupt practices. A radicalized civil society has emerged in postcolonial Nigeria, driven by reasons similar to those that generated anticolonial resistance.

One key issue revealed by the rivalries between the political parties is that the struggles to define the political basis of the Nigerian union were contested and unresolved. All parties agreed about the need to have a federal system, but they disagreed about how many regions the nation should have and how to distribute power among the regions. Minority elements wanted to create more regions or states so their people could enjoy greater autonomy. This partly explains the long and complicated riots among the Tiv in the Middle Belt as they sought to end the grip of the Hausa-Fulani and the Nigerian People's Congress. Even when ethnic rivalries had legitimate causes, they illustrate the problem of how to define an acceptable basis for political union. The political leaders who controlled the big regions were not interested in creating additional states. Violence became one way to get to an answer much faster than was promised by political negotiations. In the Western Region, prolonged political agitation and the desire of the Nigerian People's Congress to weaken the Action Group led to the establishment of the Mid-West Region in 1963. In the Niger Delta, where issues regarding the rights of minorities are still not resolved, the Willink Commission of 1957 recommended that the Ijo of the Delta did not need a separate state, a conclusion that only intensified the growth of Ijo nationalism. In February 1966, a young university undergraduate, Isaac Adaka Boro, led a band of about 160 youth to initiate a violent bid for secession. The rebellion was ended by greater military power, but it has served as a preface to a never-ending cycle of violence in this region. It took the violence of a military coup to lead to the creation of new states in Nigeria in 1967, followed by a major war.

The benefits to society that the exercise of power seemed to promise complicated the ethnic divisions in Nigeria. The agents of nationalism promised that rapid changes would follow independence. For the majority of the population, the story of the march to independence was not only political but economic. They hoped that with their people in power, their standard of living would improve. When food and jobs did not come in the expected quantity and quality, many became disappointed and angry.[16] The poor become disenchanted when those in power do not enhance their living standards. Thus, they are available to leaders who want to use violence to change society, including religious leaders who have led violent uprisings. Economic development plans did not generate the anticipated progress; the government complained of inadequate funding and foreign support. The decline of agriculture led to the further impoverishment of millions of people, thereby consolidating the social pressure to demand change and rise against the political leadership. Most of the poor were able to see (and sometimes condemn) the lifestyle of the privileged few. Ostentatious politicians did not help matters. People were waiting to be mobilized to take to violence, to fight injustice, or simply complain against power. This violence was shaped in various ways. Some in the regions pressured the regional governments to become populist, for example in the antigovernment riots in the Western Region. In many other cases, demands for economic change were aligned with ethnic rivalries. Many in the south believed that northern politicians were holding them back from progress.

A small group of the radical elite were pushing for a revolutionary option. Many among them believed that ethnicity and the politics of regionalism were standing in the way of creating a united, prosperous country and began to advocate the use of violence as an option. The coup that ended the First Republic was staged by men who described themselves as revolutionaries.

The army, the police, and violence are among the legacies of colonialism. Post-independence Nigeria is bedeviled by violence and by the excesses and corruption of the police and army. The army Nigeria inherited at independence subsequently became one of the major obstacles to political and economic development. It was fragmented by ethnicity, and while it later presented itself as a "national organization," its recruitment patterns and the politics of the officers and rank and file were based on ethnicity and regionalism. Each of the three dominant regions sought representation and power, and the officers were as divided as the politicians; many expressed support for their regional leaders.

The character of the army was exposed in 1966. In January, a number of officers seized power through violence. Six months later, another group of officers staged another coup. Both coups revealed the ethnic divisions in the army and the failure of officers to contribute positively to national integration—the Igbo staged the first coup and the Hausa-Fulani the second. Coups, attempted coups, and countercoups became a predominant feature of politics. Military regimes were never popular for long, and they resorted to repressive measures to "tame" civil society. Civil-military relations were based on distrust and the use of violence. The army and the public became separated from one another—senior officers became a power elite unto themselves, and they used their power to steal public funds. Rivalries among officers led to a civil war. The declaration of the Republic of Biafra in 1967 brought home the reality of the breakup of the country and the breakdown of law and order. The ultimate act of violence was unleashed.

The country did not break up, and it actually entered a prosperous economic phase in the 1970s, thanks to the oil boom. The expectations of the 1950s began to be repeated in the 1970s. Many wanted a higher standard of living based on revenues from oil. In a jubilant mood, General Gowon, the country's head of state, declared that the country's problem was no longer how to get money but what to do with it. Before the end of the decade, however, the confidence gave way as Nigeria accepted its first external debts. The oil boom era saw a rise in armed robbery. Successful Nigerians began the process of creating an architecture of fear by building elegant houses that are no more than security cages.

By the 1980s, the country was thinking of creating various projects on peace and security precisely because the various manifestations of violence had multiplied: cultism on campuses, countless interreligious conflicts, communal clashes, and so on. The pervasiveness of insecurity was reflected in the landscape—houses now began to have fences as high as a two-story building. When the country entered the 1990s, there was more trouble along the lines of the old ethnic and political rivalries. Militia organizations emerged to use force to protect ethnic interests, including the Odua militia in the west and the Masob militia in the east, and others around the country. Each of these affirmed that violence was a legitimate strategy for protecting ethnic interests.

The issue of revenue-sharing from oil production became intensely complicated. Complaints over land shortages, water and air pollution, and unfair allocation of revenue derived from oil energized many groups in the Niger Delta. Soon there was open rebellion and multinational oil companies such as Shell became drawn into it. The violence in the Niger Delta moved close to assuming the character of a civil war. Protestors found the means to shut down oil production and destroy pipelines. Their plight and their strategies became an international issue when the military administration of General Sanni Abacha brutally murdered a number of Ogoni political activists, including Ken Saro Wiwa, who popularized the causes of injustice. State violence led only to greater ethnic solidarity and more anti-government protests and riots. Struggles over the control of resources and the sharing of federally collected revenues will continue to be a source of conflicts and violence in the country.

It is time to close a long read. For most of the twentieth century, Nigeria existed as an acquired territory. The British acquired it by force. Those inside the territory were expected to obey in order to meet the interests of those who had acquired their territory. Interests, rather than people, had to be protected by the colonial forces. If the people cooperated, there were no problems. If they did not, the army and the police would do their work. British rule created a government that could not be trusted. The lack of trust became mutual: colonial officers did not trust the citizens they governed. The successive Nigerian governments that followed the colonial government have adopted a similar approach. Violence continues to mediate the relationship between the rulers and their subjects.

NOTES

Preface

1. See G. Aijmer and J. Abbink, eds., *Meanings of Violence: A Cross-Cultural Perspective* (Oxford: Oxford University Press, 2000).

2. I have capitalized "the North" and "Northern Nigeria" for the period when the Northern Region was in existence. I have done the same for "Eastern Nigeria," "Western Nigeria," "the East," and "the West." I have also capitalized "Northern Nigeria" and "Southern Nigeria" when referring to the early colonial period, when they were two separate entities.

3. See Elizabeth Isichei, "Colonialism Revisited," in *Studies in the History of the Plateau State, Nigeria,* ed. Elizabeth Isichei, 206–223 (London: Macmillan, 1972).

4. See Terence O. Ranger, "Connections between Primary Resistance Movements and Modern Mass Nationalism in East and Central Africa," *Journal of African History* 9, no. 3 (1968): 437–453.

5. See Allen Isaacman in collaboration with Barbara Isaacman, *The Tradition of Resistance in Mozambique: The Zambezi Valley, 1850–1921* (Berkeley: University of California Press, 1976); and Allen Isaacman and Barbara Isaacman, *Mozambique: From Colonialism to Revolution, 1950–1982* (Boulder, Colo.: Westview, 1983).

6. See C.-A. Julien, ed., *Les Africains*, 8 vols. (Paris: Jeune Afrique, 1977), which links the military feats of nineteenth-century resistance heroes with colonial nationalism.

7. See J. F. Ade Ajayi, "Nineteenth Century Origins of Nigerian Nationalism," *Journal of the Historical Society of Nigeria* 2, no. 1 (December 1961): 196–210; and Ranger, "Connections between Primary Resistance Movements and Modern Mass Nationalism in East and Central Africa," 437–453 and 631–664. The connection between the resistance of the nineteenth century and the resistance of the twentieth century is not always clear. For debates about this connection, see J. Glassman, *Feasts and Riot: Revelry, Rebellion, and Popular Consciousness on the Swahili Coast, 1856–1888* (Portsmouth, N.H.: Heinemann, 1995).

8. Frantz Fanon, *The Wretched of the Earth,* trans. Constance Farrington (New York: Grove, 1963).

9. J. S. Coleman, *Nigeria: Background to Nationalism* (Berkeley: University of California Press, 1960).

10. Obaro Ikime, *Niger Delta Rivarly: Itsekiri-Urhobo Relations and the European Presence, 1884–1936* (London: Longman, 1969); A. E. Afigbo, *The Warrant Chiefs: Indirect Rule in Southeastern Nigeria, 1891–1929* (London: Longman, 1972).

11. Donald Denoon and Adam Kuper, "Nationalist Historians in Search of a Nation: The 'New Historiography' in Dar-es-Salaam," *African Affairs* 2 (1970): 329–349.

12. Toyin Falola, *Violence in Nigeria: The Crisis of Religious Politics and Secular Ideologies* (Rochester, N.Y.: University of Rochester Press, 1998).

13. See, in particular, Toyin Falola, *The History of Nigeria* (Westport, Conn.: Greenwood, 1999).

1. Violence and Colonial Conquest

The first epigraph is from the submission by the Mbaise Clan Council to the Jones Commission, April 14, 1956, quoted in Isaac M. Okonjo, *British Administration in Nigeria, 1900–1950: A Nigerian View* (New York: Nok Publishers, 1974), 57. The second epigraph is quoted in E. J. Alagoa, "Koko: Amanyanabo of Nembe," *Tarikh* 1, no. 4 (1967): 75.

1. For details of initial contacts and the interests that motivated them, see, among others, J. D. Hargreaves, *Prelude to the Partition of West Africa* (London: Macmillan, 1963); and B. I. Obichere, *West African States and European Expansion: The Dahomey-Niger Hinterland, 1885–1898* (New Haven, Conn.: Yale University Press, 1971).

2. Draft of Beecroft's Appointment, June 30, 1849, Public Record Office, London, UK (hereafter PRO), FO 84/775.

3. For details of the conquest of Lagos, see R. S. Smith, "The Lagos Consulate 1851–1861: An Outline," *Journal of African History* 15 (1974): 393–416.

4. Commander Forbes to Commodore Bruce, November 24, 1851, PRO, CO ZHC/2016.

5. E. A. Ayandele, *The Missionary Impact on Modern Nigeria 1842–1914: A Political Analysis* (London: Longman, 1966), chapter 3.

6. Anderson, memorandum, June 11, 1883, PRO, FO 403/19.

7. Olayemi Akinwumi, *The Colonial Contest for the Nigerian Region, 1884–1900: A History of the German Participation* (Hamburg: Lit Verlag, 2004).

8. Moor to Foreign Office, November 30, 1885, PRO, FO 403/267.

9. Crowther to Hutchinson, June 18, 1879, Church Missionary Society Archives, University of Birmingham Library, UK (hereafter CMS), CA3/04.

10. Colonial Office to Foreign Office, June 16, 1888, and enclosure, PRO, FO 403/76.

11. A contemporary account of some of the wars can be found in Seymour Vandeleur, *Campaigning on the Upper Nile and Niger* (London: Methuen and Co, 1898).

12. Moor to Foreign Office, November 30, 1895, PRO, FO 403/267.

13. Memorandum on MacDonald by C. H. Hill to Foreign Office, November 26, 1895, 3, PRO, FO 2/85.

14. A. E. Afigbo, "The Aro Expedition of 1901–02: An Episode in the British Occupation of Igboland," *Odu* 7 (April 1972): 3–27.

15. Ibid.

16. Elizabeth Isichei, *The Ibo People and the Europeans: The Genesis of a Relationship to 1906* (London: Faber and Faber, 1973), 131–134.

17. Moor to Colonial Office, no. 183, April 17, 1902, PRO, CO 520/14.

18. For details, see Alan F. Ryder, *Benin and the Europeans, 1485–1897* (London: Longman, 1969); Robert Home, *City of Blood Revisited: A New Look at the Benin Expedition of 1897* (London: R. Collins, 1982); and J. O. Egharevba, *A Short History of Benin*, 4th ed. (Ibadan: University of Ibadan Press, 1968).

19. Egharevba, *A Short History of Benin*, 48.

20. Philip Igbafe, "British Rule in Benin, 1897–1920: Direct or Indirect?" *Journal of the Historical Society of Nigeria* 3, no. 4 (1967): 701–717.

21. S. A. Akintoye, *Revolution and Power Politics in Yorubaland, 1840–1893: Ibadan Expansion and the Rise of Ekitiparapo* (London: Longman, 1971).

22. A. I. Asiwaju, *Western Yorubaland under European Rule, 1889–1945: A Comparative Analysis of French and British Colonialism* (London: Longman, 1976), chapter 2.

23. R. S. Smith, "Nigeria-Ijebu," in *West African Resistance: The Military Response to Colonial Occupation*, ed. M. Crowder (New York: Africana Publishing Corp., 1971), 170ff.

24. For the British side, see Carter's report on the Ijebu-Ode, May 22, 1892, PRO, CO 147/85.

25. For this turnaround, see the elaboration of the process in E. A. Ayandele, *The Ijebu of Yorubaland, 1850–1950: Politics, Economy and Society* (Ibadan: Heinemann Educational Books, 1992).

26. J. A. Atanda, *The New Oyo Empire* (London: Longman, 1973), 72.

27. Samuel Johnson, *The History of the Yorubas* (Lagos: C.S.S., 1921), 623.

28. Joseph P. Smaldone, *Warfare in the Sokoto Caliphate: Historical and Sociological Perspectives* (Cambridge: Cambridge University Press, 1977), 123.

29. D. J. M. Muffett, *Concerning Brave Captains: Being a History of the British Occupation of Kano and Sokoto and of the Last Stand of the Fulani Forces* (London: André Deutsch, 1964), 96.

30. Lieutenant (later General) F. P. Crozier, quoted in Muffett, *Concerning Brave Captains*, 132.

31. Ibid., 161–162.

32. Quoted in ibid., 181.

33. Elizabeth Isichei, *A History of Nigeria* (London: Longman, 1983), 376–377.

34. Bruce Vandervort, *Wars of Imperial Conquest in Africa, 1830–1914* (Bloomington: Indiana University Press, 1998).

35. D. R. Headrick, *The Tools of Empire: Technology and European Imperialism in the Nineteenth Century* (New York: Oxford University Press, 1981).

36. Vandeleur, *Campaigning on the Upper Nile and Niger*, 272.

37. Report of the Commissioners of African Inquiry, Use of the Navy 1811, PRO, CO 267/29.

38. S. C. Ukpabi, "Military Recruitment and Social Mobility in Nineteenth Century West Africa," *Journal of African Studies* 2, no. 1 (Spring 1975): 87–107.

39. S. C. Ukpabi, "The Origins of the West African Frontier Force," *Journal of the Historical Society of Nigeria* 3, no. 3 (December 1966): 485–501.

40. Ibid.

41. Isichei, *A History of Nigeria*, 372.

42. Margery Perham, *Lugard: The Years of Authority, 1898–1945* (London: Collins, 1960), 45.

43. Muffett, *Concerning Brave Captains*, 114.

44. T. Pakenham, *The Scramble for Africa: The White Man's Conquest of the Dark Continent from 1876 to 1912* (London: Weidenfeld and Nicolson, 1991), 652.

45. Goldie to Salisbury, August 8, 1895, PRO, FO 403/71.

46. Johnson, *The History of the Yorubas*, 622.

47. House of Commons, Debates, 4th Ser., Vol. 91, Column 349, PRO.

2. Resistance by Violence

1. Telegram from Lieutenant-Governor to Governor, December 15, 1929, Nigerian National Archives, Enugu, Nigeria (hereafter NAE), CSE SP 1/93.

2. F. K. Ekechi, "Portrait of a Colonizer: H. M. Douglas in Colonial Nigeria, 1897–1920," *African Studies Review* 26 (March 1983): 25–50. The personality that I present here relies on this essay as well as on archival sources.

3. District Officer's Report, July 10, 1903, Nigerian National Archives, Ibadan, Nigeria (hereafter NAI), Cal Prof 10/3.

4. Ekechi, "Portrait of a Colonizer," 26.

5. See Report of the Owerri Division for the Half Year Ending 30th June, 1917, NAE, OW346/17, Riv Prof 8/5/353.

6. Colonial Office List, 1921, NAI.

7. S. N. Nwabara, *Igboland: A Century of Contact with Britain, 1860–1960* (New York: Humanities Press, 1977), 122–123.

8. Report, July 10, 1905, NAI, Cal Prof 10/3.

9. Quoted in Ekechi, "Portrait of a Colonizer," 34.

10. Report on the Owerri Division for the Half Year Ending 30th June, 1917, NAE, OW346/17, Riv Prof 8.5.353.

11. See Report on the Owerri Division, January–June 1920, NAE, OW Dist 9/6/3.

12. Iwuana to District Officer, March 8, 1950, NAE, OW Dist 7/1/8.

13. Lord Frederick Lugard, *The Dual Mandate in British Tropical Africa* (London: William Blackwood, 1922), 132.

14. Margery Perham, *Native Administration in Nigeria* (London: Oxford University Press, 1937).

15. Lugard to Colonial Office, May 29, 1915, NAI, CSO 26/33/28160.

16. See Roland Oliver and John D. Fage, *A Short History of Africa* (Harmondsworth, UK: Penguin, 1968), 302.

17. Ronald Robinson and John Gallagher, *Africa and the Victorians: The Official Mind of Imperialism* (London: Macmillan, 1961). For a summary of the African role, although its conclusions are hard to sustain, see Ronald Robinson, "Non-European Foundations of European Imperialism: Sketch for a Theory of Collaboration," in *Studies in the Theory of Imperialism*, ed. R. Owen and B. Sutcliffe (Harlow, UK: Longman, 1975).

18. For details, see Murray Last, *The Sokoto Caliphate* (London: Longman, 1967).

19. Colonel G. V. Kembell, response to E. A. Steel, "Exploration in Southern Nigeria," *Journal of the Royal United Services Institution* (1910): 446.

20. Moor to Colonial Office (Confidential), August 31, 1895, PRO, CO 520/18.

21. Don C. Ohadike, *The Ekumeku Movement: Western Igbo Resistance to the British Conquest of Nigeria, 1883–1914* (Athens: Ohio University Press, 1991), 12–13.

22. Philip Igbafe, "Western Igbo Society and Its Resistance to British Rule: The Ekumeku Movement, 1898–1911," *Journal of African History* 12, no. 3 (1973): 441–459.

23. Ohadike, *The Ekumeku Movement*, 16.

24. Report by Trenchard, December 22, 1905, PRO, CO 520/35.

25. Moor to Colonial Officer, No. 16, January 7, 1903, PRO, CO 520/18.

26. For details, see Obaro Ikime, *Niger Delta Rivalry: Itsekiri-Urhobo Relations and the European Presence 1884–1936* (London: Longman, 1969), chapter 2.

27. P. Lloyd, "The Itsekiri in the 19th Century: An Outline Social History," *Journal of African History* 4, no. 2 (1963): 207–231; P. Lloyd, "Nana the Itsekiri," in *Eminent Nigerians of the Nineteenth Century, a Series of Studies Originally Broadcast by the Nigerian Broadcasting Corporation* (Cambridge: Cambridge University Press, 1960), 79–86.

28. Ikime, *Niger Delta Rivalry*, chapters 2 and 3.

29. E. J. Alagoa, *Small Brave City-State* (Ibadan: University of Ibadan Press, 1964); Alagoa, *The Akassa Raid, 1895* (Ibadan: University of Ibadan Press, 1960).

30. See K. Onwuka Dike, *Trade and Politics in the Niger Delta, 1830–1885: An Introduction to the Economic and Political History of Nigeria* (Oxford: Clarendon Press, 1956).

31. R. A. Adeleye, *Power and Diplomacy in Northern Nigeria, 1800–1906: The Sokoto Caliphate and Its Enemies* (London: Longman, 1971), 179–189.

32. Ibid., 233–237.

33. R. A. Adeleye, "Rabih Fadlallah 1879–1893: Exploits and Impact on Political Relations in Central Sudan," *Journal of the Historical Society of Algeria* 5, no. 2 (June 1970): 223–242.

34. E. W. Bovill, *Missions to the Niger*, vol. 2, *Denham's Narrative* (London: Hakluyt Society, 1966), 478.

35. H. Clapperton, *Journal of a Second Expedition into the Interior of Africa, from the Bight of Benin to Soccatoo* (London: J. Murray, 1829), 199.

36. J. B. King, "Details of Explorations of the Old Calabar River, in 1841 and 1842," *Journal of the Royal Geographical Society* (1844): 260.

37. Robinson to Lang, September 14, 1887, CMS, G3/A3/1887/109.

38. For details of the Maji Maji, see Arnold J. Temu, "Tanzanian Societies and Colonial Invasion, 1875–1907," in *Tanzania under Colonial Rule,* ed. H. Y. Kaniki (London: Longman, 1979), 90–120; and John Iliffe, "The Organization of the Maji-Maji Rebellion," *Journal of African History* 8, no. 3 (1967): 495–512.

39. Alan F. Ryder, *Benin and the Europeans, 1485–1897* (London: Longman, 1969), 290.

40. See Adiele E. Afigbo, "Patterns of Igbo Resistance to British Conquest," *Tarikh* 4, no. 3 (1973): 20.

41. Quoted as part of a letter originally written in Arabic in 1903, in *The Occupation of Hausaland,* ed. H. F. Backwell (Lagos: Government Printer, 1927), 67–74.

42. Ibid.

43. Ibid.

44. Tew to Provincial Commissioner, Eastern Provinces, October 10, 1910, NAE, OWDIST 24/1/2.

45. R. A. Adeleye, *Power and Diplomacy in Northern Nigeria, 1804–1906* (London: Longman, 1971), 242–43.

46. Samuel Johnson, *The History of the Yorubas* (Lagos: C.S.S., 1921), 619.

47. F. Hives and G. Lumley, *Ju Ju and Justice in the Jungle* (Harmondsworth, UK: Penguin, 1940), 69–81.

48. Heneker to High Commissioner, December 26, 1902, PRO, CO 520/18.

49. Tew to Captain Ambrose, September 20, 1910, NAE, OWDIST 24/1/2.

50. Tew to Provincial Commissioner, October 10, 1910.

51. Quoted in Thomas Hodgkin, *Nigerian Perspectives: An Historical Anthology* (London: Oxford University Press, 1960), 323.

52. Ibid., 322.

53. Backwell, *The Occupation of Hausaland,* 67–74.

54. R. A. Adeleye, "Mahdist Triumph and British Revenge in Northern Nigeria, Satiru, 1906," *Journal of the Historical Society of Nigeria* 6, no. 2 (1972): 193–214.

3. Violence and Colonial Consolidation

1. *West Africa* 2, no. 82 (August 24, 1918): 493.

2. Margery Perham, *Lugard: The Years of Authority, 1898–1945* (London: Collins, 1960), 542.

3. For the history of this period, see Akinjide Osuntokun, *Nigeria in the First World War* (London: Longman, 1979).

4. Pagans Living on the Hills, Nigerian National Archives, Kaduna, Nigeria (hereafter NAK), SNP 17/24247.

5. Akinjide Osuntokun, "Disaffection and Revolts in Nigeria during the First World War, 1914–1918," *Canadian Journal of African Studies* 5, no. 2 (1971): 174.

6. Duncombe's letter, enclosed in Lugard to Colonial Office, June 12, 1915, PRO, CO 583/33/3243.

7. Ibid.

8. Young to Colonial Office, August 9, 1915, PRO, CO 583/43/36642.

9. Bishop Herbert Tugwell of Lagos to Lugard, September 9, 1914, PRO, CO 583/25/34071; Young to Lugard, December 24, 1914, PRO, CO 583/25/3407.

10. Perham, *Lugard: The Years of Authority*, 434–436.

11. Lugard's minute, September 30, 1914, PRO, CO 583/19/42181; quoted in Osuntokun, *Nigeria in the First World War*, 106.

12. Osuntokun, "Disaffection and Revolts in Nigeria during the First World War," 176.

13. Lugard to Colonial Office, June 21, 1915, PRO, CO 583/34/32247.

14. Young to Lugard, December 24, 1914, PRO, CO 583/25/34071; quoted in Osuntokun, *Nigeria in the First World War*, 109.

15. A. K. Ajiasafe, *History of Abeokuta* (Abeokuta: Fola Publishing Co., 1984), 194–195.

16. Osuntokun, "Disaffection and Revolts in Nigeria during the First World War," 177.

17. Boyle to Colonial Office, November 7, 1916, NAI, CSO 26/583/23453.

18. Report of the Kwale Rising by F. S. James (Administrator of Lagos Colony) to Lt.-Governor, Southern Provinces, November 30, 1914, NAI, CSO 20/783.

19. Report by Assistant Police Commissioner R. C. Cavendish, November 4, 1915, NAI, CSO 583/55086.

20. F. S. James to Lugard, November 7, 1914, NAI, CSO 26/48783.

21. Olufemi Vaughan, *Nigerian Chiefs: Traditional Power in Modern Politics, 1890s–1990s* (Rochester, N.Y.: University of Rochester Press, 2000).

22. F. K. Ekechi, "Portrait of a Colonizer: H. M. Douglas in Colonial Nigeria, 1897–1920," *African Studies Review* 26 (March 1983): 25–50.

23. Report on the Kwale Rising by F. S. James, November 30, 1914.

24. *Daily Times*, November 15, 1929, 3.

25. *Times* (London), October 12, 1908, 7.

26. A. W. H. Haywood and F. A. S. Clarke, *The History of the Royal West African Frontier Force* (Aldershot, UK.: Gale and Polden, 1964), 68–69.

27. Frank Hives, *Juju and Justice in Nigeria* (London: John Lane, 1930), 106.

28. Report by Captain P. K. Carre, July 10, 1905, enclosure in Carre to Divisional Commissioner, July 30, 1905, NAI, Calprof 10/3.

29. Report of the Norie Operation by Lieutenant Half-Penny, 1905, PRO, CO 520/31.

30. For details, see F. K. Ekechi, "The Igbo Response to British Imperialism: The Episode of Dr. Stewart and the Ahiara Expedition, 1905–1916," *Journal of African Studies* 1, no. 2 (Summer 1974): 145–157.

31. Haywood and Clarke, *The History of the Royal West African Frontier Force*, 80.

32. Egerton to Crewe (Confidential), September 22, 1909, PRO, CO 520/81.

33. "Inquiry under Collective Punishment Ordinance: Ikot Abassi, Ikot Ekpene Division, 1930," NAE, EP 6863/CSE, 1/85/36546.

34. Ibid.

35. Ibid.

36. Ibid.

37. Ibid.

38. For details, see F. K. Ekechi, "The War to End All Wars: Perspectives on the British Assault on a Nigerian Oracle," *Nigeria Magazine* 53 (January–March 1985): 59–68; and F. K. Ekechi, "The British Assault on the Ogbunorie Oracle," *Journal of African Studies* 14 (Summer 1987): 69–77.

39. *African Mail* (Lagos), June 30, 1916, 5.

40. Ibid.

41. For a study of the police from a historian's view, see Tekena Tamuno, *The Police in Modern Nigeria, 1861–1965: Origins, Development, and Role* (Ibadan: Ibadan University Press, 1970).

42. "Police Transport," 1918, NAI, Ben Prof 1/1170/4.

43. "Breach of Peace at Aba," 1941, NAI, CSO 26/41837.

44. Superintendent of Police, Warri-Benin Province, to Office of the Superintendent, Nigerian Police, November 6, 1943, NAI, CSO 26/4183.

45. Minor Disturbances in Southern Provinces (Secretary, Southern Provinces to Chief Secretary to the Government, Lagos, September 17, 1936), NAI, CSO 26/26208, vol. III.

46. Ibid.

47. "Disturbance at Uyo Market," 1938, NAE, CSE 1/85/ 7617.

48. Ibid.

49. "Prison Disturbances," 1933, NAI, CSO 26/28472.

50. Director of Prisons, Southern Provinces, Enugu, to the Honourable Secretary, Southern Provinces, Enugu, June 16, 1933, NAI, CSO 26/28472.

51. "Disturbance at Owo Prison," 1933, NAI, CSO 26/54484.

52. "Riots in ENA Prison," 1933, NAI, Abe Prof 2/1222/1.

4. TAXATION AND CONFLICTS

1. See Janet Roitman, *Fiscal Disobedience: An Anthropology of Economic Regulation in Central Africa* (Princeton, N.J.: Princeton University Press, 2005); and Barbara Bush and Josephine Maltby, "Taxation in West Africa: Transforming the Colonial Subject into the 'Governable Person,'" *Critical Perspectives on Accounting* 15, no. 1 (2004): 5–34.

2. For details on indirect rule, see, among others, F. D. Lugard, *The Dual Mandate in British Tropical Africa*, 5th ed. (1922, repr., London: Frank Cass, 1965); R. Heussler, *The British in Northern Nigeria* (Oxford: Oxford University Press, 1968); Margery Perham, *Native Administration in Nigeria* (London: Oxford University Press, 1937); Margery Perham, "A Restatement of Indirect Rule," *Africa* (July 1954): 321–334; Obaro Ikime, "Reconsidering Indirect Rule: The Nigerian Example," *Journal of the Historical Society of Nigeria* 4, no. 4 (December 1968): 421–438; and J. A. Atanda, *The New Oyo Empire* (London: Longman, 1973).

3. Moor to Colonial Office, July 1, 1903, NAI, CSO 1/13, 1903.

4. Michael Mason, "The Jihad in the South: An Outline of the Nineteenth Century Nupe Hegemony in Northeastern Yorubaland and Afenmai," *Journal of the Historical Society of Nigeria* 5, no. 2 (1970): 193–209.

5. Lugard, *The Dual Mandate in British Tropical Africa*, 219.

6. Secret file, Lugard to Secretary of State for the Colonies, March 13, 1915, NAI, CSO 9/1/8.

7. Dispatches to the Colonial Office, no. 64, January 1917, enclosure in Goldsmith to Lugard, NAI, CSO 1/17.

8. *Report of the Commission of Inquiry Appointed to Inquire into the Disturbances in the Calabar and Owerri Provinces, December 1929* (Lagos, Nigeria: Government Printer, 1930), 2.

9. Secret file no. 35, 1915, NAI, CSO 9/1/8.

10. Annual Reports, Kabba Province, 1914, para. 40, NAK, Loko Prof ACC21, no. 75.

11. *Report by the Hon. W. G. A. Ormsby-Gore, M.P. (Parliamentary Under-Secretary of State for the Colonies), on His Visit to West Africa during the Year 1926* (London: H.M. Stationery Office, 1926), 116; see also Jeremy White, *Central Administration of Nigeria, 1914–1948: The Problem of Polarity* (London: Frank Cass & Company, 1981), 142–143.

12. *Report of the Commission of Inquiry into the Disturbances in the Calabar and Owerri Provinces, December 1929,* 3.

13. Ibid.

14. A. E. Afigbo, "The Native Treasury Question under the Warrant Chief System in Eastern Nigeria, 1899–1929," *Odu: University of Ife Journal of African Studies* 4, no. 1 (July 1967): 29–43.

15. *Report of the Commission of Inquiry into the Disturbances in the Calabar and Owerri Provinces, December 1929,* 7.

16. A. K. Ajisafe, *History of Abeokuta* (Abeokuta: Fola Publishing Co., 1984), 200.

17. W. C. Syer's memorandum, enclosed in Boyle to Milner, January 21, 1919, PRO, CO 583/68/59455. Syer was the resident of Egbaland.

18. Boyle to Milner, January 21, 1919, PRO, CO 583/68/59455.

19. Ibid.

20. Ibid.

21. Nigerian official to Walter Long, August 28, 1918, PRO, CO 583/71/41944.

22. Lugard to Colonial Office, June 21, 1918, PRO, CO 583/66/35056.

23. W. C. Syer (Resident of Egbaland) to Lugard, August 6, 1918, PRO CO 583/66/24819.

24. H. J. Read to Secretary, Liverpool Chamber of Commerce, December 5, 1918, PRO, CO 583/69/44321.

25. T. J. Waters to Lugard, June 20, 1918, PRO, CO 583/66/35056.

26. Harding's minute, September 16, 1918, PRO, CO 583/67/44700.

27. Brigadier General Cunliffe to Lugard, December 9, 1918, PRO, CO 583/68/59455.

28. Ajiasafe, *History of Abeokuta,* 202–203.

29. *West Africa,* August 24, 1918, 493.

30. Boyle to Milner, January 21, 1919, PRO, CO 583/68/59455.

31. Syer to Lugard, August 6, 1918.

32. Report of Commission of Enquiry into the Egba Rebellion 1918, enclosed in Boyle to Milner, January 21, 1919, PRO, CO 583/72/12803.

33. *West Africa* 2, no. 82 (August 24, 1918): 493.

34. I have used archival records to supplement the accounts in Obaro Ikime, "The Anti-Tax Riots in Warri Province, 1927–1928," *Journal of the Historical Society of Nigeria* 3, no. 3 (December 1966): 559–573.

35. Annual Reports, Warri Province, 1927, NAI, CSO 26/2/11857, vol. 5, 1927.

36. Ibid.

37. Ibid.

38. Obaro Ikime, "Chief Dogho: The Lugardian System in Warri, 1917–1932," *Journal of the Historical Society of Nigeria* 3, no. 2 (December 1965): 313–333.

39. Ikime, "The Anti-Tax Riots in Warri Province," 561.

40. Ibid.

41. Annual Reports, Warri Province, 1927, NAI, CSO 26/2/11857, vol. 5, 1927.

42. Ibid.

43. Ibid.; Annual Report, Ase Sub-District, 1927, NAI, Ugheli District 41/1928.

44. Annual Reports, Kabba Province, 1914, para. 7, NAK, Loko Prof ACC21, no. 75.

45. Assessment Report, 9–10, NAI, CSO 26/21546.

46. Ibid., p. 3.

47. Agbor should not be confused with Aboh. They were both Ika Igbo-speaking precolonial kingdoms; Aboh was a coastal kingdom, Agbor was in the hinterland. People in both kingdoms speak related languages but not necessarily the same language.

48. Annual Report, 1940, NAI, Benin Prof 1/BP 1893.

49. Ibid.

50. Ibid.

51. Ibid.

52. Ibid.

53. Ibid.

54. Lord Frederick Lugard, *The Dual Mandate in British Tropical Africa* (London: William Blackwood, 1922), 241.

55. Bassa Komo District Disturbances, Telegram no. 68, NAK, SNP 7/5881/1911.

56. Minutes Paper 5881/1911, NAK, SNP 7/5881/1911.

57. District Officer to Commander, Lokoja, November 1911, Telegram no. 87, NAK, SNP 7/5881/1911.

58. Captain Byng-Hall, enclosure in Lugard to Colonial Office, CO 583/20/810, quoted in Akinjide Osuntokun, *Nigeria in the First World War* (London: Longman, 1979), 145.

59. Lugard to Colonial Office, December 16, 1914, PRO, CO 583/20/810.

60. "Munshi Province, Dekina Division, Dekina District Assessment Report" (compiled by Captain F. F. W. Byng Hall), 1918, NAK, SNP10/564/1918.

61. "District Head Dekina," 1926, NAK, Loko Prof 187/1926.

62. Perham, *Lugard: The Years of Authority*, 448.

63. Syer to Lugard, August 6, 1918.

64. Ibid.

5. Gendered Violence

1. *Report of the Commission of Inquiry Appointed to Inquire into the Disturbances in the Calabar and Owerri Provinces, December 1929* (Lagos, Nigeria: Government Printer, 1930).

2. See J. C. Anene, *Southern Nigeria in Transition 1885–1906* (Cambridge: Cambridge University Press, 1966).

3. On Macdonald's administration, see Obaro Ikime, "Sir Claude Macdonald in the Niger Coast Protectorate—A Reassessment," *Odu*, n.s., no. 3 (April 1970): 22–44.

4. A. E. Afigbo, "The Eastern Provinces under Colonial Rule," in *Groundwork of Nigerian History*, ed. Obaro Ikime (Ibadan: Heinemann, 1980), 418.

5. Ibid., 418–419. Afigbo's use of "political officers" refers to British administrators.

6. The best sources of information on the 1929 war are two long and detailed official documents: Nigeria, *Report of the Aba Commission of Inquiry* (Lagos: Government Printer, 1930); and Nigeria, *Notes of Evidence. Report of the Aba Commission of Inquiry* (Lagos: Government Printer, 1930).

7. Nigeria, *Report of the Aba Commission of Inquiry*, 13.

8. Ibid., 13.

9. Elizabeth Isichei, *History of the Igbo People* (London: Macmillan, 1976), 151–152.

10. District Officer's report, 1925, NAE, Ogoja Province 391/1925.

11. Quoted in Isichei, *A History of Nigeria*, 400.

12. Nigeria, *Report of the Aba Commission of Inquiry*, 17–18.

13. Ibid., 14.

14. Ibid., 10. Gray baft is a semi-finished cotton product used to manufacture printed textiles.

15. Ibid., 24–28.

16. Ibid., 14.

17. S. N. Nwabara, *Igboland: A Century of Contact with Britain, 1860–1960* (New York: Humanities Press, 1977), 85.

18. Nigeria, *Report of the Aba Commission of Enquiry*, 16.

19. Ibid., memorandum, 2.

20. The members of the commission of inquiry later said that his sentencing was high-handed and was based on "biased evidence of the women and [that] insufficient weight [was given] to the probabilities of the case." Nigeria, *Report of the Aba Commission of Enquiry*, 16.

21. Peggy Sanday, *Female Power and Male Dominance: On the Origins of Sexual Inequality* (Cambridge: Cambridge University Press, 1981), 136; Lorna Lueker Zukas, "Women's War of 1929," in *International Encyclopedia of Revolution and Protest* (Blackwell Publishing, forthcoming), available at http://www.revolution protestencyclopedia.com/pdfs/IEO_Womens_War_of_1929.pdf.

22. Telegrams from F. Ferguson, Political Officer of the Northern Column, to Resident of Owerri, December 17, 1929, NAE, CSE 1/85/3538, SP 6/6659.

23. Nigeria, *Report of the Aba Commission of Enquiry*, 79–81.

24. These included various collective punishment inquiries that met in January 1930 and the commission of inquiry of the same month.

25. Nigeria, *Report of the Aba Commission of Enquiry*, 27.

26. "Inquiry under the Collective Punishment Ordinance," 2, NAE, EP 6784, CSE 1/85/32624.

27. Ibid.

28. Nigeria, *Report of the Aba Commission of Enquiry*, 119–120.

29. E. Falk, Senior Resident of Calabar, to Secretary of the Southern Provinces, January 27, 1930, NAE, SP 7/3.

30. Nigeria, *Report of the Aba Commission of Enquiry*, 1.

31. Ibid., 121.

32. Ibid.

33. For the influential studies emanating from this era, see Margery Perham, *Native Administration in Nigeria* (London: Oxford University Press, 1937); Ida C. Ward, *An Introduction to the Ibo Language* (Cambridge: Heffer, 1935); C. K. Meek, *Law and Authority in a Nigerian Tribe: A Study in Indirect Rule* (London: Oxford University Press, 1937); and Sylvia Leith-Ross, *African Women: A Study of the Ibo of Nigeria* (London: Faber, 1939).

34. Native Courts Ordinance no. 12 of 1930, NAE.

35. Ibid., section 2.

36. The long list included child-stealing, counterfeiting, conspiracy, corrupt practices, forgery, defamation of government documents, fraudulent accounting, homicide, judicial corruption, obtaining goods by false pretenses, trial by ordeal, offenses against the public revenue of the government of Nigeria, offenses relating to the posts and telegraphs or the railway, official corruption, official secrets, stealing, rape, sedition, dealing in slaves, and treason.

37. Native Courts Ordinance no. 12 of 1930, NAE.

38. Sir Donald Cameron, *The Principles of Native Administration and Their Application* (Lagos: Government Printer, 1939).

39. These hopes were not fulfilled. Afigbo notes that colonial officers criticized post-1930 local governments for being loud and unwieldy. Elders who were disappointed that they did not enjoy the status and salaries of chiefs complained about the new system. By 1940, colonial officers and educated Nigerians saw the native authority system as a failure. See Afigbo, "The Eastern Provinces under Colonial Rule," 422–423.

6. Verbal Violence and Radical Nationalism

The epigraph is from Osita C. Agwuna, "We Are on the Road towards African Irredentism," *Nigerian Spokesman*, August 31, 1946, 7.

1. Hakeem Tijani, *Britain, Leftist Nationalists and the Transfer of Power in Nigeria, 1945–1965* (New York: Routledge, 2005).

2. Ikenna Nzimiro, "Zikism and Social Thought in the Nigerian Pre-Independence Period, 1944–1950," in *Themes in African Political and Social Thought*, ed. Onigu Otite (Enugu: Fourth Dimension Publishers, 1978), 300.

3. Toyin Falola, *Violence in Nigeria: The Crisis of Religious Politics and Secular Ideologies* (Rochester, N.Y.: University of Rochester Press, 1998).

4. Toyin Falola, *Nationalism and African Intellectuals* (Rochester, N.Y.: University of Rochester Press, 2001); and Thomas Hodgkin, *Nationalism in Colonial Africa* (London: Muller, 1956).

5. Kalu Ezera, *Constitutional Developments in Nigeria* (Cambridge: Cambridge University Press, 1964).

6. Claude S. Phillips, Jr., "Nigeria and Pan-Africanism," *Ibadan: A Journal Published at University College*, no. 14 (October 1962): 8.

7. Among others, see James Coleman, *Nigeria: Background to Nationalism* (Berkeley: University of California Press, 1958); Richard Sklar, *Nigerian Political Parties* (Princeton, N.J.: Princeton University Press, 1963); and G. O. Olusanya, "Nationalist Movements," in *Groundwork of Nigerian History*, ed. Obaro Ikime (Ibadan: Heinemann, 1980), 545–569.

8. *Nigerian Spokesman*, September 10, 1946, 11.

9. Mokwugo Okoye, *Vistas of Life: A Survey of Views and Visions* (Enugu: Eastern Nigerian Printing Corp., 1962).

10. O. C. Agwuna, *Inside Africa (A Study of the Colour Bar Problem)* (Yaba: Zik's Press, 1947).

11. See K. W. J. Post, "Nationalism and Politics in Nigeria: A Marxist Approach," *Nigerian Journal of Economics and Social Studies* 6, no. 2 (July 1964): 167–176.

12. See G. O. Olusanya, *The Second World War and Politics in Nigeria, 1939–1953* (Ibadan: Evans Brothers, 1973).

13. Toyin Falola, *Development Planning and Decolonization in Nigeria* (Gainesville: University Press of Florida, 1996).

14. Only the examples of nationalism expressed in a violent manner and violent words are examined here. For historical context, see Olusegun Osoba, "Ideological Trends in the Nigerian National Liberation Movement and the Problems of National Identity, Solidarity, and Motivation, 1934–1965: A Preliminary Assessment," *Ibadan: A Journal Published at University College*, no. 27 (October 1969): 26–38.

15. See V. C. Iketuonye, *Zik of New Africa* (London: Macmillan, 1961).

16. K. A. B. Jones-Quartey, *A Life of Azikiwe* (Baltimore, Md.: Penguin Books, 1965).

17. Nnamdi Azikiwe, *Renascent Africa* (Accra, 1937; repr., London: Frank Cass, 1968).

18. Ehiedu E. G. Iweriebor, *Radical Politics in Nigeria, 1945–1950: The Significance of the Zikist Movement* (Zaria: Ahmadu Bello University Press, 1996).

19. Among others, see A. O. Njoku, "Zikism: A Forgotten Philosophy of African Liberation," *Negro Digest* 16, no. 8 (1967): 30–38; and Edward H. Schiller, "Nnamdi Azikiwe: The Man and His Ideas," *Black Academy Review* 1, no. 1 (Fall 1970): 11–25.

20. Anthony Enahoro, *Nnamdi Azikiwe: Saint or Sinner?* (Lagos: Zik's Press, 1947).

21. M. C. K. Ajuluchukwu (alias Monger), "Zik of Africa," in *Zik of Africa: His Political Struggles for the Freedom of the Black Race*, ed. Akinola Lasekan (Lagos: Zik's Press, 1947).

22. G. O. Olusanya, "India and Nigerian Nationalism," *Africa Quarterly*, 5, no. 3 (October–December 1965): 188–191.

23. The lecture was later printed as *What Nigeria Wants: A Close Study of Indian Struggles with Special Reference to Nigeria* (Yaba: Chuks Printer, 1947).

24. Nnamdi Azikiwe, *Suppression Story: True or False?* (Warri, 1946), 1.

25. A. A. Nwafor Orizu, *Without Bitterness: Western Nations in Post-War Africa* (New York: Creative Age Press, 1944).

26. *West African Pilot*, March 2, 1946, 1.

27. Ibid.

28. Iweriebor, *Radical Politics in Nigeria*, 37.

29. See O. Akinsuroju, *Nigerian Political Theatre, 1923–1953* (Lagos: City Publishing Association, 1953).

30. Mokwugo Okoye, *Storms on the Niger* (Enugu: Eastern Nigerian Printing Corporation, 1965), 106.

31. *West African Pilot*, March 2, 1946, 2.

32. Ibid., 5.

33. *Nigerian Spokesman*, July 22, 1946, 5.

34. Ibid., 3.

35. C. O. Agwuna, *What Is the Zikist Movement? A Brief Sketch of the Work and Organisation of the Zikist Movement* (Lagos: Adedimeta Press, 1949), 6.

36. *Nigerian Spokesman*, July 23, 1947, 4.

37. *West African Pilot*, October 25, 1946, 7.

38. *Nigerian Spokesman*, November 17, 1947, 2.

39. Raji Abdallah, "Time to Fight," *West African Pilot*, August 13, 1947, 3.

40. K. O. K. Onyioha, *The National Church of Nigeria: Its Catechism and Credo* (Lagos: National Church Publishing Agency, 1951), 3–5.

41. Ibid.; "Nigerian Political Summary, January–March 1949," PRO, CO 537/4727.

42. Mbonu Ojike, *My Africa* (New York: John Day, 1946); and M. Ojike, *The Road to Freedom* (Yaba: Chuks, 1947).

43. *Nigerian Spokesman*, May 7, 1947, 2.

44. *West African Pilot*, June 3, 1947, editorial.

45. *West African Pilot*, June 3, 1947, 3.

46. *West African Pilot*, June 22, 1946, 5.

47. John Flint, "Scandal at the Bristol Hotel: Some Thoughts on Racial Discrimination in Britain and West Africa and Its Relationship to the Planning of Decolonization, 1939–1947," *Journal of Imperial and Commonwealth History* 12, no. 1 (October 1983): 74–93.

48. *West African Pilot*, March 5, 1947, 1.

49. "Racial Discrimination," circular no. 25, 221.3.47, Government Printer, Lagos, 1947.

50. Habib Raji Abdallah, "Zikism as I Understand It," *West African Pilot*, August 14, 1947, 1.

51. Habib Raji Abdallah, "The Cloud Bursts," *West African Pilot*, January 19, 1948, 8.

52. G. O. Olusanya, "India and Nigerian Nationalism," *African Quarterly* 5, no. 3 (October–December 1965): 188–191.

53. *West African Pilot*, October 9, 1947, 1.

54. Nduka Eze, "Memoirs of a Crusader," mimeograph, 1952 (in author's possession).

55. *West African Pilot*, October 29, 1948, 1.

56. *African Echo*, November 6, 1948, 1–2.

57. *West African Pilot*, January 13, 1949, 1.

58. Osita Agwuna, "To All the People of Nigeria and All Zikists," *West African Pilot*, January 27, 1949, 1.

59. *West African Pilot*, November 22, 1948, 1.

60. *West African Pilot*, November 23, 1948, 1–2.

61. "Political Intelligence Reports, West Africa," secret file no. 28, PRO, CO 537/4727.

62. *West African Pilot*, April 5, 1949, 1.

63. "The Zikist Movement," PRO, CO 537/5807, 30824.

64. "West Africa, Nigerian Political Summaries," PRO, CO 537/5806.

65. See Hugh Foot's account in his memoir, *A Start in Freedom* (New York: Harper and Row, 1964), 109–111.

66. *Nigerian Gazette Extraordinary* (Lagos: Government Printer, 1950), 381–382.

67. Billy J. Dudley, *Parties and Politics in Northern Nigeria* (London: Frank Cass, 1968), 72–115.

68. C. S. Whitaker, *The Politics of Tradition: Continuity and Change in Northern Nigeria, 1946–1966* (Princeton, N.J.: Princeton University Press, 1970), 355–359.

7. Labor, Wages, and Riots

1. A. G. Hopkins, "The Lagos Strike of 1897: An Exploration in Nigerian Labour History," *Past and Present* 35 (December 1966): 133–155.

2. Wogu Anababa, *The Trade Union Movement in Nigeria* (New York: Africana Publishing Co., 1969), 15.

3. *Lagos Weekly Record*, January 17, 1920, 5.

4. Nigerian Railway, *Annual Report, 1920* (Lagos: Government Printer, 1921).

5. Nigerian trade unions always looked for ways to connect themselves with the international labor movement, from which they borrowed ideas on bargaining and political participation. See Dafe Otobo, *Foreign Interests and Nigerian Trade Unions* (Ibadan: Heinemann, 1986).

6. Falola, *Development Planning and Decolonization in Nigeria.*

7. Government Notice no. 75 of 1941, NAI.

8. M. A. Tokunboh, *Labour Movement in Nigeria: Past and Present* (Lagos: Lantern Books, 1985), 41.

9. Department of Labour, *Annual Report, 1944* (Lagos: Government Printer, 1945), 15.

10. Department of Labour, *Quarterly Report, June 1944* (Lagos: Government Printer, 1945), 7.

11. *West African Pilot,* June 6, 1945, 1.

12. Department of Labour, *Annual Report, 1946* (Lagos: Government Printer, 1947), 8–9.

13. Robin Cohen, *Labour and Politics in Nigeria* (London: Heinemann, 1974), 160–163.

14. Wale Oyemakinde, "Michael Imoudu and the Emergence of Militant Trade Unionism in Nigeria, 1940–1942," *Journal of the Historical Society of Nigeria* 37, no. 3 (December 1974): 541–561.

15. Cohen, *Labour and Politics in Nigeria,* 159–165.

16. Ibid. See also Robin Cohen, "Nigeria's Labour Leader No. 1: Notes for a Biographical Study of M. A. O. Imoudu," *Journal of the Historical Society of Nigeria* 5, no. 2 (1970): 303–308.

17. Azikiwe wrote a series entitled "If I Were Governor of Nigeria" during this time. See *West African Pilot,* July 4, 1945.

18. Nnamdi Azikiwe, *Suppression of the Press in British West Africa* (Onitsha: African Book Co., 1946).

19. *West African Pilot,* April 1 and 2, 1946, 1, 3.

20. William Tudor Davies, *Enquiry into the Cost of Living and Control of the Cost of Living in the Colony and Protectorate of Nigeria* (London: HMSO, 1946).

21. On the issue of controlling food prices as part of an effort to minimize labor protests, see Wale Oyemakinde, "The Pullen Marketing Scheme: A Trial in Food Price Control in Nigeria, 1941–1947," *Journal of the Historical Society of Nigeria* 6, no. 4 (June 1973): 413–423.

22. Nigeria, *Report of the Commission of Enquiry into the Disturbances which Occurred at Burutu on the 21st of June, 1947* (Lagos: Government Printer, 1948).

23. *West African Pilot,* May 6, 1949.

24. "Nigerian Political Summary, April–May 1949," secret file no. 30, PRO, CO 537/4727.

25. "Nigerian Political Summary, Governor to Secretary of State, August 26, 1949," PRO, CO 537/4727.

26. *West African Pilot,* September 3, 1949, 2.

27. For details on labor-government relations in the Iva Valley area, see Carolyn A. Brown, *"We Were All Slaves": African Miners, Culture, and Resistance at the Enugu Government Colliery* (Portsmouth, N.H.: Heinemann, 2003).

28. Agwu Akpala, "The Background of the Colliery Shooting Incident in 1949," *Journal of the Historical Society of Nigeria* 3, no. 2 (December 1965): 335–363.

29. *Nigeria: Annual Report, Department of Labour, 1949–50* (Lagos: Government Printer, 1952), 23–24.

30. Anababa, *The Trade Union Movement,* 104–105.

31. *Nigeria: Annual Report, Department of Labour, 1949–50,* 21–23.

32. See Onogbo Achogbo, *The Iva Valley Tragedy: A Memorable Incident in Nigerian National and Trade Union History* (Enugu: Published by the author, 1953).

33. *West African Pilot,* November 24 and 25, 1949, 1–2.

34. *Nigeria: Annual Report on the Police Force, 1949–50* (Lagos: Government Printer, 1951), 23–25.

35. Ibid., 24.

36. *West African Pilot*, November 26, 1949, 4.

37. *West African Pilot*, November 28, 1949, 11.

38. Ibid., 2.

39. Colonial Office, *Report of the Commission of Enquiry into the Disorders in the Eastern Provinces of Nigeria, November 1949* (London: HMSO, 1950).

40. *West African Pilot*, July 5, 1950, 13.

41. Mbazulike Amechi, *The Forgotten Heroes of Nigerian Independence* (Onitsha: Etukokwu Publishers, 1985).

42. For the connections between unions and politics, see B. C. Roberts, *Labour in the Tropical Territories of the Commonwealth* (London: Bell, 1964); S. C. Suffrin, *Unions in Emerging Societies* (Syracuse, N.Y.: Syracuse University Press, 1964); and M. Singh, *History of Kenya's Trade Union Movement* (Nairobi, Kenya: East Africa Publishing House, 1969).

43. Kola Balogun, *As Youth Sees It* (Lagos: Zik's Press, 1947), 4.

44. Mokwugo Okoye, *Storms on the Niger* (Enugu: Eastern Nigerian Printing Corporation, 1965), 106.

45. See Kola Balogun, *My Country Nigeria* (Yaba: Sankey Printing Works, 1955).

46. See M. C. K. Ajuluchuku, *Imoudu versus Governor* (Lagos: Broadway Printers, 1947); and M. C. K. Ajuluchuku, *Workers versus Whitelegs* (Port Harcourt: Published by the author, 1951).

47. See Abiodun Aloba, *Zik: The Imperfect* (Lagos: Published by the author, 1946).

48. See the writings of Nduka Eze, a Zikist, in the *Nigerian Spokesman*, September 11, 1946.

49. See J. Weeks, "The Impact of Economic Conditions and Institutional Forces on Urban Wages in Nigeria," *Nigerian Journal of Economic and Social Sciences* 13, no. 3 (1971): 313–339.

50. See W. M. Warren, "Urban Real Wages and the Nigerian Trade Union Movement," *Economic Development and Cultural Change* 15, no. 1 (1966): 22–36; and J. Weeks, "Wage Policy and the Colonial Legacy," *Journal of Modern African Studies* 9, no. 3 (1971): 361–387.

51. *Daily Service*, December 27, 1945.

52. See statements by Osita Agwuna in the *West African Pilot*, December 31, 1947, 8.

53. Bola Ige, *People, Politics and Politicians of Nigeria* (Ibadan: Heinemann, 1995), 22.

CONCLUSION

1. See, for instance, Cheryl Johnson-Odim and NinaEmma Mba, *For Women and the Nation: Funmilayo Ransome-Kuti of Nigeria* (Urbana: University of Illinois Press, 1997).

2. Ali Mazrui, "The Resurrection of the Warrior Tradition in African Political Culture," *Journal of Modern African Studies* 13, no. 1 (1975): 84.

3. Bruce Vandervort, *Wars of Imperial Conquest in Africa, 1830–1914* (Bloomington: Indiana University Press, 1998), 219.

4. Toyin Falola, *Violence in Nigeria: The Crisis of Religious Politics and Secular Ideologies* (Rochester, N.Y.: University of Rochester Press, 1998), chapter 5.

5. Toyin Falola, *The History of Nigeria* (Westport, Conn.: Greenwood Press, 1999), chapters 12 and 13.

6. R. A. Adeleye, *Power and Diplomacy in Northern Nigeria, 1800–1906: The Sokoto Caliphate and Its Enemies* (London: Longman, 1971), 179–189.

7. David Pratten, *The Man-Leopard Murders: History and Society in Colonial Nigeria* (Edinburgh, UK: Edinburgh University Press for the International African Institute, 2007).

8. S. Ellis, "African Wars of Liberation: Some Historiographical Reflections," in *Trajectoires de Libération en Afrique Contemporaine*, ed. P. Konings, W. van Binsbergen, and G. Hesseling (Paris, 2000), 69–91.

9. Oke Onigbin Court, NAK, Ilorin Prof 2230.

10. J. M. Lee, *African Armies and Civil Order* (New York: Praeger, 1969), 45. See also T. H. Parsons, *The African Rank and File: Social Implications of Colonial Military Service in the King's African Rifles, 1902–1964* (Portsmouth, N.H.: Heinemann, 1999).

11. Mazrui, "The Resurrection of the Warrior Tradition in African Political Culture," 71.

12. See L. H. Gann and Peter Duignan, *The Rulers of British Africa, 1870–1914* (Stanford, Calif.: Stanford University Press, 1978), 231.

13. See Philip D. Curtin, *The Image of Africa: British Ideas and Action, 1780–1850* (Madison: University of Wisconsin Press, 1964); and William B. Cohen, *The French Encounter with Africans: White Response to Blacks, 1530–1880* (Bloomington: Indiana University Press, 1980).

14. A. Boyle, *Trenchard* (New York: Norton, 1979), 79.

15. See the illuminating and vigorous debates in three books: P. Richards, *Fighting for the Rain Forest: War, Youth and Resources in Sierra Leone* (Portsmouth, N.H.: Heinemann, 1996); M. Kaldor, *New and Old Wars: Organized Violence in a Global Era* (Stanford, Calif.: Stanford University Press, 1999); and E. Braathen, M. Bøås, and G. Sæther, *Ethnicity Kills? The Politics of War, Peace and Ethnicity in Sub-Saharan Africa* (New York: St. Martin's, 2000).

16. The connection between poverty and politics is common to all African countries. See F. D. Colburn, *The Vogue of Revolution in Poor Countries* (Princeton, N.J.: Princeton University Press, 1994).

BIBLIOGRAPHY

PRIMARY SOURCES

Archives

Church Missionary Society Archives, University of Birmingham Library, UK (CMS)
Nigerian National Archives, Ibadan (NAI)
Nigerian National Archives, Enugu (NAE)
Nigerian National Archives, Kaduna (NAK)
Public Record Office, London, UK (PRO)

Newspapers and Magazines (all published in Lagos, Nigeria)

African Echo, 1948–1950
Daily Comet, 1947–1950
Daily Service, 1945–1950
Daily Times, 1945–1960
Lagos Weekly Record, 1920
Nigerian Spokesman, 1946–1953
Southern Nigerian Defender, 1948–1950
West African Pilot, 1945–1950
West African Review, 1945–1950

Official Documents

Annual Reports on Nigeria, 1946–1950. London: HMSO, 1946–1950.
Callwell, C. E. *Small Wars: Their Principles and Practice.* London, HMSO, 1906.
   Repr. (with a new introduction by D. Porch), Lincoln: University of Nebraska
   Press, 1996.
Cameron, Sir Donald. *The Principles of Native Administration and Their Application.*
   Lagos: Government Printer, 1939.
Clifford, H. "United Nigeria." *Journal of the Royal African Society* 21 (1921–1922):
   1–14.

Colonial Office. *Enquiry into the Cost of Living and Control of the Cost of Living in the Colony and Protectorate of Nigeria.* London: HMSO, 1946.

———. *Enquiry into the Disorders in the Eastern Provinces of Nigeria: Proceedings of the Commission.* Vols. 1–2. London: HMSO, 1950.

———. *Report of the Commission of Enquiry into the Disorders in the Eastern Provinces of Nigeria, November 1949.* London: HMSO, 1950.

Davies, William Tudor. *Enquiry into the Cost of Living and the Control of the Cost of Living in the Colony and Protectorate of Nigeria.* London: HMSO, 1946.

Department of Labour. *Annual Reports, 1943–1950.* Lagos: Government Printer, 1943–1950.

———. *Quarterly Report, June 1944.* Lagos: Government Printer, 1945.

———. *Quarterly Review, 1944–50.* Lagos: Government Printer, 1944–1950.

The Independent Nigeria: 1 October, 1960. Lagos: Government Printer, 1960.

Macdonald, Major C. M. *Report of the Visit of Her Majesty's Commission to the Niger and Oil Rivers.* London: Colonial Office Library, 1890.

Memorandum on the Subject of Native Land Tenure in the Colony and Protectorate of Southern Nigeria. Nigerian Pamphlet, F. 36. Lagos: Government Publisher, 1911.

Nigeria. *Annual Report, Department of Labour, 1949–50.* Lagos: Government Printer, 1952.

———. *Annual Reports of the Nigeria Police Force, 1945–1950.* Lagos: Government Printer, 1945–1950.

———. *Laws of the Colony of Southern Nigeria, 1908.* London: Stevens and Sons, 1910.

———. *The Laws of Nigeria, 1923, 1944–1950, 1961.* Lagos: Government Printer, 1923, 1944–50, 1961.

———. *Legislative Council Debates, 1945–50.* Lagos: Government Printer, 1945–1950.

———. *Notes of Evidence. Report of the Aba Commission of Inquiry.* Lagos: Government Printer, 1930.

———. *Report of the Aba Commission of Inquiry.* Lagos: Government Printer, 1930.

———. *Report of the Commission of Inquiry Appointed to Inquire into the Disturbances in the Calabar and Owerri Provinces, December 1929.* Lagos, Nigeria: Government Printer, 1930.

———. *Report of the Commission of Enquiry into the Disturbances Which Occurred at Burutu on the 21st of June, 1947.* Lagos: Government Printer, 1948.

Nigeria Gazette, 1945–1950. Lagos: Government Printer, 1945–1950.

Nigerian Gazette Extraordinary 37, no. 21, April 13, 1950. Lagos: Government Printer, 1950.

Nigerian Railway. *Annual Report, 1920.* Lagos: Government Printer, 1921.

"Racial Discrimination." Circular no. 25, 221.3.47. Lagos: Government Printer, 1947.

Regulations Including the Nigerian Defence Regulations. Lagos: Government Printer, 1944.

U.S. Adjutant-General's Office, Military Information Division. *Colonial Army Systems of the Netherlands, Great Britain, France, Germany, Portugal, Italy, and Belgium.* Washington, D.C.: Government Printing Office, 1901.

Books, Tracts, Pamphlets, and Essays

Achogbo, Onogbo. *The Iva Valley Tragedy.* Enugu: Published by the author, 1953.

Agwuna, C. O. *Go with the Masses: Studies on Essential Tactics in National and Colonial Struggles.* Vol. 1. Enugu: EPS, 1953.

————. *Inside Africa (A Study of the Colour Bar Problem).* Yaba: Zik's Press, 1947.

————. *What Is the Zikist Movement? A Brief Sketch of the Work and Organisation of the Zikist Movement.* Lagos: Adedimeta Press, 1949.

Ajuluchukwu, M. C. K. *Imoudu versus Governor.* Lagos: Broadway Printers, 1947.

————. *Inner Party Criticism.* Nos. 1–2. Lagos: Published by the author, 1954.

————. *Tits-Bits Here and There.* Lagos: Published by the author, 1946.

————. *Workers versus Whitelegs.* Port Harcourt: Published by the author, 1951.

Akinsuroji, O. *Nigerian Political Theatre (1923–1953).* Lagos: City Publishing Association, 1953.

————. *Zik in Nigeria's Ship of Destiny.* Lagos: City Publishing Association, 1951.

Akunneto, I. *Tribalism in Nigeria.* Lagos: Published by the author, 1947.

Allen, Captain W. "Excursion up the River of Cameroons and the Bay of Ambiosis." *Journal of the Royal Geographical Society* 13 (1843): 1–17.

Allen, J. G. C. *Native Policy in Nigeria.* Lagos: Twentieth Century Press, 1943.

Aloba, Abiodun. *Zik: The Imperfect.* Lagos: Published by the author, 1946.

Amechi, Mbazulike. *Forgotten Heroes of Nigerian Independence.* Onitsha: Etukokwu Publishers, 1985.

Anyiam, F. U. *Among Nigerian Celebrities.* Lagos: Published by the author, 1960.

————. *Men and Matters in Nigerian Politics, 1934–1958.* Yaba: John Okwesa, 1959.

Balogun, Kola. *As Youth Sees It.* Yaba: Zik Press, 1947.

————. *Century of the Common Man.* Osogbo: Published by the author, 1954.

————. *Home Rule Now.* Lagos: Obajimmi Printing Works, 1952.

————. *Ideals of a Zikist.* Lagos: Published by the author, 1946.

————. *My Country Nigeria.* Yaba (Lagos): Sankey Printing Works, 1955.

————. *A Precedent for Future Regrets: Shall We Nigerians Let This Be?* Zikist Tract no. 2. Lagos: The Zikist Movement, 1946.

————. *Tax More Abundant or Life More Abundant.* Osogbo: Published by the author, 1954.

————. *Village Boy: My Own Story.* Ibadan: Africanus Publishers, 1969.

————. *What Nigeria Wants.* Yaba: Chuks, 1947.

Enahoro, Anthony. *Nnamdi Azikiwe: Saint or Sinner?* Lagos: Published by the author, 1947.

Ita, Eyo. *The Assurance of Freedom.* Calabar: West African People's Institute Press, 1949.

————. *Crusade for Freedom.* Calabar: West African People's Institute Press, 1949.

————. *Sterile Truths and Fertile Lies.* Calabar: West African People's Institute Press, 1949.

Izuogu, O. *Heroes of New Africa: Zik Genius of Today.* Lagos: Published by the author, 1960.

Juwe, S. M. *Margaret Ekpo in Nigerian Politics: Behold the Mother of the Son of New Nigeria.* Kafanchan: Published by the author, 1954.

————. What Is the National Church of Nigeria and the Cameroons and the God of Africa? Port Harcourt: Goodwill Press, n.d. [1953?]

King, J. B. "Details of Explorations of the Old Calabar River, in 1841 and 1842." Journal of the Royal Geographical Society (1844): 260.

Lasekan, Akinola, ed. Zik of Africa: His Political Struggles for the Freedom of the Black Race. Lagos: Zik's Press, 1947.

Lugard, Lady Flora. A Tropical Dependency. London: James Nisbet, 1905.

Lugard, Lord Frederick. The Dual Mandate in British Tropical Africa. London: William Blackwood, 1922.

Macaulay, Herbert. An Antithesis on the Public Lands (Amendments) 1945. Lagos: National Council, 1945.

Mbah, A. N. The Life Story of Zik. Onitsha: Appolos Brothers, 1960.

National Church of Nigeria and the Cameroons. The Constitution of the National Council of Nigeria and Cameroons. Lagos: Published by the author, 1945.

————. Freedom Charter. Lagos: Published by the author, 1948.

————. Hymns and Prayers. Aba: Published by the author, 1950.

Ogbalu, F. C. Zik: Biography and Selected Speeches. Onitsha: University Publishing Co., 1955.

Ohiare, P. A. Late Alhaji Raji Abdullah's Memorial Pamphlet. Ilorin: Published by the author, 1983.

Ojike, Mbonu. My Africa. New York: John Day, 1946.

————. The Road to Freedom. Yaba: Chuks, 1947.

Ojiyi, Okwudili. The British Political Shooting of Nigerian Coalminers on November 18, 1949. Onitsha: Goodway Printing Press, 1965.

Okoye, Mokwugo. African Cameos. Port Harcourt: Amacs, 1954.

————. Against Tribe. Enugu: Zik's Press, 1962.

————. Blackman's Destiny. Port Harcourt: Amacs, 1956.

————. Fullness of Freedom. Onitsha: Chinyelu, 1953.

————. The Rebel Line. Onitsha: Etudo Ltd., 1962.

————. Some Facts and Fancies. Lagos: Ifeolu, 1953.

————. Some Men and Women. Onitsha: New Era, 1956.

————. Storms on the Niger. Enugu: Eastern Nigerian Printing Corp., 1965.

Olaogun, E. E. The Building of the National Council of Nigeria and the Unity of Nigeria. Lagos: Published by the author, 1947.

Onyioha, K. O. K. National Church of Nigeria: Its Catechism and Credo. Lagos: National Church Publishing Agency, 1951.

Orizu, A. A. Nwafor. Original Zikism. Onitsha: United Brothers Press, n.d.

————. Without Bitterness: Western Nations in Post-War Africa. New York: Creative Age Press, 1944.

Robinson, C. H. Nigeria: Our Latest Protectorate. London: Marshall, 1900.

Steel, E. A. "Exploration in Southern Nigeria." Journal of the Royal United Services Institution (1910): 446.

What Nigeria Wants: A Close Study of Indian Struggles with Special Reference to Nigeria. Yaba: Chuks Printer, 1947.

SECONDARY SOURCES

Abdulraheem, Tajudeen, and Adebayo Olukoshi. "The Left in Nigerian Politics and the Struggle for Socialism, 1945–1985." *Review of African Political Economy* 13, no. 37 (December 1986): 64–80.

Adams, R. F. G. "The Arochuku Dialect of Ibo." *Africa* 11, no. 1 (January 1929): 57–70.

Adejuyigbe, O. *Boundary Problems in Western Nigeria: A Geographical Analysis.* Ile-Ife: University of Ife Press, 1975.

———. "Ife/Ijesa Boundary Problem." *Nigerian Geographical Journal* 13 (1970): 23–38.

Adeleye, R. A. "Mahdist Triumph and British Revenge in Northern Nigeria: Satiru, 1906." *Journal of the Historical Society of Nigeria* 6, no. 2 (1972): 193–214.

———. *Power and Diplomacy in Northern Nigeria, 1804–1906.* London: Longman, 1971.

Ademoyega, Wole. *The Federation of Nigeria.* London: George Harrap, 1962.

Afigbo, A. E. "The Aro Expedition of 1901–1902: An Episode in the British Occupation of Igboland." *Odu*, n.s., no. 7 (April 1972): 3–27.

———. "The Consolidation of British Imperial Administration in Nigeria, 1900–1918." *Civilizations* 21, no. 4 (1971): 436–458.

———. "The Eastern Provinces under Colonial Rule." In *Groundwork of Nigerian History*, ed. Obaro Ikime. Ibadan: Heinemann, 1980.

———. "The Native Treasury Question under the Warrant Chief System in Eastern Nigeria, 1899–1929." *Odu: University of Ife Journal of African Studies* 4, no. 1 (July 1967): 2943.

———. "Patterns of Igbo Resistance to British Conquest." *Tarikh* 4, no. 3 (1973): 20.

———. *The Warrant Chiefs: Indirect Rule in Southeastern Nigeria.* London: Longman, 1972.

Ajayi, J. F. A. *Christian Missions in Nigeria 1841–1891.* London: Longman, 1965.

———. "Nigerian Nationalism." *Ibadan: A Journal Published at University College*, no. 10 (November 1960): 16–18.

———. "Nineteenth Century Origins of Nigerian Nationalism." *Journal of the Historical Society of Nigeria* 2, no. 1 (December 1961): 196–210.

———, and M. Crowder, eds. *History of West Africa.* Vol. 2. London: Longman, 1973.

Ajuluchukwu (alias Monger), M. C. K. "Zik of Africa." In *Zik of Africa: His Political Struggles for the Freedom of the Black Race*, ed. Akinola Lasekan. Lagos: Zik's Press, 1947.

Akintoye, S. A. *Revolution and Power Politics in Yorubaland 1840–1893: Ibadan Expansion and the Rise of Ekitiparapo.* London: Longman, 1971.

Akinwumi, Olayemi. *The Colonial Contest for the Nigerian Region, 1884–1900: A History of the German Participation.* Hamburg: Lit Verlag, 2004.

Akpala, Agwu. "The Background to the Colliery Shooting Incident in 1947." *Journal of the Historical Society of Nigeria* 3, no. 2 (December 1965): 335–363.

Alagoa, E. J. *The Akassa Raid, 1895.* Ibadan: University of Ibadan Press, 1960.

————. "Koko: Amanyanabo of Nembe." *Tarikh* 1, no. 4 (1967): 75.

————. *The Small Brave City-State: A History of Nembe-Brass in the Niger Delta.* Ibadan: University of Ibadan Press, 1964.

Ananaba, Wogu. *The Trade Union Movement in Nigeria.* New York: African Publishing Co., 1969.

Anene, J. C. *Southern Nigeria in Transition, 1885–1906.* Cambridge: Cambridge University Press, 1966.

Arikpo, Okoi. *The Development of Modern Nigeria.* Harmondsworth, UK: Penguin, 1967.

Arlinghaus, B., and P. H. Baker, eds. *African Armies, Evolution and Capabilities.* Boulder, Colo.: Westview, 1986.

Asiwaju, A. I. *Western Yorubaland under European Rule, 1889–1945: A Comparative Analysis of French and British Colonialism.* London: Longman, 1976.

————, ed. *Partitioned Africans: Ethnic Relations across Africa's International Boundaries, 1884–1984.* New York: St. Martin's Press, 1985.

Atanda, J. A. *The New Oyo Empire.* London: Longman, 1973.

August, T. G. *The Selling of the Empire: British and French Imperialist Propaganda, 1890–1940.* Westport, Conn.: Greenwood Press, 1985.

Awa, Eme. *Federal Government in Nigeria.* Berkeley: University of California Press, 1964.

Awolowo, O. *Assassination Story: True or False.* Onitsha: Published by the author, 1946.

————. *AWO: The Autobiography of Chief Obafemi Awolowo.* Cambridge: Cambridge University Press, 1960.

————. *Land Tenure in Northern Nigeria: A Study of Treaty Rights of the Royal Niger Company, Chartered and Limited.* Yaba: African Book Co., 1942.

————. *Path to Nigerian Freedom.* London: Faber, 1947.

————. *Zik: A Selection of the Speeches of Dr. Nnamdi Azikiwe.* Cambridge: Cambridge University Press, 1961.

Ayandele, E. A. *The Missionary Impact on Modern Nigeria 1842–1914: A Political Analysis.* London: Longmans, 1966.

Azikiwe, Nnamdi. *Renascent Africa.* Accra: Published by the author, 1937; repr., London: Frank Cass, 1968.

————. *Suppression of the Press in British West Africa.* Onitsha: African Book Co., 1946.

————. *Suppression Story: True or False.* Warri: Published by the author, 1946.

Backwell, H. F., ed. *The Occupation of Hausaland, 1900–1904.* Lagos: Government Printer, 1927; reprint London: Frank Cass, 1969.

Bailes, H. "Technology and Imperialism: A Case Study of the Victorian Army in Africa." *Victorian Studies* 24, no. 1 (1980): 82–104.

Bart, William N. M. G. *Nigeria under British Rule.* London: Methuen, 1927.

Basden, G. T. *Among the Ibos of Nigeria.* London: Seeley, Service & Co., 1921; repr., London: Frank Cass, 1966.

————. *Niger Ibos.* London: Seeley, Service & Co., 1938; repr., London: Frank Cass, 1966.

————. "Notes on the Ibo Country and the Ibo People, Southern Nigeria." *Geographical Journal* 39 (1912): 241–247.

Bello, Ahmadu. *My Life*. Cambridge: Cambridge University Press, 1962.

Birmingham, D. *The Decolonization of Africa*. Athens: Ohio University Press, 1996.

Bolt, C. *Victorian Attitudes to Race*. London: Routledge and Kegan Paul, 1971.

Bond, B., ed. *Victorian Military Campaigns*. London: Hutchinson, 1967.

Bovill, E. W. *Missions to the Niger*. Vol. 2, *Denham's Narrative*. London: Hakluyt Society, 1966.

Boyle, A. *Trenchard*. New York: Norton, 1979.

Braathen, E., M. Bøås, and G. Sæther. *Ethnicity Kills? The Politics of War, Peace, and Ethnicity in SubSaharan Africa*. New York: St. Martin's, 2000.

Bradford, James C., ed. *The Military and the Conflict between Cultures: Soldiers at the Interface*. College Station: Texas A&M University Press, 1977.

Bradley, K. *Once a District Officer*. New York: St. Martin's Press, 1966.

Brounger, S. G. "Nigeria Past and Present." *Journal of the African Society* 47, no. 12 (April 1913): 249–255.

Brown, C. A. *"We Were All Slaves": African Miners, Culture, and Resistance at the Enugu Government Colliery*. Portsmouth, N.H.: Heinemann, 2003.

Burns, Sir A. *Colonial Civil Servant*. London: Allen and Unwin, 1949.

————. *In Defence of Colonies*. London: Allen and Unwin, 1957.

Bourdillon, Sir Bernard. "The Future of Native Authorities." *Africa* 15 (July 1945): 124–128.

Carman, W. Y. *A History of Firearms from Earliest Times to 1914*. London: Routledge, 1955.

Cary, Joyce. *Britain and West Africa*. London: Longman, Green and Co., 1947.

Clapperton, H. *Journal of a Second Expedition into the Interior of Africa, from the Bight of Benin to Soccatoo*. London: J. Murray, 1829.

Clayton, A., and D. Killingray, eds. *Khaki and Blue: Military and Police in British Colonial Africa*. Athens: Ohio University Press, 1989.

Clowes, W. L. *The Royal Navy: A History from the Earliest Times to the Death of Queen Victoria*. 7 vols. London: Sampson, Low, Martson, 1903.

Cohen, Robin. *Forced Labour in Colonial Africa*. London: Zed, 1979.

————. *Labour and Politics in Nigeria*. London: Heinemann, 1974.

————. "Nigeria's Labour Leader No. 1: Notes for a Biographical Study of M.A.O. Imoudu." *Journal of the Historical Society of Nigeria* 5, no. 2 (1970): 303–308.

————, and R. Sandbrook. *The Development of an African Working Class*. Toronto: University of Toronto Press, 1975.

Cohen, William. B. *The French Encounter with Africans: White Response to Blacks, 1530–1880*. Bloomington: Indiana University Press, 1980.

Colburn, F.D. *The Vogue of Revolution in Poor Countries*. Princeton, N.J.: Princeton University Press, 1994.

Cole, P. D. *Modern and Traditional Elites in the Politics of Lagos*. Cambridge: Cambridge University Press, 1975.

Coleman, J. S. *Nigeria: Background to Nationalism*. Berkeley: University of California Press, 1958.

Crocker, W. R. *Nigeria: A Critique of British Colonial Administration.* London: George Allen, 1936.

Crowder, M. *West Africa under Colonial Rule.* Evanston, Ill.: Northwestern University Press, 1968.

———, ed. *West African Resistance: The Military Response to Colonial Occupation.* London: Hutchinson and Co., 1971.

Curtin, P. D. *The Image of Africa: British Ideas and Action, 1780–1850.* Madison: University of Wisconsin Press, 1964.

Davidson, B. *The People's Cause: A History of Guerillas in Africa.* Harlow, UK: Longman, 1981.

De Moor, J. A., and H. L. Wesseling, eds. *Imperialism and War: Essays on Colonial War in Asia and Africa.* Leiden: E. J. Brill, 1989.

Dike, K. O. *Trade and Politics in the Niger Delta, 1830–1885.* Oxford: Clarendon Press, 1956.

Dudley, Billy J. *Parties and Politics in Northern Nigeria.* London: Frank Cass, 1968.

Dusgate, R. H. *The Conquest of Northern Nigeria.* London: Frank Cass, 1985.

Earle, E. M., ed. *Makers of Modern Strategy: Military Thought from Machiavelli to Hitler.* Princeton, N.J.: Princeton University Press, 1943.

Egharevba, J. O. *A Short History of Benin.* 4th ed. Ibadan: University of Ibadan Press, 1968.

Ekechi, F. K. "The British Assault on the Ogbunorie Oracle." *Journal of African Studies* 14 (Summer 1987): 69–77.

———. "The Igbo Response to British Imperialism: The Episode of Dr. Stewart and the Ahiara Expedition, 1905–1916." *Journal of African Studies* 1, no. 2 (1974): 145–157.

———. *Missionary Enterprise and Rivalry in Igboland, 1857–1914.* London: Frank Cass, 1972.

———. "Portrait of a Colonizer: H. M. Douglas in Colonial Nigeria, 1897–1920." *African Studies Review* 26 (March 1983): 25–50.

———. "The War to End All Wars: Perspectives on the British Assault on a Nigerian Oracle." *Nigeria Magazine* 53 (January–March 1985): 59–68.

Eldridge, C. C. *England's Mission: The Imperial Idea in the Age of Gladstone and Disraeli, 1868–1880.* Chapel Hill: University of North Carolina Press, 1974.

Ellis, S. "African Wars of Liberation: Some Historiographical Reflections." In *Trajectories de Libération en Afrique Contemporaine,* ed. P. Konings, W. van Binsbergen, and G. Hesseling. Paris: Karthala, 2000.

Ezera, Kalu. *Constitutional Developments in Nigeria.* Cambridge: Cambridge University Press, 1964.

Falola, Toyin. *Development Planning and Decolonization in Nigeria.* Gainesville: University Press of Florida, 1996.

———. *Nationalism and African Intellectuals.* Rochester, N.Y.: University of Rochester Press, 2001.

———. *Violence in Nigeria: The Crisis of Religious Politics and Secular Ideologies.* Rochester, N.Y.: University of Rochester Press, 1998.

Fanon, Frantz. *The Wretched of the Earth*. Translated by Constance Farrington. New York: Grove Press, 1996.

Fisher, H. J., and V. Rowland. "Firearms in the Central Sudan." *Journal of African History* 12, no. 2 (1971): 215–239.

Flint, John E. *Sir George Goldie and the Making of Nigeria*. London: Oxford University Press, 1960.

———. "Scandal at the Bristol Hotel: Some Thoughts on Racial Discrimination in Britain and West Africa and Its Relationship to the Planning of Decolonization, 1939–1947." *Journal of Imperial and Commonwealth History* 20, no. 1 (October 1983): 74–93.

Foerster, S., W. J. Mommsen, and R. Robinson, eds. *Bismarck, Europe, and Africa: The Berlin Africa Conference of 1884–1885 and the Onset of Partition*. Oxford: Oxford University Press, 1988.

Foot, Hugh. *A Start in Freedom*. New York: Harper and Row, 1964.

Forde, Daryll, and G. I. Jones. *The Ibo and Ibibio-Speaking Peoples of South-Eastern Nigeria*. London: International African Institute, 1950.

Fortes, Meyer. "The Impact of the War on British West Africa." *International Affairs* 21, no. 2 (April 1945): 206–219.

Gailey, H. A. *The Road to Aba: A Study of British Administrative Policy in Eastern Nigeria*. London: University of London Press, 1971.

Gann, L. H., and P. Duignan, eds. *African Proconsuls: European Governors in Africa*. Stanford, Calif.: Hoover Institution, 1979.

———. *The Rulers of British Africa, 1870–1914*. Stanford, Calif.: Stanford University Press, 1978.

Green, M. M. *Ibo Village Affairs*. London: Sidgwick and Jackson, 1947.

———. *Land Tenure in an Ibo Village in South-Eastern Nigeria*. London: Humphries, 1941.

Hammond, Dorothy, and Alta Jablow. *The Myth of Africa*. New York: Library of Social Science, 1977.

Hanson, James. "Nationalism and Socialism in Nigeria." *The Canadian Forum* 13, no. 325 (February 1948): 249–251.

Hargreaves, J. D. *Prelude to the Partition of West Africa*. London: Macmillan, 1963.

———. *West Africa Partitioned*. Vol. 1, *The Loaded Pause, 1885–1889*. London: Macmillan, 1974.

Hayes, Carlton J. *Nationalism: A Religion*. New York: Macmillan, 1960.

Haywood, A., and F. A. S. Clarke. *The History of the Royal West African Frontier Force*. Aldershot, UK: Gale and Polden, 1964.

Headrick, D. R. *The Tools of Empire: Technology and European Imperialism in the Nineteenth Century*. New York: Oxford University Press, 1981.

Heggoy, A. A., and J. M. Haar, eds. *The Military in Imperial History: The French Connection*. New York: Garland, 1984.

Hensley, F. M. *Niger Dawn*. North Devon, UK: Arthur H. Stockwell, 1948.

Hetherington, Penelope. *British Paternalism and Africa, 1920–1940*. London: Frank Cass, 1978.

Heussler, Robert. *The British in Northern Nigeria*. Oxford: Oxford University Press, 1968.

———. *Yesterday's Rulers: The Making of the British Colonial Service*. Syracuse, N.Y.: Syracuse University Press, 1963.

Higham, R., ed. *A Guide to the Sources of British Military History*. London: Routledge, 1972.

Hiskett, M. *The Sword of Truth: The Life and Times of the Shehu Usman dan Fodio*. New York: Oxford University Press, 1973.

Hives, F. *Juju and Justice in Nigeria*. London: John Lane, 1930.

———, and G. Lumley. *Ju Ju and Justice in the Jungle*. Harmondsworth, UK: Penguin, 1940.

Hobsbawm, Eric, and Terence O. Ranger, eds. *The Invention of Tradition*. Cambridge: Cambridge University Press, 1983.

Hodgkin, Thomas. *Nationalism in Colonial Africa*. London: Muller, 1956.

———. *Nigerian Perspectives: An Historical Anthology*. London: Oxford University Press, 1960.

Home, Robert. *City of Blood Revisited: A New Look at the Benin Expedition of 1897*. London: R. Collins, 1982.

Hopkins, A. K. "The Lagos Strike of 1897: An Exploration in Nigerian Labour History." *Past and Present* 35 (December 1966): 133–155.

Igbafe, Philip. *Benin under British Administration*. London: Longman, 1979.

———. "British Rule in Benin, 1897–1920: Direct or Indirect?" *Journal of the Historical Society of Nigeria* 3, no. 4 (1967): 701–717.

———. "Western Igbo Society and Its Resistance to British Rule: The Ekumeku Movement, 1898–1911." *Journal of African History* 12, no. 3 (1973): 441–459.

Ige, B. *People, Politics and Politicians of Nigeria*. Ibadan: Heinemann, 1995.

Iketuonye, V. C. *Zik of New Africa*. London: Macmillan, 1961.

Ikime, Obaro. "The Anti-Tax Riots in Warri Province, 1927–1928." *Journal of the Historical Society of Nigeria* 3, no. 3 (December 1966): 559–573.

———. "The British in Bauchi, 1901–1908: An Episode in the British Occupation and Control of Northern Nigeria." *Journal of the Historical Society of Nigeria* 7, no. 2 (June 1974).

———. "The British 'Pacification' of the Tiv." *Journal of the Historical Society of Nigeria* 7, no. 1 (December 1973) 103–109.

———. "Chief Dogho: The Lugardian System in Warri, 1917–1932." *Journal of the Historical Society of Nigeria* 3, no. 2 (December 1965): 313–333.

———. "Colonial Conquest and Resistance in Southern Nigeria." *Journal of the Historical Society of Nigeria* 6, no. 3 (December 1972).

———. *The Fall of Nigeria: The British Conquest*. London: Heinemann, 1977.

———. *Merchant Prince of the Niger Delta*. London: Heinemann, 1968.

———. "Reconsidering Indirect Rule: The Nigerian Example." *Journal of the Historical Society of Nigeria* 4, no. 4 (December 1968): 421–438.

———. "Sir Claude Macdonald in the Niger Coast Protectorate—A Reassessment." *Odu*, n.s., no. 3 (April 1970): 22–44.

———, ed. *Groundwork of Nigerian History*. Ibadan: Heinemann, 1980.

Iliffe, John. "The Organization of the Maji-Maji Rebellion." *Journal of African History* 8, no. 3 (1967): 495–512.

Isichei, Elizabeth. *A History of Nigeria.* London: Longman, 1983.

———. *History of the Igbo People.* London: Macmillan, 1976.

———. *The Ibo People and the Europeans: The Genesis of a Relationship to 1906.* London: Faber and Faber, 1973.

Iweriebor, Ehiedu G. *Radical Politics in Nigeria, 1945–1950: The Significance of the Zikist Movement.* Zaria: Ahmadu Bello University Press, 1996.

Johnson-Odim, C., and N. E. Mba. *For Women and the Nation: Funmilayo Ransome-Kuti of Nigeria.* Urbana: University of Illinois Press, 1997.

Johnson, Samuel. *The History of the Yorubas.* Lagos: C.S.S., 1921.

Jones, G. I. "Dual Organization in Ibo Social Structure." *Africa* 19, no. 2 (April 1949): 150–156.

———. *The Trading States of the Oil Rivers: A Study of Political Development in Eastern Nigeria.* London: Oxford University Press, 1963.

———. "Who Are the Aro?" *Nigerian Field* 8, no. 3 (July 1939): 100–103.

Jones-Quartey, K. A. B. *A Life of Azikiwe.* Baltimore, Md.: Penguin Books, 1965.

Kaldor, M. *New and Old Wars: Organized Violence in a Global Era.* Stanford, Calif.: Stanford University Press, 1999.

Kaniki, H. Y., ed. *Tanzania under Colonial Rule.* London: Longman, 1979.

Keith, A. B. "Land Tenure in Nigeria." *Journal of the African Society* 11 (April 1912): 325–331.

Last, M. *The Sokoto Caliphate.* London: Longman, 1967.

Latham, A. J. H. *Old Calabar, 1600–1891.* Oxford: Oxford University Press, 1973.

Law, Robin. "Horses, Firearms and Political Power in Pre-Colonial West Africa." *Past and Present* 72 (1976): 112–132.

Lee, J. M. *African Armies and Civil Order.* New York: Praeger, 1969.

Leith-Ross, S. *African Women: A Study of the Ibo of Nigeria.* London: Faber, 1939.

Le Vine, V. T. *Political Leadership in Africa: Post-Independence Generational Conflict in Upper Volta, Senegal, Niger, Dahomey, and the Central African Republic.* Stanford, Calif.: Hoover Institute, 1967.

Lloyd, P. "The Itsekiri in the 19th Century: An Outline Social History." *Journal of African History* 4, no. 2 (1963): 207–231.

———. "Lugard and Indirect Rule." *Ibadan: A Journal Published at University College,* no. 10 (November 1960): 18–22.

Lorimer, D. A. *Colour, Class and the Victorians: English Attitudes to the Negro in the Mid-Nineteenth Century.* Leicester, UK: Leicester University Press, 1978.

MacKenzie, J. M., ed. *Popular Imperialism and the Military, 1850–1950.* Manchester, UK: Manchester University Press, 1992.

MacPhee, Alan. *The Economic Revolution in British West Africa.* London: George Routledge & Sons, 1926.

Maddox, G., and T. K. Welliver, eds. *Colonialism and Nationalism in Africa.* 4 vols. New York: Garland, 1993.

Meek, C. K. *Law and Authority in a Nigerian Tribe: A Study in Indirect Rule.* London: Oxford University Press, 1937.

Morel, E. D. *Nigeria: Its Peoples and Its Problems*. London: John Murray, 1912.

Muffett, D. J. M. *Concerning Brave Captains: Being a History of the British Occupation of Kano and Sokoto and of the Last Stand of the Fulani Forces*. London: André Deutsch, 1964.

Murray, W., M. Knox, and A. Bernstein, eds. *The Making of Strategy: Rulers, States, and War*. Cambridge: Cambridge University Press, 1994.

Nair, K. K. *Politics and Society in South Eastern Nigeria, 1841–1906*. London: Frank Cass, 1972.

Nicholson, I. F. *The Administration of Nigeria, 1900–1960*. Oxford: Clarendon Press, 1969.

Nnoli, Okwudiba. *Ethnic Politics in Nigeria*. Enugu: Fourth Dimension Publishers, 1978.

Nwabara, S. N. "British Foundation of Nigeria: A Saga of Hardship, 1788–1914." *Civilizations* 13, no. 3 (1963): 308–317.

———. "Encounter with the Long Ju-Ju, November 1901 to May 1902—A Prelude to British Military Expeditions in Iboland." *Transactions of the Historical Society of Ghana* 9 (1968): 79–89.

———. *Igboland: A Century of Contact with Britain, 1860–1960*. New York: Humanities Press, 1977.

———. "Nana the Itsekiri." In *Eminent Nigerians of the Nineteenth Century, a Series of Studies Originally Broadcast by the Nigerian Broadcasting Corporation*. Cambridge: Cambridge University Press, 1960.

Mason, M. "The Jihad in the South: An Outline of the Nineteenth Century Nupe Hegemony in Northeastern Yorubaland and Afenmai." *Journal of the Historical Society of Nigeria* 5, no. 2 (1970): 193–209.

Mazrui, A. "The Resurrection of the Warrior Tradition in African Political Culture." *Journal of Modern African Studies* 13, no. 1 (1975): 84.

Newbury, Colin. "Trade and Technology in West Africa: The Case of the Niger Company, 1900–1920." *Journal of African History* 14, no. 4 (1978): 551–575.

Njoku, A. O. "Zikism: A Forgotten Philosophy of African Liberation." *Negro Digest* 16, no. 8 (1967): 30–38.

Nzimiro, Ikenna. "Zikism and Social Thought in the Nigerian Pre-Independence Period, 1944–1950." In *Themes in African Political and Social Thought*, ed. Onigu Otite. Enugu: Fourth Dimension Publishers, 1978.

Obichere, B. I. *West African States and European Expansion: The Dahomey-Niger Hinterland, 1885–1898*. New Haven, Conn.: Yale University Press, 1971.

Ohadike, Don C. *The Ekumeku Movement: Western Igbo Resistance to the British Conquest of Nigeria, 1883–1914*. Athens: Ohio University Press, 1991.

Okonjo, Isaac M. *British Administration in Nigeria, 1900–1950: A Nigerian View*. New York: Nok Publishers, 1974.

Okoye, M. *Storms on the Niger: A Short Story of Nigeria's Struggle from the Arab Influx to the Election Crisis*. Enugu: Nigeria Printing Corp., n.d.

———. *Vistas of Life: A Survey of Views and Visions*. Enugu: Eastern Nigerian Printing Corp., 1962.

Oliver, Roland, and John D. Fage. *A Short History of Africa.* Harmondsworth, UK: Penguin, 1968.

Olorunshola, V. O. *The Politics of Cultural Sub-Nationalism in Africa.* Garden City, N.Y.: Anchor Books, 1972.

Olusanya, G. O. "India and Nigerian Nationalism." *African Quarterly* 5, no. 3 (October–December 1965): 188–191.

———. "Nationalist Movements." In *Groundwork of Nigerian History,* ed. Obaro Ikime. Ibadan: Heinemann, 1980.

———. *The Second World War and Politics in Nigeria, 1939–1953.* Ibadan: Evans Brothers, 1973.

———. "The Zikist Movement: A Study in Political Radicalism, 1946–1950." *Journal of Modern African Studies* 4, no. 3 (1966): 323–333.

Osoba, S. A. "Ideological Trends in the Nigerian National Liberation Movement and the Problems of Identity, Solidarity, and Motivation, 1934–1965: A Preliminary Assessment." *Ibadan: A Journal Published at University College,* no. 27 (October 1969): 26–38.

———. "The Nigerian Power Elite, 1952–1965." In *African Social Studies: A Radical Reader,* ed. Peter Gutkind and Peter Waterman, 368–382. New York: Monthly Review Press, 1977.

Osuntokun, Akinjide. *Nigeria in the First World War.* London: Longman, 1979.

Otobo, D. *Foreign Interests and Nigerian Trade Unions.* Ibadan: Heinemann, 1986.

Owen, R., and B. Sutcliffe, eds. *Studies in the Theory of Imperialism.* Harlow, UK: Longman, 1972.

Oyemakinde, Wale. "Michael Imoudu and the Emergence of Militant Trade Unionism in Nigeria, 1940–1942." *Journal of the Historical Society of Nigeria* 7, no. 3 (December 1974): 541–561.

———. "The Pullen Marketing Scheme: A Trial in Food Price Control in Nigeria, 1941–1947." *Journal of the Historical Society of Nigeria* 6, no. 4 (June 1973): 413–423.

Pakenham, T. *The Scramble for Africa: The White Man's Conquest of the Dark Continent from 1876 to 1912.* London: Weidenfeld and Nicolson, 1991.

Paret, P., ed. *Makers of Modern Strategy: From Machiavelli to the Modern Age.* Princeton, N.J.: Princeton University Press, 1986.

Parsons, T. H. *The African Rank and File: Social Implications of Colonial Military Service in the King's African Rifles, 1902–1964.* Portsmouth, N.H.: Heinemann, 1999.

Pearce, R. D. "Governors, Nationalists and Constitutions in Nigeria, 1935–1951." *Journal of Imperial and Commonwealth History* 9, no. 3 (May 1981): 289–307.

Perham, Margery. *Lugard: The Years of Adventure, 1858–1898.* London: Collins, 1956.

———. *Lugard: The Years of Authority, 1898–1945.* London: Collins, 1960.

———. *Native Administration in Nigeria.* London: Oxford University Press, 1937.

———. "A Restatement of Indirect Rule." *Africa* (July 1954): 321–334.

———, and M. Bull, eds. *The Diaries of Lord Lugard.* London: Faber and Faber, 1963.

Phillips, Claude S., Jr. "Nigeria and Pan-Africanism." *Ibadan: A Journal Published at University College,* no. 14 (October 1962): 8–13.

Post, K. W. J. "Nationalism and Politics in Nigeria: A Marxist Approach." *Nigerian Journal of Economic and Social Studies* 6, no. 2 (July 1964): 167–176.

Ranger, Terence O. "Connections between Primary Resistance Movements and Modern Mass Nationalism in East and Central Africa." Parts 1 and 2. *Journal of African History* 9, nos. 3 and 4 (1968): 437–453, 631–641.

———. "White Presence and Power in Africa." *Journal of African History* 20, no. 4 (1979): 463–469.

Rich, P. *Race and Empire in British Politics.* Cambridge: Cambridge University Press, 1986.

Roberts, B. C. *Labour in the Tropical Territories of the Commonwealth.* London: Bell, 1964.

Robinson, R. "Non-European Foundations of European Imperialism: Sketch for a Theory of Collaboration." In *Studies in the Theory of Imperialism*, ed. R. Owen and B. Sutcliffe. Harlow, UK: Longman, 1975.

———, and J. Gallagher. *Africa and the Victorians: The Official Mind of Imperialism.* London: Macmillan, 1961.

Rotberg, R. I., and A. Mazrui, eds. *Protest and Power in Black Africa.* New York: Oxford University Press, 1970.

Ryder, A. F. *Benin and the Europeans, 1485–1897.* London: Longman, 1969.

Sheperd, G. *The Politics of African Nationalism.* New York: Frederick Praeger, 1963.

Schiller, E. H. "Nnamdi Azikiwe: The Man and His Ideas." *Black Academy Review* 1, no. 1 (Fall 1970): 11–25.

Singh, M. *History of Kenya's Trade Union Movement.* Nairobi: East Africa Publishing House, 1969.

Sklar, Richard. *Nigerian Political Parties.* Princeton, N.J.: Princeton University Press, 1963.

Smaldone, Joseph P. *Warfare in the Sokoto Caliphate: Historical and Sociological Perspectives.* Cambridge: Cambridge University Press, 1977.

Smith, Anthony, ed. *Nationalist Movements.* London: Macmillan, 1976.

Smith, R. S. "The Lagos Consulate 1851–1861: An Outline." *Journal of African History* 5 (1974): 393–416.

———. "Nigeria-Ijebu." In *West African Resistance: The Military Response to Colonial Occupation*, ed. M. Crowder. New York: Africana Publishing Corp., 1971.

———. *Warfare and Diplomacy in Pre-Colonial West Africa.* London: Methuen, 1976.

Strachan, H. *European Armies and the Conduct of War.* London: Allen and Unwin, 1983.

Suffrin, S. C. *Unions in Emerging Societies.* Syracuse, N.Y.: Syracuse University Press, 1964.

Talbot, P. A. *The Peoples of Southern Nigeria.* 4 vols. London: Humphrey Milford, 1926.

———. "Some Foreign Influences on Nigeria." *Journal of the Royal African Society* 24 (April 1925): 178–199.

Tamuno, T. N. *The Evolution of the Nigerian State: The Southern Phase, 1898–1914.* London: Longman, 1973.

———. *The Police in Modern Nigeria.* Ibadan: Ibadan University Press, 1966.

Thompson, Sir G. "Some Problems of Administration and Development in Nigeria." *Journal of the African Society* 26 (July 1927): 305–322.

Tokunboh, M. A. *Labour Movement in Nigeria: Past and Present.* Lagos: Lantern Books, 1985.

Ukpabi, S. C. "Military Recruitment and Social Mobility in Nineteenth Century West Africa." *Journal of African Studies* 2, no. 1 (Spring 1975): 87–107.

———. "The Origins of the West African Frontier Force." *Journal of the Historical Society of Nigeria* 3, no. 3 (December 1966): 485–501.

———. *Strands in Nigerian Military History.* Zaria: Gaskiya, 1986.

Uzoigwe, G. N. *Britain and the Conquest of Africa.* Ann Arbor: University of Michigan Press, 1975.

Vandeleur, S. *Campaigning on the Upper Nile and Niger.* London: Methuen and Co, 1898.

Vandervort, B. *Wars of Imperial Conquest in Africa, 1830–1914.* Bloomington: Indiana University Press, 1998.

Vaughan, O. *Nigerian Chiefs: Traditional Power in Modern Politics, 1890s–1990s.* Rochester, N.Y.: University of Rochester Press, 2000.

Ward, I. C. *An Introduction to the Ibo Language.* Cambridge: Heffer, 1935.

Warren, W. M. "Urban Real Wages and the Nigerian Trade Union Movement." *Economic Development and Cultural Change* 15, no. 1 (1966): 22–36.

Weeks, J. "The Impact of Economic Conditions and Institutional Forces on Urban Wages in Nigeria." *Nigerian Journal of Economic and Social Sciences* 13, no. 3 (1971): 313–339.

———. "Wage Policy and the Colonial Legacy." *Journal of Modern African Studies* 9, no. 3 (1971): 361–387.

Weigert, S. L. *Traditional Religion and Guerrilla Warfare in Modern Africa.* Houndmills, Basingstoke, Hampshire: Macmillan Press, 1995.

Wesseling, H. I., ed. *Expansion and Reaction.* Leiden, Netherlands: Leiden University Press, 1978.

Whitaker, C. S. *The Politics of Tradition: Continuity and Change in Northern Nigeria, 1946–1966.* Princeton, N.J.: Princeton University Press, 1970.

White, G. "Firearms in Africa: An Introduction." *Journal of African History* 12 (1971): 173–183.

Wright, Richard. *White Man, Listen!* New York: Doubleday, 1964.

INDEX

Aba market, 74

Aba Women's War, 108, 114, 115–16, 117–23, 124, 174; commission to investigate, 126–29; fines for, 124, 125, 126

Abacha, General Sanni, 184–85

Abak, 119

Abassi, Mbiafun Ikot, 70–71

Abayomi, Kofo, 169–70

Abdallah, Habib Raji, 143–44, 145, 146–47, 151, 157

Abeokuta, 1, 56–61, 91

Aboh, 3, 39–40

Action Group, 182

activists: anti-colonial, 133, 134, 145–47; arrests of, 146; post-colonial, 184–85; prison and, 149; trials of, 147, 149. *See also* Azikiwe, Nnamdi; resistance, anti-colonial

Adubi War, 84

"affrays," 74

Afigbo, A. E., 111

Afikpo, 38, 39

African Civil Service Technical Workers Union (ACSTWU), 156, 158, 160, 162

African Clerical Workers Union, 162

African Echo, 145–46

African General Workers Union, 162

African Mercantile Workers Union, 162

African rulers, 49, 65–66; British intentions and, 46–47; coercion and, 176; power and the colonial government, 32, 86; reprisals for riots and, 125 (*see also* Collective Punishment Ordinance); revolts and, 88–89; and taxation, 79–80, 98–101; treatment of defeated, 22. *See also* headmen; warrant chiefs

Agbor, 99

Agwuna, Osita, 144–45, 146–47

Ahiara, 69

Ahmadu, 102–103

Ajasi, Sir Kitoyi, 126

Ajasse, 98

Ajuluchukwu, M. C. K., 136, 138, 139–40

Akinsanya, Samuel, 170

Akitoye, King, 4

Akoko, 97

Alagoa, E. J., 42

alake, 56–58, 59, 61, 89, 91

Alder, Soyemi, 60

Al-Kanemi, 46

alliance failures, 23

Aloba, Abiodun, 138

amanyanabo (king), 33

TOYIN FALOLA

is the Frances Higginbotham Nalle Centennial Professor in History
and University Distinguished Teaching Professor at The University of
Texas at Austin. He is editor (with Matt D. Childs) of *The Yoruba
Diaspora in the Atlantic World* (2005); (with Akinwumi Ogundiran)
of *Archaeology of Atlantic Africa and the African Diaspora* (2007);
(with Kevin D. Roberts) of *The Atlantic World: 1450–2000* (2008); and
(with Joel E. Tishken and Akíntúndé Akínyẹmí) of *Ṣàngó in Africa and
the African Diaspora* (2009), all published by Indiana University Press.